60386046

S0-BSA-240

8-10-2005

SUCCESS WITH STRUGGLING READERS

SOLVING PROBLEMS IN THE TEACHING OF LITERACY

Cathy Collins Block, Series Editor

Wayne
LB
1050.5
.G36
2005

Success with Struggling Readers

THE **BENCHMARK SCHOOL** APPROACH

Irene West Gaskins

FOREWORD BY MICHAEL PRESSLEY

THE GUILFORD PRESS
New York   London

© 2005 The Guilford Press
A Division of Guilford Publications, Inc.
72 Spring Street, New York, NY 10012
www.guilford.com

All rights reserved

Except as noted, no part of this book may be reproduced, translated, stored in a retrieval system, or transmitted, in any form or by any means, electronic, mechanical, photocopying, microfilming, recording, or otherwise, without written permission from the Publisher.

Printed in the United States of America

This book is printed on acid-free paper.

Last digit is print number: 9 8 7 6 5 4 3 2 1

LIMITED PHOTOCOPY LICENSE

These materials are intended for use only by qualified professionals.

The Publisher grants to individual purchasers of this book nonassignable permission to reproduce the numbered figures in this book. This license is limited to you, the individual purchaser, for use with your own clients or students. It does not extend to additional professionals in your institution, school district, or other setting, nor does purchase by an institution constitute a site license. This license does not grant the right to reproduce these materials for resale, redistribution, or any other purposes (including but not limited to books, pamphlets, articles, video- or audiotapes, and handouts or slides for lectures or workshops). Permission to reproduce these materials for these and any other purposes must be obtained in writing from the Permissions Department of Guilford Publications.

Library of Congress Cataloging-in-Publication Data

Gaskins, Irene West.
  Success with struggling readers: the Benchmark School approach / Irene West Gaskins; foreword by Michael Pressley.
      p. cm. — (Solving problems in the teaching of literacy)
  Includes bibliographical references and index.
  ISBN 1-59385-169-3 (pbk.) — ISBN 1-59385-170-7 (cloth)
  1. Reading—Remedial teaching. I. Benchmark School (Media, Pa.) II. Title. III. Series.
LB1050.5.G36 2005
372.43—dc22

                                                                                    2004027993

For my children, Richard Charles Gaskins, Jr.,
and Robert West Gaskins,
and for my grandchildren, Helen Emily Gaskins, Audrey Jane Gaskins,
Susan Ruth Gaskins, William Benjamin Gaskins II,
Lindsay Catherine Chan Gaskins, Geoffrey Chan Gaskins,
and Joan McCammon Gaskins,
who provided the impetus for my addiction to bookstores
and to the most enchanting read-aloud books,
and who reinforced for me that children do indeed
learn to read in different ways

About the Author

Irene Gaskins leads students through the new classrooms in the Hamilton Wing.

Irene West Gaskins, EdD, is a school administrator and founder, in 1970, of Benchmark School, a school for struggling readers located in suburban Philadelphia. Her 45-year career in education began in the public schools of Virginia and Pennsylvania, after which she taught at the Graduate School of Education at the University of Pennsylvania, from 1968 to 1983.

Collaborating with the energetic and dedicated faculty of Benchmark School, as well as with major consultants from around the country, Gaskins has worked on such significant problems as designing word recognition instruction that works for students who previously had made little progress in this area, improving reading performance by increasing students' awareness and control of cognitive styles and other personal factors, and designing programs that teach strategies for understanding and learning from texts. During the years 1988–1994 the strategies research at Benchmark was funded by a cognitive studies grant from the James S. McDonnell Foundation, and Benchmark was the foundation's national demonstration school. One of the aspects of her job that Gaskins likes most is being the teacher, or co-teacher, who pilots and fine-tunes the new programs being developed at Benchmark.

The results of this work have been published in such journals as *The Reading Teacher, Reading Research Quarterly, Journal of Reading Behavior, Language Arts, Elementary School Journal, Remedial and Special Education*, and *Journal of Learning Disabilities*. Gaskins is also the author of three books about teaching reading, seven decoding programs, and 56 children's books that accompany a beginning decoding program. Gaskins is a frequent speaker at state, national, and international conferences and workshops. In 1986 Benchmark School was selected for recognition by the U.S. Department of Education as an elementary school that exemplified excellence in education. In addition, Benchmark's reading program is one of six exemplary programs featured on videotapes developed by the Center for the Study of Reading located at the University of Illinois. Benchmark's summer program received recognition in 1999 as *Philadelphia* magazine's Best of Philly© Summer Camp, Intellectual. Recently Gaskins was a member of the Rand Study Group and of the planning committee for the 2009 National Assessment of Educational Progress. In 1998 Gaskins was honored as a Distinguished Educator by *The Reading Teacher* and in 2001 received the International Reading Association's William S. Gray Citation of Merit for lifetime achievement. The School of Education of Michigan State University honored her in 2003 with a Crystal Apple in recognition of her achievements in education.

Foreword

I first visited Benchmark School in the late 1980s. After one day I was convinced that, with respect to reading, it was the most evidence-based, innovative educational approach I had ever seen. A few years later, I would collaborate with Irene Gaskins and her staff to investigate how they developed active comprehension in Benchmark students. That work has gone far to promote a new vision about how comprehension instruction can be developed in schools—a vision that I helped to document at Benchmark and that was largely invented by Irene and her Benchmark associates (Pressley et al., 1992). I spent enough time in the school 15 years ago to notice any warts. There were few, with every hour spent at the school illuminating something innovative that I had not noticed before. For a psychologist convinced that education can be improved by applying research findings in school settings, Benchmark in the early 1990s was a dream come true to me—but not a dream, a reality—existing proof that impressive education can follow from intelligent awareness and interpretation of research by educators dedicated to developing educational programming that works even with the most challenged learners.

As this foreword is being written, I am collaborating with Irene again to do a new documentary of Benchmark, this time focusing on the entire school experience. Benchmark is so much better in 2005 than it was in the late 1980s and early 1990s. In the old days, Benchmark used a homegrown approach to word recognition known as Word ID. Since then, the approach has been revised and improved. Comprehension instruction has continued to evolve, so that it now naturally occurs across years and across the curriculum, folding in much of the new thinking about comprehension developed since the early 1990s. Impressive science, social studies, and mathematics curricula have been devised and implemented. There is now much more complete and impressive attention given to the socioemotional needs of Benchmark students, again incorporating much of what is known about motivating students and developing in them realistic conceptions about how far they can go in life and how they can meet their academic and personal goals. Finally, the cramped building that housed the school in the early 1990s has been expanded considerably. More than just new space, this expansion is functionally supportive of Benchmark education in many ways. I was always impressed by the design of the little classrooms that served the school 15 years ago. There are more little classrooms now, incorporating technology better and arranging space for the many grouping and instructional options that occur at Benchmark. The building is an architectural jewel. I see many new school buildings; I have never seen one so attractive or one so well conceived for its purpose.

Most impressive now is the staff that is the school. Every teacher is on board with the Benchmark approach, delivering the curriculum, doing it well, trying to do it better all the time. This dedication reflects not only the appealing and compelling curricula developed by Irene and her associates but also an impressive program of professional development. Professional development takes place all the time, as does new curriculum development. Benchmark teachers are always inventing new units, new ways of applying the science of education in their classrooms. They do so with enthusiasm, sharing and cooperating with their colleagues to provide the very best educational experience they can to Benchmark students.

Benchmark students land in the school because of early school failure, typically in reading. Most learn how to read at Benchmark. All learn how to cope with a world of texts. So, to be certain, much of the language arts instruction, especially in the first few years, is more remedial, explicit, and complete instruction than occurs in regular education. Even so, it never seems like remedial education, because as students learn to read, they read and think about very sophisticated content. So, the first-year middle school students in the program did quite a bit of reading and thinking about the role of women in the U.S. democratic experience. The curriculum at every grade level is saturated with U.S. history. What impresses me is that I always learn something new, often quite a bit, when I experience a Benchmark social studies discussion. The same is true when I sit in science and math classes. Even in language arts, the discussions in the middle school often deal with topics and writers that I only encountered in college. Benchmark students experience a conceptually rich curriculum that has been well thought out by Irene and her colleagues.

As you read this book, many of you will decide that a visit to the school is a must. I agree; the school receives many visitors. If you decide to visit, do so for at least a week, for even at the end of that week, you will not have seen it all. This school is overflowing with new thinking, so much so that I continue to learn much about the school despite my many visits. This is the most sophisticated educational environment I have ever experienced. Even the pedagogy in higher education settings that have taken seriously the development of impressive teaching (e.g., the case method teaching at Harvard Business School) is pretty simple compared to the complex articulation of methods and content at Benchmark. If the book you are about to read has a shortcoming, it is that it cannot do justice to a school that is much too sophisticated to be depicted completely in a single volume. Read this book—as every person who is interested in how to construct excellent education should—and then, come for a visit. Then you will know what I mean.

The only fitting way to close this preface is to say a few words about the qualifications of the author, Irene Gaskins. Irene was educated as a school psychologist at the University of Pennsylvania, where she developed a sophisticated understanding of reading. Following the Penn experience, she and some friends opened the first version of Benchmark in a church basement, with the goal of teaching reading to local students who were just not "getting it" in their schools. Their success led to the expansion of their institution, including amassing the capital to build their own school building. From the earliest years of the institution, Irene led the Benchmark faculty to rely on research for guidance, inviting the best and the brightest in reading research to inform the school, including, for example, Joanna Williams and Richard Anderson. The commitment to research-based instruction expanded, with many top-drawer reading and education researchers visiting and contributing to Benchmark over the years. Irene has served many roles over the years and contributed in countless ways—she is the founder, chief curriculum developer, principal, professional development leader, fund raiser, and I could go on and on. Her spouse, Dick Gaskins, also is involved with the school in many ways, in particular, attending to financial issues as well as inventing a physical plant that is as good as a school physical plant can get.

Irene and Dick Gaskins are an omnipresence in this institution, and their combined brilliance results in a school that is without peer, as far as I can tell, with respect to the total education of children who struggled to achieve in regular education. When I sit in a third-year middle school class at Benchmark, the impact of their contributions really hits home. The class I watch is not just a good middle school class session, it is a great one, as good as the best middle school hours I have ever watched. The students are thinking big thoughts, organizing those thoughts into impressive compositions, and clearly ready to attend a demanding, main-line Philadelphia high school . . . with success there virtually certain. Turning kids' lives around so well is an enormous accomplishment. The book you are about to read will provide some insights about how such education can happen. As you read the book, think about how its vision might become that of many more schools across the United States, including your own. I am always impressed that a year at Benchmark costs no more than a year of special education in a Pennsylvania public school. The Benchmark folks spend the money well, with every minute of every school day producing results. I hope that Irene's vision becomes the vision of many more educators.

MICHAEL PRESSLEY, PhD

REFERENCE

Pressley, M., El-Dinary, P. B., Gaskins, I., Schuder, T., Bergman, J. L., Almasi, J., & Brown, R. (1992). Beyond direct explanation: Transactional instruction of reading comprehension strategies. *Elementary School Journal*, 92, 511–554.

Acknowledgments

For so many of us, learning to read opens the door to an exciting world of ideas—a world that no child should have to miss. However, when that door is held shut by struggles in learning to read, a child's opportunities to become all that he or she might be are sorely limited. For 45 years I have had the good fortune to be part of the lives of students who are struggling to learn to read. To protect their identities as I tell their stories, I have used pseudonyms. I am thankful to these students and their parents for generously sharing their lives with me as, together, we endeavored to open the door to the world of ideas. I applaud the tenacity of these parents for seeking learning support for their children, and I congratulate their children for their willingness to persevere and become readers, despite the fact that learning to read was more labor intensive for them than for others.

Successes in this same endeavor during the 35-year history of Benchmark School have been due, in large part, to an extraordinary staff. I have learned so very much from them. A few of their stories are told in this book. In addition, I have had the privilege to sit at the feet of the giants in the fields of reading education and cognitive psychology. You will hear much more about these giants in the pages that follow, for they have inspired my work.

This project—to write about what I have learned—has been lovingly supported by my family, my staff, my university colleagues, my church, and the extended Benchmark family, all of whom have listened with patience as I have talked through my experiences to discover what seems important to share. While I wrote, my super-efficient administrative assistant, Regina Smith, and the very conscientious assistant director of Benchmark School, Sally Laird, kept things running smoothly at Benchmark. At home my husband not only made sure that meals were prepared and the TV and other interruptions were kept low, but he also made sure that I was whisked off periodically to be with our ever-supportive boys, Rick and Robb, their gracious wives, Bronwyn and Jennifer, and their very special children, our grandchildren.

Because I wanted to represent accurately what happens at Benchmark, whether it was in classrooms, offices, mentor rooms, playgrounds, or in between, I asked staff members to read and react to chapters as they were written. I am tremendously fortunate to work with a group of professionals who enthusiastically embraced this project. The following staff members each read and reacted to at least one chapter in the book: Sue Arabia, Susan Audley, Maria Berger, Karen Berry, Dawn Christopher, Sherry Cress, Alexandra Cummin, Betsy Cunicelli, Amy Cuthbertson, Joan Davidson, Susie Delemitas, Barbara Demos, Denise DiCocco, Eleanor Gensemer, Lynn Gonzalez, Tom Hurster, Edie Isaacson, Kathy Junod, Ruth Kelemen, Sally Laird, Helen Lawrence, Deborah Lee, Adam Lemisch, Eric MacDonald, Sandy Madison, Drew McCorkell, Barbara Mistichelli, Kim Munday, Susan North, Deedie O'Donnell, Colleen O'Hara, Joyce Ostertag, Ethan Pennington, Val Polaha, Nancy Powell, Beverly Prince, Melinda Rahm, Jami Reish, Kristina Reisinger, Janice Sands, Eric Satlow, Theresa Scott, Judy Sennett, Jackie Sheridan, Linda Six, Marianne Smith, Zeffie Spirokostas, Megan Walter, and Cindy Whittle.

I am especially grateful to Eric Satlow, my research associate, who read and reread specific chapters as I tried to clearly express the influence of research and theory on how we teach and interact with students at Benchmark. My son Robert Gaskins, a reading educator at the University of Kentucky, was also drafted to provide feedback on a few of the most challenging chapters, and I greatly value his reflective responses. Thorne Elliot, a now-retired but long-time Benchmark teacher, also was most helpful in sharing her genius for written expression regarding several perplexing issues.

Two members of the Benchmark family read, reacted to, and proofread every word of this book: Lynn Gonzalez, one of Benchmark's development directors, and Dick Gaskins, the president of Benchmark's Board of Directors, who also happens to be my number-one helpmate and loving husband. Their kindness and support went above and beyond! A special thanks to Lynn Gonzalez for also completing many of the graphics. In this department Lynn was assisted by Layne Graff, whom we called upon to complete the most intricate of the graphics. Allison Dagen and Kathleen A. J. Mohr, selected as reviewers by Chris Jennison, my editor at The Guilford Press, provided excellent suggestions. Finally, I would like to express my appreciation to Chris, who gently persisted until he persuaded me to take on this book project, then deftly guided me through the process with sage counsel and exquisite timing, as well as Anna Brackett, editorial project manager, and Margaret Ryan, copyeditor, who worked so conscientiously and thoughtfully to make this book as perfect as possible.

Contents

PART II

CONTEXT AND THEORIES OF LEARNING

PART III

CLASSROOM IMPLEMENTATION

SUCCESS WITH STRUGGLING READERS

PART I

STRUGGLING READERS

When instruction occurs in an inviting setting with a caring and knowledgeable staff, struggling readers are more likely to be interested in the learning opportunities that are provided.

CHAPTER 1

Searching for Answers to the Why and How of Struggling Readers

In this book I take the reader with me on a 45-year odyssey in search of answers to two questions:

1. Why do some bright students fail to learn to read, despite receiving the same instruction, from the same teachers, in the same classrooms in which their classmates succeed?
2. What, if anything, works when teaching struggling readers to read?

The answer to the first question, I suspect, has to do with the fact that no two people are alike—that it is our differences that define who we are. In this book we explore those differences and their implications for instruction. One implication I suggest is that as long as educators believe they have discovered *the* one best approach for teaching all students, it is a certainty that the instructional match will be a poor one for some students. When this is the case, students will struggle and fail. When educators understand differences among learners and adjust instruction accordingly, students succeed.

The abbreviated answer to "What works?" is: a caring teacher who knows a lot about current research and theory in education and psychology and, as a result, is an expert at such tasks as managing a classroom, teaching students explicitly how to accomplish school tasks, and scaffolding instruction to support students where they are. In this book I elaborate on what the Benchmark School staff and I have discovered about what works as well as why students fail to learn to read and how this failure can be turned into success. As a backdrop for answering my opening questions, in this chapter I provide background information about my personal experiences in teaching struggling readers and how these experiences led to the founding of Benchmark School. I also introduce Benchmark's students, staff, parents, and programs.

3

HISTORY

Teaching and Learning to Teach

An overriding concern I had during the 1960s was the tendency of educators and psychologists to look for the reason for poor reading within the child. The rationale seemed to be, if everyone else in the class, except Johnny, is learning to read as a result of what is happening in the class, then there must be something wrong with Johnny. Rarely was the instructional approach questioned. My hypothesis, however, was that perhaps most students were learning *in spite of* teachers or programs. Looking back on the first elementary school reading class I taught, I certainly suspect that was the case. I now believe that the successful students in my class either adjusted their way of learning to match the way I taught, or they figured out how to read on their own. If I am right, the very students who were unable to adjust to the way I taught and who needed instruction tailored to the way they learned were the ones who did not get taught. Certainly the easy-to-teach students were in the majority in suburban schools, and many teachers like myself may have deluded themselves into thinking they were teaching. In actuality, the very students who needed teaching may not have been taught, because they needed something different from what I knew how to present. As I continued to work with struggling readers, I also continued to wonder if the reason some students struggled in learning to read might lie in how we taught them, and I pondered whether all children might succeed in learning to read in the early grades if we changed our instruction to meet each child where he or she was at in the reading process.

As a result of these wonderings, two activities occupied much of my time during the 1960s: one was trying to teach all my students to read, and the other was attending graduate school to acquire the knowledge of research and theory that would help me reach that goal. The two questions above (Why do some students fail? What works?) provided the purpose and focus for my ongoing knowledge quest.

It was exciting to be a student, and later a research assistant, at the University of Pennsylvania in the 1960s. Penn had received one of the First Grade Reading Studies grants, and I loved being in on the comments Wesley Schnyer, Penn's principal investigator, made after his visits to the Philadelphia classrooms that were using one of the two reading methods he was comparing. The methods being compared in the Penn study were a traditional basal reader approach and a linguistic approach. Charles Fries, the author of the linguistic approach the Philadelphia schools were using, was at Penn at the time and one of my professors. One of his instructional axioms was that beginning readers' texts should contain no pictures because students need to focus on the minimal differences in words, rather than rely on pictures for clues. The texts for the linguistic program contained few high-frequency words (e.g., *the, are*) unless the high-frequency words contained a common spelling pattern (e.g., *in, at*). This alone, I thought, made for some pretty bland and awkward reading, made even less appealing by a lack of illustrations. However, much to my surprise, not all struggling readers agreed with me.

As part of a two-semester clinical course, Penn's reading majors tutored struggling readers using Fries's approach, among other approaches (e.g., Fernald, basal, synthetic phonics, language experience). I can remember thinking, "How will I ever motivate students to become excited about a character named Dan, who is asked to fan the man in the tan van?" However, unexpectedly for me, a few of my students thrived using this approach, apparently as a result of the comfort they derived from being able to decode all of the words in the text, due to the words' consistent rhyming structure. Some students actually deemed the linguistic approach as the method that helped them the most. This estimation, however, was not expressed by most of my students, some of whom seemed not to notice the minimal visual differences between words such as *man* and *men* or *let* and *lit*. I was learning that different approaches work for different students, and that student differences affect success in learning to read. Researchers at the 27 universities that conducted First Grade Reading Studies concluded that no one method was significantly superior to the others. It appeared that it was the teacher who made the difference, not the method or materials (Bond & Dykstra, 1967). I was delighted. This huge study confirmed what I suspected—it is how knowledgeable a teacher is in meeting students where they are that really counts.

During the 10 years in which I was completing graduate work, I also gained experience teaching struggling readers in public and private schools, as well as in a growing private practice in my home. In 1968, in addition to teaching in my private practice, I began teaching several reading methods courses at Penn. By that time I had grown dissatisfied with the instructional options and prognosis for struggling readers prevalent in the 1960s. With few exceptions, the programs then in place did not produce students who eventually returned to regular classes and functioned academically on a level commensurate with their abilities, or even on a level equal to average students in their grade placement. As we entered the 1970s, it was clear to many parents, and to me, that the programs for remediating reading problems and preparing poor readers for successful school experiences were not working. There had to be a better way. That better way, I knew, would be based on the realization that there is not one best way to teach children to read, to learn, or to think. Instead, instruction needed to be grounded in research-based principles of instruction, one principle being that *children learn differently*. I found myself sharing theories with my Penn students about reading instruction that were based on findings I had gleaned from the research but not actually tried in a classroom. I longed for a school where I could try out my theories about research-based instruction for struggling readers.

Founding a School

I did not have to wait long for that school. In 1970 several events conspired to force me to step out on faith and make my dream for a school a reality. One event was that the church to which my husband and I belonged had just finished a beautiful new educational building, and our pastor, George Eppehimer, asked if I would like to start a school there. That opportunity got me thinking seriously about starting a school. The deciding event was a visit from the manager of the township in which our home was located. He knocked on my door in the spring of 1970 and informed me that my neighbors had complained about my running a school in my home, something not allowed in our Pennsylvania township. Their evidence was the two to four cars that were frequently parked in front of our house. I countered that I was not running a school. I only tutored students, some individually and some in small groups. He asked how many students I worked with each week. I mentally counted my students and surprised even myself when I discovered that I was teaching 42 students a week. The township manager said that 42 students constituted a school. He suggested I find another location for my school.

Seventeen of those 42 students formed the nucleus for what was to become Benchmark School. Benchmark began as a half-day, released-time school, with students returning in the afternoon to their neighborhood schools. Before long those of us teaching at the school realized that struggling readers need support throughout the school day in all of their courses. By 1973 Benchmark was able to offer both a half-day and a full-day program. Both options included a daily 2½-hour reading block that featured a great deal of reading and responding to what was read (Gaskins, 1980). The half-day program was phased out during the early years of the school because it separated the teaching of reading from the rest of the curriculum. Now all children who attend Benchmark School receive a full elementary and middle school curriculum. We have grown from a school of 17 students to our present enrollment of 204. Currently, the student body consists of 130 lower school students and 74 middle school students.

As it began, Benchmark remains an independent school for children who read below grade level, have average or above-average intelligence, and whose reading delay cannot be attributed to primary emotional or obvious neurological problems. Many of our students enter the school as nonreaders, with the remaining students entering the school reading below fourth-grade reader level. Our goal as we began the school was to guide poor readers in grades 1–8 to read on a par with their potential. Those who worked with me agreed that children learn differently, and that a one-program-fits-all approach to teaching would not be appropriate for, or fair to, our students. We believed that students who had not experienced success in learning to read had been victims of instruction that did not match the way they learned. As a result, Benchmark's teachers had to know how to teach using many different approaches or methods and to adjust these, as well as the skills and strategies they taught, to the needs of individual students.

Although Benchmark began as a school whose major focus was teaching reading to struggling readers, the school's interest from the start was the total child. We wanted each student to experience success and, as a result, develop a sense of self-worth and self-confidence that we knew were prerequisites for their being willing to take the risks that are necessary for further academic success. Our goal was not only to provide each student we accepted with a successful academic experience during the student's stay at Benchmark, but also to equip him or her with the heuristics (informal methods for learning independently), strategies, and skills needed to cope with the demands of the educational settings students would encounter after Benchmark.

Our early years were exhilarating; we could see that we were achieving these goals, despite many obstacles. For one thing, as a new, unknown school we had to accept students on whom others had given up, often students whose difficult behavior appeared more prominent than their reading difficulties. Yet Benchmark teachers were able to love those students who rejected their love, to see positive attributes in each student, and to persist in finding a way to reach each one. The staff planned extensively, worked as a team, and studied hard to grow professionally. Their rewards came in the form of each tiny step forward, each sign of interest, each acknowledgment that learning to read was possible, and, most of all, each student we caught mesmerized by a book.

Growing a School

The Physical Plant

Benchmark opened its doors as an incorporated, independent school in the fall of 1970. We began classes in a damp church basement not far from the Wallingford train station rather than in the country church's new educational building, as originally planned (but that is a story for another day). As a result of an influx of state-funded students, we grew quickly, necessitating the rental of additional space from the Wallingford–Swarthmore School District. We even dared to think about building our own building.

In the spring of 1974, a 10-year-old Benchmark applicant led me to an idyllic piece of land for a school: 68 mostly wooded acres in the middle of the hubbub of suburban Delaware County. The goal was to scrape up the money for 7 acres and hope that, over time, we could acquire more acres. Lyman Perry, a newly minted architect and husband of a Benchmark teacher, was drafted to design the building—and what a design it was! Ten classrooms opened into a large library with a cathedral ceiling and skylight. A mezzanine surrounded the library, looking down on the library and classrooms. My office and those of other administrators would be situated on the mezzanine. The design was simple, functional, and breathtaking. Builders bid on constructing it and came in with bids well beyond the mortgage any bank would give us. One builder agreed to build as much of the building as we could afford, and walk away from the building when we reached that amount. And that is exactly what happened.

In August 1975 we called the 128 parents of Benchmark students and asked them to volunteer to help us finish the building, so that we could begin school in the building

Building community is particularly important for struggling readers who participate in programs that draw students from many locales. In this picture students and staff enjoy an assembly in the Carrington Commons.

the day after Labor Day. Each family was given a specific responsibility and worked at the school with my husband, boys, and me every night and weekend until the building was fit for occupancy. That was another amazing story! School began, as scheduled, in the new building.

In 1978 we added a second building, a gymnasium designed in the same contemporary style as the classroom building. The enrollment of the school continued to grow, and we added four classrooms and a large science room in the basement of the original classroom building. Next, in 1982, we built the Perot Wing, which added four classrooms, six offices for psychologists and counselors, an art room, and a conference room, followed in 1992 by the addition of the three-story Preston Wing, containing a curriculum library on the top floor, 12 offices and a science room on the middle floor, and an auditorium and kitchenette on the bottom floor—1992 was the year that I swore I would never build another building, but I had to eat my words.

In the fall of 2002 the middle school moved into a spacious, new, two-story wing, the Dorrance Hill Hamilton Wing, with six classrooms and a huge commons area on one floor and, above it, two office suites totaling 14 offices, plus a second and larger conference room to better accommodate our ever-growing staff. Probably the most remarkable building feat at Benchmark is our A. Palmer West Performing Arts Center, which opened just in time to host a series of lectures by Howard Gardner in March of 2003. The architecture is, again, breathtaking. Its most noticeable feature is the mammoth glass window located behind the stage that runs the full length and height of the stage and allows guests to view the heavily wooded setting of the school.

Along with the construction of new buildings, we have also renovated older building spaces. As just one example, the 10 lower school classrooms were most recently renovated by adding 12 additional feet to each classroom, primarily to accommodate the increased staff in each classroom as well as the addition of many computers.

The grounds, too, have increased. We now have 23 acres of woods, buildings, playgrounds, challenge courses, and playing fields. Unfortunately, the remainder of the original 68 wooded acres located on the shore of a beautiful reservoir was snapped up by developers before we could acquire it.

The Students

Since the founding of Benchmark, our students have had two things in common: They struggle in reading and/or writing, and they have average or above-average ability. Although in our early years most of our students were state funded, this has not been the case since the early 1980s. During the most recent years, Benchmark students have tended to be predominantly white, middle-class students with an average Wechsler Intelligence Scale for Children (WISC-III or -IV) Full Scale IQ of 110–115. A few students each year are African American and Asian American, as well as children of recent immigrants to the United States. Most of our students are privately funded with about 10% receiving tuition assistance and 3% receiving state funds. During school year 2004–2005, 204 students arrived at the school each day from as far away as New Jersey and Delaware, as well as Philadelphia and areas north of Philadelphia. Others live on the main line in the townships of Delaware County, Montgomery County, and Chester County

Most students have higher Verbal intelligence scores than Performance scores and tend to have low Information, Arithmetic, Digit Span, and Coding scores as compared to their other subtest scores on the WISC-III. This pattern may change as more children are evaluated using the WISC-IV.

Most students enter Benchmark when they are between 7 and 10 years of age, and most enter as virtual nonreaders. Most students remain at the school through the age of 14, although no new students are accepted who are older than 11 years, 11 months. All students who enter the school are performing below expectation for their age in reading and writing, with most exhibiting poor decoding and spelling skills. A few of the characteristics most often mentioned in reference to entering Benchmark students are inattentive, disorganized, passive, impulsive, rigid, not persistent, intellectually curious, verbal, and charming.

characteristics of students

During recent years students' average length of stay has been 6 years, after which most enter a full-time regular school setting, reading at or above the mean percentile in reading of the receiving school's student body. Our placement and follow-up department tracks the progress of our graduates for at least 5 years after they leave Benchmark. Our data suggest that almost 100% of our former students attend college and most graduate from college, with a surprising number going on to graduate school to complete, for example, law degrees or PhDs.

The Staff

The original staff of Benchmark School joined me because of the prospect of an exciting project and belief in the school's mission. For the most part the staff included parents of students in my tutoring practice, graduate and undergraduate students whom I taught at the University of Pennsylvania, and friends from church. The teachers all had master's degrees in reading and, like me, enjoyed professional growth and challenging students. Staff members' interest in professional growth, which has continued to the present day, is one of the secrets behind our success with struggling readers. We never believe that we have "arrived." We know there is always more to learn, so that we can better meet the needs of our students.

The school began with three dedicated teachers who were graduates of Penn's reading program. Kate Perry worked with the youngest students, Barbara Grove taught the middle group, and I taught the oldest students. In the next 10 years we added more outstanding graduates from Penn's reading program. They proved, time and again, that a school is as good as its teachers. They were what made the school great. Among those teachers from Penn were Thorne Elliot, Norma Notzold, Barbara Barus, Janet Rogers, Sally Ross Laird, Suzie Perot, Penny Moldofsky, Michelle Hoffman, Rebecca Hemphill, Judy Beck, Caroline Curtis, Emily Moorhead, Valerie Maerker, Ellen Reider, Nancy Stevens Powell, and Mary Beth Casey Humbert. All brought to their teaching rich theoretical and research knowledge about teaching reading, and during their time at the school, that knowledge continued to grow. Many have now moved on to positions of leadership in other schools, taking a bit of Benchmark with them. I am very proud of what they have accomplished. In addition to recruiting my Penn students, I found fabulous teachers at such unexpected places as the Little League field where my boys played baseball (Marj Downer and Nancy Brown).

A multidimensional approach recognizes that students learn differently and will need instruction matched to the approach and level that works best for each of them.

Most head teachers began at the school as student interns or aides. It has been our practice since the beginning of the school for each teacher to have an assistant, either an aide or a co-teacher. In more recent years the aides have been called *support teachers*. Support teachers are college graduates, sometimes with a master's degree, who are exploring the possibility of becoming teachers at Benchmark. During the recent past, each of our 10 lower school head teachers has had two assistants. Sometimes both are support teachers, and in other classrooms the teacher's assistants may be a support teacher and a co-teacher. In the middle school, some classes have two assistants, others have one. We view these assistant positions as a way of training staff to become head teachers.

The current staff of 90 includes 17 head teachers, 30 co-teachers and support teachers, 5 mathematics teachers, 5 special subjects teachers, 7 support services staff (psychologists, counselors, social workers), 1 reading tutor, 2 librarians, 7 academic coaches/supervisors, 4 development personnel, 2 bookkeeping, 4 front office, 1 Word Detectives sales, 1 drama club coach, 1 speech and language therapist, 1 information technology coordinator, 1 building and grounds maintenance employee, and the director of the school—the role I fill.

The Parents

Benchmark's parents come from all walks of life. In the majority of cases, both parents work outside the home. Since the founding of the school, parents of Benchmark students have signed a contract that commits them to supporting their child's program at the school by supervising 2 hours of homework each evening, as well as taking part in parent conferences, educational parent evenings, and volunteer activities. Most of our parents are actively involved in these endeavors and run many volunteer projects at the school. For example, to mention only a few of the volunteer projects, the Benchmark Parent Association (BPA) provides daily assistance in shelving books in the library, runs a pizza and milk program for students, provides children's programs, collects bonus coupons, sponsors a 3-day book fair, tape-records books, plans social functions, and raises money for special projects.

Homework checklists, with space for notes to and from parents, are sent home nightly by the teachers of the younger students, and assignment books are used with older students. Parents of students in the younger classes at Benchmark are asked to read to their child for 20–30 minutes each evening in a read-aloud book provided by the school that is at their child's intellectual and interest level. In addition, parents agree to supervise their child's 30 minutes of reading in a text at his or her independent level. At the lowest reading levels, parents listen to their child read to them, or they may choral or echo read with their child. At higher reading levels, parents help children schedule a regular time for homework and arrange for a quiet place for their child to work independently. Parents are asked to check to see that their child has satisfactorily completed the written response to reading that accompanies nightly reading. Parents also may be asked to work with children on math flash cards or to check math computation. Additionally, parents are expected to take an interest in social studies, science, and health projects and support these in any way they can. For children at the beginning stages of reading, meetings are held to train parents in how to support the Word Detectives decoding program taught at Benchmark (Gaskins, 1998).

Communication between teachers and parents is frequent. The homework checklist is a daily means of communication and phone calls to and from home are commonplace on an almost weekly basis. In addition, communication by e-mail is becoming popular. Parent conferences are held each trimester, as well as additionally as requested. Teachers of the younger students usually send home a monthly newsletter that reports events of the past month and previews what will be studied in the coming month. Each Wednesday the school sends home what has become known as "the Wednesday announcements" to keep parents aware of events happening at the school. The Benchmark staff takes communication with parents very seriously.

THE SCHOOL'S ORGANIZATION, PROGRAM'S, AND PROFESSIONAL DEVELOPMENT

Organization of the School

For the past 15 years the school has been organized into a lower school and a middle school. The lower school is composed of students in grades 1–6, although grade levels are not used to determine placement at Benchmark; instead students are grouped based on their reading levels and ages. Classes are composed of between 11 and 13 students who are reading at two or three contiguous reading levels (e.g., 2-2, 3-1, 3-2). Students in each class would be those generally thought of as first/second graders, second/third graders, and so on.

Lower School

Lower school students receive literacy instruction from 8:15 until 11:00 each day. At 11:00 students begin their afternoon schedule, which includes 40-minute periods: lunch and recess (daily), math (daily), science (two or three times weekly), social studies (three or four times weekly), physical education (two times weekly), music (one time weekly), art (one time weekly), health (one time weekly), handwriting (two times weekly), and class meeting (one time weekly). A read-aloud period is also worked into each day's afternoon schedule. The head teacher teaches the literacy block and social studies and oversees the lunch/recess block. Generally, special teachers and support services are in charge of the remaining blocks. In the youngest class the head teacher also teaches science, as well as writing in the afternoon. Thus, the youngest students receive one period a day more of literacy instruction than students in the other lower school classes.

Middle School

Middle school students are designated as first-year, second-year, and third-year students. The first-year classes are composed mostly of seventh graders, with a few sixth graders. Second years are mostly eighth graders, and third years are students who have not yet turned 15 and who choose to remain for an extra year to better prepare for entry the following year into a traditional high school.

Middle school students change classes every 40 minutes, except for the 80-minute literacy period prior to lunch. Middle school students all have 40 minutes of science and 40 minutes of social studies each morning, followed by a 30-minute mentor period before the 80-minute literacy block. Next, there is a 40-minute period for lunch and socializing, followed by 40 minutes of more literacy instruction. The final two periods of the day are devoted to math and special subjects.

Support Services

The seven professionals in this department, composed of psychologists, counselors, and social workers, are assigned as consultants to lower school classrooms; they have a caseload of approximately two classes. Their job is to get to know the students, parents, and teachers associated with their classes and to provide any services that will support the children in the classes to which they are assigned. For example, these professionals facilitate weekly class meetings, mediate discipline problems, run small groups, provide parent programs, see students individually, organize case conferences, and collaborate with teachers in planning for each student. Each support services member is an integral part of several classroom teams.

Curriculum and Instruction

Much of Benchmark's curriculum and instruction is homegrown; it is based on research, theory, and what works with Benchmark students. How we teach and what we teach are continually evolving as we study the professional literature and gather data about the progress of our students. This book tells the story of curriculum and instruction at Benchmark, and I leave it to the reader to seek out information in the following chapters that is relevant to his or her students.

Special Programs

In addition to teaching the traditional elementary and middle school curriculum in a not-so-traditional way, Benchmark offers many extras for its students. Some lower school students participate in a taped-repeated-reading program, and some middle school students use taped books to support the voluminous reading done in the middle school. For our youngest readers we have a books-in-bags program, in which children take home a bag of three to five "little books" for the week, then are "checked out" by our reading tutor, usually referred to as the books-in-bags lady. Other special programs are readers theater, drama club, and after-school guided study. One of our most exciting events is the production of a Broadway musical each year by the middle school, including making sets and running the technology booth. In addition, after-school activities include an outstanding soccer program, a ropes course challenge club, girls' club, chess club, basketball, golf, chorus club, and much more.

Professional Development

For 35 years long-term, in-depth professional development has been the foundation upon which Benchmark teachers have built a top-notch program. Professional development is a way of life at Benchmark. The school is characterized by staff inquiry, collaboration, and continuous improvement. It is a learning organization. The staff believes that, if the goal of schooling is knowing how to learn and understand, then it follows that teacher training should be grounded in the knowledge of how students learn and understand. Our inservice programs, retreats, seminars, and workshops throughout the year explore the what, why, and how of classroom presentations—presentations that are tailored to the characteristics of learners and emphasize major concepts and principles, together with strategies for learning and understanding.

To achieve satisfactory progress, struggling readers not only need to experience high-quality, explicit instruction and maximum time on task, but they also need to be in an environment that supports their social needs.

Events that facilitate professional development are monthly inservice meetings, often led by a well-known educator or psychologist and sometimes led by our own in-house experts; weekly research seminars co-led by the director and research associate; weekly meetings with academic coaches/supervisors; and team and department-level meetings. An interactive journal, passed between a teacher and academic coach as they observe each other teach, is a great facilitator of professional growth. Professional development is augmented by a large professional library of up-to-date books and professional journals, which are kept in circulation by the school's librarian. In addition, there is always at least one research project and one curriculum development project being carried out at Benchmark. For example, currently Eric Satlow, our research associate, Linnea Ehri, our word-identification consultant, and I are analyzing 11 years of Benchmark word-identification data, whereas others are conducting an ethnographic study with Michael Pressley about the workings of Benchmark School. With respect to curriculum development the staff has developed programs for process writing, word identification, and strategies across the curriculum. In addition, the staff has collaborated to develop conceptually based instruction in mathematics, social studies, and science. Without a strong emphasis on professional development, Benchmark would not be able to present a schoolwide, coordinated program that allows our students a chance to be the best they can be.

OVERVIEW OF WHAT IS TO COME

The remainder of this book attempts to answer, in depth, the questions posed at the beginning of this chapter:

1. Why do some bright students fail to learn to read, despite receiving the same instruction, from the same teachers, in the same classrooms in which their classmates succeed?
2. What, if anything, works when teaching struggling readers to read?

Benchmark's Interactive Learning Model is discussed in Chapters 2–6 as a way of examining the variables that the Benchmark staff believes interact to determine the ease with which children learn to read. Chapters 3 and 4 explore characteristics of struggling readers and how we help students cope with characteristics that may prove to be roadblocks to learning. Chapters 5 and 6 deal with situation, task, and text variables that influence learning to read and with which students and teachers need to be aware.

Chapters 7–9 introduce the learning principles that guide instruction in Benchmark classrooms, whereas Chapters 10–13 illustrate how the Benchmark staff applies these principles to teach students procedural knowledge, including how to decode and complete other school tasks such as comprehending text and organizing long-term projects. Chapter 14 describes how we teach declarative knowledge by emphasizing concepts, essential understandings, and knowledge structures. The final chapter is a summary of some of the insights I have gained from 45 years of teaching struggling readers.

A library at the center of the school is a daily reminder that reading many books at an appropriate level is the key to success as a reader.

At Benchmark we have discovered that struggling readers not only can be taught to read, but they can be taught to succeed well in schools that place a high premium on learning, thinking, and problem solving. We believe this goal is achieved because Benchmark teachers understand individual students and apply student-centered, research-based principles. To achieve this accomplishment requires a great deal of knowledge. The goal of this book is to share some of the knowledge that the Benchmark staff has acquired over many years.

CHAPTER 2

Introduction to Benchmark's Interactive Learning Model and Person Variables

The history of Benchmark is the story of the evolution of a model of learning and a set of principles about how struggling readers learn. The model and principles are based on our study of the professional literature in reading, education, and psychology and our experience implementing research-based practices in Benchmark classrooms. Our study and experience, which began with the inception of the school, are at the core of our practice.

In its early years, when Benchmark was a "released-time school," students attended the school for 2½ hours for reading and language arts instruction and returned to their regular schools in the afternoon. This part-time schedule allowed the teaching staff of this nascent school to engage in hours of bag-lunch seminars. The topic of discussion was always the same: What do research and theory have to say about how children learn, and how can we apply our findings to helping our struggling readers learn to read?

It was an exciting time at Benchmark and in the history of learning theory. Behaviorism was fading in popularity and cognitive science was emerging to fill the void. We pored over professional journals and texts and discussed what we were learning. These discussions developed into a formalized practice known as "research seminar," a practice that continues today as an integral part of life at Benchmark. Today the focus of research seminar is as it began: What do research and theory have to say about how children learn, and how can we apply our findings to helping our struggling readers learn to read?

THE INTERACTIVE LEARNING MODEL (ILM)

Benchmark's Interactive Learning Model (ILM) grew out of our research seminar and serves as our foundation for decisions and actions regarding individual students. It is not, however, a static model. The ILM has evolved throughout the school's history and undoubtedly will continue to evolve in response to new research and theory. In this chapter I provide an overview of the ILM to set the course for the remainder of the book. (See Figure 2.1 for the four basic elements of the ILM and Figure 2.2 for a more elaborated version of the model.) I also provide a historical perspective on person variables, the within-person variables that are discussed in depth in Chapter 3.

Over the years, our ILM has been influenced by a variety of perspectives, including those of Patricia Alexander (e.g., 2000), Richard Anderson and David Pearson (e.g., 1984), Michael Pressley (e.g., 1995, 2002), Richard Snow (e.g., Snow, Corno, & Jackson, 1996), and others of the cognitive, constructivist, social-constructivist, and situational perspectives (e.g., Anderson, Greeno, Reder, & Simon, 2000; Lambert & McCombs, 1998; Shepard, 2000). We agree with Sarason (2004) that "learning is a process that occurs in an interpersonal and group context, and it is always composed of an interaction of factors to which we append labels such as *motivation, cognition, emotion* or *affect*, and *attitude*" (p. vii).

During the 1980s, based on the research seminar's study of the work of Ann Brown and John Bransford, among others, the Benchmark ILM became a tetrahedral model of learning (see Gaskins & Elliot, 1991). Our model stressed the complex interactions among *person, situation, task,* and *text* variables that affect learning. Our current model still features these same four variables; however, over the years the model has become more elaborated, especially as we have come to appreciate the impact that society, culture, and context have on "knowing and knowledge" (Alexander, 2000). In an earlier work (Gaskins, 2003), this model was outlined as it applies to reading comprehension.

The ILM serves as the foundation for making decisions and determining actions regarding individual students. (See Figure 2.3 for a sample of person and situation variables.) Using the ILM, the teacher assesses, usually in collaboration with parents and/

FIGURE 2.1. Four basics elements of the Benchmark Interactive Learning Model: Learning is the result of interactions between text, task, person, and situation variables.

From *Success with Struggling Readers* by Irene Gaskins. Copyright 2005 by The Guilford Press. See copyright page for photocopying limitations.

FIGURE 2.2. Elaborated version of the Benchmark Interactive Learning Model.

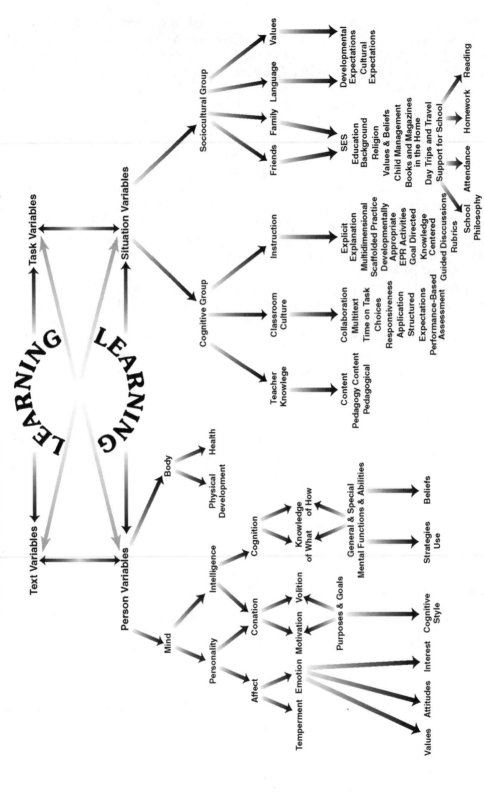

From *Success with Struggling Readers* by Irene Gaskins. Copyright 2005 by The Guilford Press. See copyright page for photocopying limitations. Portions are adapted from Snow, Corno, and Jackson (1996).

FIGURE 2.3. Person and situation variables
in the Benchmark Interactive Learning Model.

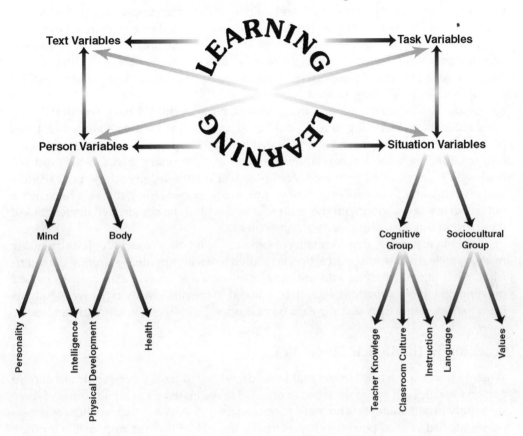

From *Success with Struggling Readers* by Irene Gaskins. Copyright 2005 by The Guilford Press. See copyright page for photocopying limitations.

or other staff members, the strengths and challenges a student exhibits with regard to person, situation, task, and text variables. Specifically, we consider:

1. Which person variables support or impede learning?
2. Which situation variables maximize learning?
3. For which task and text variables should the student be made aware and taught strategies?

Following that analysis, an action plan is created that supports the student's development as a reader and a learner.

To begin the process of exploring Benchmark's ILM, I provide a historical perspective about the person variables, which is followed in Chapters 3 and 4 with Benchmark's current thinking about this class of variables. In Chapters 5 and 6, I discuss the other three ILM variables, the outside-the-person variables found in the learning environment: the situation, task, and text variables.

PERSON VARIABLES: A HISTORICAL PERSPECTIVE

Over the course of my experience, and sometimes counter to prevailing theory and practice, I have become convinced that bright struggling readers can learn to be competent readers if teachers are aware of the person variables that are unique to each student and design reading instruction in light of these differences. In support of that conviction, I present a historical perspective of the interrelationship between person variables and difficulties in learning to read and write.

Since the first day I stepped into a classroom as a child, I have wondered why some students find learning to read so difficult. By the time I was in sixth grade, I was acutely aware of students who often seemed brilliant during discussions yet who were also regarded by some teachers and classmates as "not smart" because they did not read well. I was puzzled by the paradox—the world knowledge of these poor readers was often broader than mine, yet their written work earned failing marks. I have never outgrown my fascination with the contradictions within the personal characteristics of these bright but struggling readers and writers.

Early in my career, three domains of experience led me to conclude that struggling readers can learn to read if instruction is tailored to each individual's unique characteristics: teaching, researching, and testing. How these three experiential domains helped me conclude that instruction needs to be tailored to the differences in the way students learn to read, rather than searching for what is wrong with them, is summarized below.

Teaching in the Deficit Model Era

When I became a teacher, I found that I was drawn to students whose contradictions in person variables did not make sense to me. As I investigated the school records of these seemingly bright students who were poor readers, I discovered that teachers and psychologists had posited personal characteristics for each of them as responsible for their difficulties in reading. Some thought a particular student's poor reading was related to a below-average IQ score, some identified personality factors as the problem, and some believed that lack of effort was the missing ingredient. Still others postulated more dire etiologies that did not sit well with me. These were based on the explanations for reading difficulties popular in the 1960s: delayed development of laterality, mixed dominance, omission of the crawling stage in a child's development, and perceptual-processing difficulties. These explanations were frequently summarized as "minimal brain damage" or "minimal brain dysfunction."

The 1960s were a time of testing for, and adjusting teaching to accommodate for, visual–motor and memory deficits that coexisted with difficulty in learning, particularly learning to read. Leaders of the newly founded field of learning disabilities (LD), such as William Cruickshank, Marianne Frostig, Newell Kephart, and Samuel Kirk, looked for patterns among the deficits they observed in the test profiles of children who were bright but had difficulty learning, and then designed programs to teach children with these processing deficits. Optometrists joined the "off-task" training movement and added visual training to their practices to meet the prescribed need for children's eyes to be trained. These training programs were labeled "off task" because they trained students in the deficit areas that correlated with poor reading, rather than in the "on-task" skills and strategies of reading, such as decoding and comprehension.

I was convinced that there was nothing so different about the brains or eyes of the nonreading students with whom I worked that they could not be taught to read. I was also convinced that students would improve in whatever skill that was trained, so better to teach to the area of concern—reading. In the hope of better understanding the person variables that contributed to a child's difficulty in learning to read, I decided to pursue advanced degrees in reading and psychology.

During my early years of graduate school, I continued as a reading teacher in several schools. What always struck me when I began working with students was how different each one was. Some exhibited excellent listening comprehension, accompanied by severe decoding problems, whereas others read words effortlessly but did not understand what they read. Some were regarded as behavior problems in their regular classrooms, whereas others were shy and passive. Some bluffed and relied on their good background knowledge, whereas others had totally given up trying and were often labeled lazy. However, with daily success in reading at an appropriate instructional level, especially in the cases of my elementary students, all began to blossom, and self-concepts improved.

Researching Dyslexia

In 1965 I became a research assistant for the University of Pennsylvania's Reading Clinic dyslexia study. About the same time, I was designing and gathering data for my own dissertation research about fourth graders who were bright but virtually nonreaders. I labeled them *dyslexics*. Ralph Preston, then director of Penn's Reading Clinic, described dyslexics as students who were "stuck at the primer level." The goal of both studies was to discover the discriminating person-related variables of bright children who had extreme difficulty in learning to read, despite the same instruction that worked for their peers, and who also had no primary difficulties such as obvious brain damage or emotional, visual, or hearing problems. I hoped the discovery of discriminating variables would lead to a method or methods of teaching reading that would break these children loose from their position as older students who were stuck at the beginning levels of reading.

Results of the Reading Clinic study suggested that the neurologists, psychologists, and psychiatrists who evaluated both the students labeled *dyslexic* and the average readers in the control group were unable to distinguish between the two groups based on neurological tests, psychological tests, or psychiatric interviews. They found variability of mental functioning (e.g., memory for designs, number sequencing) and ability in both groups.

In my own research I was able to distinguish between a group of fourth-grade boys labeled *dyslexic* and another group labeled *nondyslexic poor readers*. The three factors making the largest contribution to discriminating between groups were type of spelling errors, sentence-copying errors, and time and space orientation (e.g., ability to tell time using an analog clock, interpret phrases such as "15 minutes till," know date of birth, know which months are summer and which are winter, locate the United States on a world map, know name of the state in which one lives, etc.; Gaskins, 1970). Other researchers at the time tended to label these factors as visual–perceptual or perceptual–motor deficits. I thought that the first two differences could be explained by the fact that the nondyslexics had a larger sight vocabulary; therefore, differences in spelling and copying errors should be expected because the so-called dyslexic students had not looked at, let alone learned, as many words as the comparison group. (Based on research of the past decade, I now realize that the differences in type of spelling errors reflected differences in the ability to segment words into their component sounds and match letters to those sounds.)

The third difference (time and space orientation) may be explained by the tendency of students who are experiencing extreme difficulty in learning to read to not recognize the need to actively create associations or mental anchors to something familiar as a way of orienting themselves in time and space (e.g., remember summer months by thinking: *June, July,* and *August* are short words, just as summer vacation is too short). Consistent with the Penn study, I found no differences between the two groups of poor readers on visual-, auditory-, or motor-processing measures, nor on tests of laterality. (Laterality assesses patterns of hand, eye, and foot preferences. Mixed handedness occurs when a child uses the right hand for some tasks, but the left hand for others. An example of crossed dominance occurs when a child is right-handed but left-eyed or left-footed.)

Testing Struggling Readers

As part of my graduate work, I completed the course work and internship to become a school psychologist. I had pursued this certification so that I would be able to administer the tests that would pinpoint the person variables that explained what was hampering struggling readers. What I realized after administering these tests for several years was that I learned more about the person variables that are important for learning to read when I was in the classroom teaching struggling readers than during the time I spent testing or labeling them. I was beginning to develop the theory that the vast majority of children who experienced difficulty in learning to read had no one common etiology, such as visual-, auditory-, or motor-processing difficulties. Perhaps their only common problem was that they learned words differently from the way they were taught.

Just as I was changing my view regarding testing, so were a few others in the field. At just about the same time Benchmark School opened its doors to struggling readers, a new group of LD scholars emerged, including Donald Hammill and his associates. They published research that placed in doubt the value of searching for, and teaching to, perceptual–motor and other processing differences (Hammill, 1972; Hammill, Goodman, & Wiederholt, 1974). Based on their research, and that of others, it appeared that teaching in response to perceptual and memory deficits that had been exhibited on tests (i.e., off-task characteristics) was not improving students' abilities to read and write. The prescription of this new group of LD researchers was to teach what you wanted the child to learn (how to read) rather than teaching in response to correlates of learning difficulties (e.g., poor replication of designs). For at least a decade, however, this message did not gain wide acceptance within the LD community or among parents of children labeled LD. Instead, searching for panaceas or quick fixes to learning problems was the norm in the 1970s (e.g., Feingold diet, Frostig Visual Perceptual Training), despite convincing research suggesting that time and money would be better spent in teaching struggling students how to read and write.

CHARACTERISTICS OF STUDENTS
IN A SCHOOL FOR STRUGGLING READERS

Armed with the growing hypothesis that struggling readers learned words differently from the way they had been taught previously, the fledgling staff of Benchmark School began in earnest to teach our bright underachievers to read. Our original students came in all ages, reading levels, and temperaments, as they continue to do today. Few initially exhibited enthusiasm for a second chance at learning to read. Most had become masters at work avoidance, even when the reading and writing tasks were tailored to their appropriate instructional levels. Most were either non-readers, "stuck at the primer level," or barely instructional at the second half of first-grade level. Some were as old as 12. One was a first grader who had been unsuccessful during his kindergarten experience in learning the letters of the alphabet and in learning to write his name. If there was a generality to be made about our early students, it was that the younger they were, the more easily we could engage them in learning, despite the labels that had been pinned on them that might have predicted otherwise.

Labels Don't Help Much

By the fall of 1975, there were 128 children enrolled at Benchmark School; most of them attended Benchmark for a full-day elementary curriculum, at no cost to their parents, with only a few attending on released time from their regular schools. At that time, state and school district funding was available for struggling readers if they were referred by their school district and if they were "properly labeled" for special education funding by a psychologist and either a neurologist or psychiatrist. The referral process and labeling focused on inferences that were made about the functioning of students' brains based on their performance on tests and their behavior in the classroom. Clearly, government policymakers employed a deficit/damage model. Benchmark did not. However, we *did* want to help poor readers, however they were labeled. Fortunately, because Benchmark had an excess of applicants, we were able to select and accept only children for whom our expertise in teaching reading was a good match. We limited our enrollment to students who demonstrated primary reading problems. By *primary reading problems* we mean that the reading difficulty is not secondary to serious emotional issues, acquired neurological damage, or extreme sensory deprivation, such as deafness or blindness. This is not to say we did not believe poor readers have some neurological and emotional differences. We expected that the students we admitted to Benchmark might have subtle, difficult-to-measure differences in the structures of their brains, as well as some emotional overlay from the trauma of being bright but unable to keep pace with their peers in reading and writing.

Applicants for admission were required to attend our summer program. Those who responded well to this 6-week reading and writing program were accepted for the regular school year. The person variables that all these students had in common were the same ones that had intrigued me as a child and throughout graduate school: (1) average or above-average intelligence and (2) failure to learn to read in classrooms in which their classmates succeeded in learning to read. Some of our students had been labeled dyslexic, yet the only common factor among these "dyslexics" was poor reading. The label provided no help in defining a child's learning needs or in teaching him or her. Those labeling these children as dyslexic seemed to have been using different definitions of dyslexia. Because the term *dyslexia* means different things to different people, we discourage parents and staff from using this label. However, there is no doubt in the staff's mind that dyslexia exists and that dyslexia varies on a continuum from severe to moderate to minimal. The defining characteristics are difficulty, as compared to their peers, in (1) segmenting words into sounds, (2) matching letters to sounds, (3) decoding words efficiently, and (4) reading fluently (Shaywitz, 2003). We further define dyslexia as a learning difference with lifelong residuals, such as slow reading pace and difficulty spelling, even when the dyslexic student, is quite capable of learning to read on par with his or her peers, having used a program that addresses his or her learning differences.

Formal Efforts to Understand Person Variables

Roadblocks

Although Benchmark staff members were convinced that all children learn differently and that it was our job to adapt instruction to these differences, we wanted to identify more formally the personal characteristics that our students exhibited, especially those characteristics that presented roadblocks to learning. Thus in 1978 we began the yearly administration of the Benchmark School Roadblocks Questionnaire (Gaskins, 1984).

Using this questionnaire (Figure 2.4), Benchmark teachers documented the factors that seemed to interfere with their students' academic progress. Some of the difficulties that teachers identified were related to such processing differences as organization, work pace (too fast or too slow), attention, and memory (for words and facts). However, the difficulty most often cited at all age levels was written expression (a process that seems to be an interaction between difficulties in fine motor coordination; memory for sound–letter matches in words; flow of ideas, strategy, and content knowledge; and probably other variables as well). Year after year teachers reported that almost half of Benchmark's students had either major or minor difficulty expressing themselves in writing. Despite this one similarity on the Roadblocks Questionnaire, we discovered, as we systematically gathered data across the school over many years, that no single difficulty was cited as *the* major roadblock for the majority of our students (Gaskins, 1984; Gaskins & Satlow, 2004). Despite the fact that our admission policies had become more stringent over the years, our population of struggling readers continued to display diverse difficulties. These data provided support for our hypothesis that struggling readers have different strengths and challenges, and, therefore, need the option of more than one way to learn to read. It is for this reason that we provide a multidimensional approach to teaching reading.

Further support for the contention that struggling readers have diverse profiles is found in a study by Joanne Murphy (1996), who followed up 108 young adults who had attended Benchmark School 10 years earlier, as struggling readers in elementary and middle school. She found that although some processing characteristics (i.e., poor

FIGURE 2.4. Benchmark School Roadblocks Questionnaire.

Student's Name:_____ Date_____

Person Supplying Information:_____

Instructions: Put a check in front of the items that you believe will pose the most serious roadblocks to this student's success in a regular classroom. Put a double check in front of any item that you judge to be especially detrimental to this student's ultimate progress in a regular school setting.

Academic Roadblocks

____Poor sight vocabulary　　　　____Poor listening skills

____Poor comprehension　　　　　____Poor math skills

____Poor oral expression　　　　　____Poor reading in the content areas

____Poor written expression　　　　____Poor phonemic awareness

　　　　　　　　　　　　　　　　____Poor decoding

　　Other academic factors: _____

____*At the start of the year* how would you have rated this student for phonemic awareness?
　　(Either give no check, a single check, or a double check.)

____*At the start of the year* how would you have rated this student for decoding?
　　(Either give no check, a single check, or a double check.)

Nonacademic Roadblocks

____Poor organization　　　　　____Numerous avoidance tactics

____Poor self-control　　　　　　____Poor attention and/or concentration

____Poor frustration tolerance　　____Unstable or distraught emotional state

____Works too fast　　　　　　　____Poor peer interaction

____Works too slowly　　　　　　____Little curiosity or interest

____Too teacher dependent　　　____Negative attitude

____Poor effort, not persistent　　____Poor self-concept

____Inflexible, not adaptable

　　Other behavioral factors: _____

Home and Physical Factors

____Poor physical health　　　　　____Poor quality homework

____Limited intellectual potential　____Infrequently completed homework

____Poor vision or hearing　　　　____Insufficient home reading

____Frequent absences　　　　　　____Poor child management by parents

____Poor background of knowledge　____Poor support for school by parents

____Poor gross or fine motor coordination

　　Other home and/or physical factors:_____

____No roadblocks

From *Success with Struggling Readers* by Irene Gaskins. Copyright 2005 by The Guilford Press. See copyright page for photocopying limitations.

attention and concentration) still remained after these students had attended Bench-mark, those students who had exhibited the fewest roadblocks at the conclusion of their education at Benchmark School were the most successful 10 years later. Exhibiting few or no roadblocks at the time of departure from Benchmark was more predictive of success than a student's reading level at the time of departure. Given the predictive ability of the roadblocks, these person variables are clearly an important focus of instruction.

Cognitive Styles

Other person variables became the focus of our attention during the 1980s. My interest in mental processing and style issues was piqued by the results of the Roadblocks Questionnaire and by a lecture on cognitive style given by Jonathan Baron, a professor at the University of Pennsylvania. Baron uses the term *cognitive style* to refer to consistencies in mental processing. I wondered whether or not those person variables that are variously labeled temperament, processing style, and thinking dispositions could be changed. Baron was also interested in the same question. Therefore, in the early 1980s we collaborated on a cognitive style study at Benchmark. We chose to address three of our students' problematic cognitive styles: impulsivity, inflexibility, and nonpersistence. During the first several months of the study, the students in the experimental group were instructed in small groups about how to take charge of their maladaptive styles. Upon the conclusion of that training and for the remainder of the school year, students in the experimental group met once a week with a trainer to review the goal cards that their teachers completed daily and to receive coaching about taking charge of their styles. At the conclusion of 8 months of small-group and individual training, students in the experimental group demonstrated significantly more awareness and control over their maladaptive styles than did students in the control group (Gaskins & Baron, 1985). There was a definite benefit to teaching struggling readers the metacognitive skills to cope with maladaptive styles of thinking. These results bolstered the belief at Benchmark that even something as fundamental as cognitive style could be affected by appropriate instruction/intervention. Therefore, we continue to address these and other person variables in our programs and instruction.

PRESENT-DAY PERSPECTIVE ON PERSON VARIABLES AND RELATED INSTRUCTION

Throughout our history, the Benchmark staff has pondered the effects of each student's person variables on progress in reading and overall success in learning. We initially adapt instruction to fit the characteristics each student presents and over time guide students to become aware of characteristics that interfere with success. Finally, we explicitly teach students how to take charge of personal characteristics that interfere with success in school and in life.

In the early years of the school, our mission was to help students learn to read well enough to return to a regular school placement reading at or above grade level in reading. During the years when our students were primarily state funded (between 1973

Learning to listen attentively and actively is an important goal for all students.

and 1980), school districts tended to place students in Benchmark School for 2 or 3 years. At the end of that period, students would return to regular classroom settings, often reading at or close to grade level. We followed up these students after they left Benchmark. Many had become avid readers, some even reading when they should have been paying attention to instruction. However, too many of the students who were returned to regular classrooms after only a few years at Benchmark did not fare well in the upper elementary grades. In these grades more was expected of students than reading words correctly and understanding stories. These fourth-, fifth-, and sixth-grade students needed to apply reading skills and learning strategies to the tasks of reading in the content areas, preparing for tests and quizzes, completing long-term projects, and organizing their time to meet long- and short-term assignment deadlines.

We discovered that teaching struggling readers how to read was only the tip of the "instructional iceberg." We suspected that we needed to address the entire iceberg with our instruction—addressing the inside-the-person and outside-the-person variables that got these struggling readers in trouble in the first place. We had to help students learn the declarative (the "what") and procedural (the "how") knowledge they needed to be successful in classrooms where learning became progressively more complex each year. In addition, we needed to teach our struggling readers how to cope with their maladaptive temperaments and styles, as well as to support them in dealing with affective issues. We also needed to be aware of general and special mental functions and abilities that might be roadblocks to school success and teach students how to take charge of these roadblocks and advocate for themselves regarding their special needs, such as the need for additional time for tests or an exemption from a foreign language.

All of the pieces of the "iceberg," as represented in the ILM (Figure 2.1), are part of our current program. Additionally, because we now understand that developing the tools and strategies of learners, thinkers, and problem solvers takes many years of mediated practice, most students remain at Benchmark through eighth grade.

SUMMARY

The ILM presented here is the result of years of teaching, reading, and collaborating among Benchmark teachers, grade-level supervisors, and members of our support services department (psychologists, social workers, and counselors), as well as the observations of experts who have visited the school over the years to share their knowledge. All have contributed to what has become the Benchmark Interactive Learning Model.

In the next chapter, I discuss the many person variables that the Benchmark staff currently consider strengths that can be used to facilitate progress and the variables that must be addressed directly to improve student progress.

CHAPTER 3

Exploring the Strengths and Challenges of Struggling Readers

Personality

"Why is Carl experiencing so much difficulty in learning to read?" laments a parent. The teacher replies that the reason a child struggles in learning to read is not usually as simple as attributing the reading difficulty to one factor; rather, the reason usually lies in an interaction of factors, such as person, situation, task, and text variables. In an attempt to shed some light on the mother's question, the teacher will consider a wide array of these variables.

Along with Carl's teacher, in this chapter and Chapters 4–6 we examine variables that may interact to create roadblocks to learning to read for many of our students. We begin this examination with four person variables: *temperament, emotion, motivation,* and *volition.* As Carl and other students respond to instruction in reading, these variables interact with other variables either to support success in learning to read or to present challenges. In conceptualizing person variables, we identify them as being of the *mind* or of the *body.* More importantly, we view them as interactive, not independent, variables.

The structures of the mind shape behaviors and mental processes (Wolman, 1989) and are composed of two categories: *personality* and *intelligence* (Snow et al., 1996). Personality is comprised of *affect, temperament,* and *emotion;* intelligence brings to mind *cognition* (thinking). *Motivation* and *volition* (the will to take action) are influenced by both personality and intelligence (see Figure 3.1). Each of these mind variables may act as a strength or a challenge as students learn to read. Mind variables are discussed in this chapter and in Chapter 4.

It was the personality of Carl, our struggling reader, that captured his teacher's heart. Like many other struggling readers, Carl appeared to compensate for his school difficulties with his charming personality. When we speak of personality, we are refer-

FIGURE 3.1. Structure of the mind.

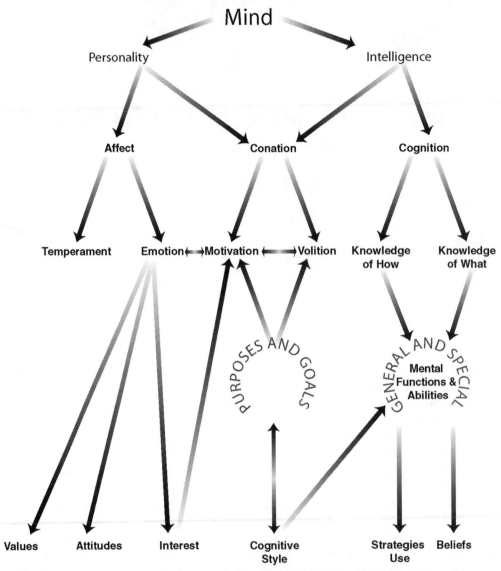

From *Success with Struggling Readers* by Irene Gaskins. Copyright 2005 by The Guilford Press. See copyright page for photocopying limitations. Portions adapted from Snow, Corno, and Jackson (1996).

ring to individual differences that are primarily noncognitive. As does Wolman (1989), we define personality as a pattern of traits that underlies a tendency to act and react consistently across time and situations. Personality includes a student's ability to interact with others—an ability that has become increasingly important in an age when no one possesses all the knowledge needed to complete complex tasks and collaboration is essential to success. Personality can be a mix of affect and conation (motivation and volition).

AFFECT

A variable frequently noted when discussing struggling readers is *affect*, or a student's usual emotional tendency. For example, during a weekly consultation with a Benchmark teacher (T), one of the school's psychologists (P) might have a conversation such as the one that follows.

P: I know you are concerned about the slow progress that Derrick is making in learning to read and that you are equally concerned about his self-concept. How would you describe Derrick's affect?

T: Derrick is usually cheerful and upbeat, which is pretty amazing in view of how difficult it is for him to decode words and the amount of reading he needs to do in and out of school.

P: I know you are also concerned about another boy in the same reading group. What can you tell me about Bill's affect?

T: Bill has *such* flat affect. He doesn't exhibit enthusiasm, nor does he complain or misbehave. He just seems resigned to the way things are.

We know that the affects exhibited by Derrick and Bill are the result of the interaction of many person, situation, task, and text variables. In working with these two students the teacher, classroom psychologist, and parents will collaborate to identify situation, task, and text variables that can be changed to improve both reading progress and the students' affective response to school tasks. In thinking about affect, they will consider its two major components: *temperament* and *emotion*.

Temperament

Based on our Interactive Learning Model (ILM), one part of affect we want to consider as we think about struggling readers is their temperament, the tendency to behave or react in a particular way. It is a style of behavior, the how of behavior, as opposed to the what or the why. Carey's (1997) longitudinal research over four decades led him to identify nine temperament traits:

1. *Activity level* (high to low)
2. *Regularity/predictability* (highly regular to irregular)
3. *Initial reaction* (bold or inhibited)
4. *Adaptability* in adjusting to the environment after the first response
5. *Intensity* (energy level of response)
6. *Mood* (from usually positive to usually negative)
7. *Persistence and attention span* (sticks with an activity)
8. *Distractibility* (easily sidetracked)
9. *Sensitivity* (the amount of stimulation necessary to rouse a response)

Temperament is quite stable over time, in contrast to emotion (the other piece of affect), perhaps because about half of a child's temperament is inherited (Carey, 1997). A variety of physical and psychological factors in the child and in the child's environment account for the other half (Carey).

It is important for parents and teachers to understand temperament, especially the inborn nature of temperament, so that they do not "unintentionally work against the child's natural behavioral style in trying to change basically unchangeable aspects of behavior" (Carey, 1997, p. *xx*). It is our belief at Benchmark that, although parents and teachers may not be able to change a child's basic temperament, they can change the way they respond to and manage it, as well as teach students how to recognize aspects of, and be in control of, their own temperaments.

As an example of temperament, let us look at category 3 in Carey's list: "initial reaction." Carl's initial reaction to any situation tends to be appropriately bold. In contrast, each Benchmark class, especially classes with new-to-Benchmark students, tends to have at least one slow-to-warm-up child. These are children who begin their stay at the school by standing on the sidelines during recess and sitting quietly at their desks, making few, if any, attempts to interact with classmates. With gentle support from their teachers over several months, these students usually make one or more friends. Teachers know that, during these early weeks at school, it is important to encourage and support these children unobtrusively, yet not to push them before they are ready to join in activities.

We have noticed, however, that for some students with slow-to-warm-up temperaments, it may take months and even several years for them to feel comfortable with the special-subjects teachers with whom they interact only once or twice a week or with the students from other classes with whom they attend a weekly double-class activity. As we have tracked these slow-to-warm-up students, we find that they do eventually become comfortable with those within the school community, although they often continue to seem withdrawn around those who are only vaguely familiar to them. This behavior is consistent with the stable nature of temperament.

Another example of temperament is a student's adaptability. Let us look at how having a nonadaptable temperament relates to success in the classroom. Typically, nonadaptable children are easily upset by changes in their routine. For example, when a teacher revises the daily schedule and decides to switch a subject usually taught in the morning to the afternoon, students with a nonadaptable temperament may react by arguing about the change or being uncomfortable or confused. Similarly, when asked to change seats with a student so that another student can see the chalkboard more clearly, a nonadaptable student may refuse to move. When a nonadaptable child's mother informs her child that the favorite shirt he or she always wears on Monday is in the laundry hamper, the child may seem to overreact to not being able to wear the shirt by pouting or throwing a tantrum. These children are not being disobedient or stubborn, although they can be taught a more appropriate means of handling their lack of adaptability. If the nonadaptable reaction is one that has been fairly common since shortly after birth, the behavior is probably due to temperament; that is, it is an innate quality of the child. The key to maintaining harmony and cooperation is to create a "goodness of fit" (a situation variable) between the child's temperament and the way the adult reacts, as illustrated in the scenario below.

T: Today we are going to change our routine so that we will be prepared for the
       social studies game we have been invited to play with Mrs. Jones's class. We
       will have social studies at 10 o'clock and continue working on our writing
       project after lunch.

S: But I can't do that. What if I forget what I was going to write?

T: Paul, you bring up a good point. Why don't you continue writing your story
       during seatwork time this morning, and you can finish your seatwork while
       the rest of us are writing this afternoon.

In this scenario, the teacher modeled being flexible while at the same time achieving
her objective of changing the schedule. Undoubtedly, if she had told Paul that he would
just have to adjust to the change in schedule, Paul's learning experiences throughout
the rest of the day might have been less productive than would be in his best interest.
At Benchmark we find that being aware of each child's typical behavioral responses
(temperament) and being willing to create a goodness of fit have a gigantic payoff: Students feel that they are in a caring environment and respond with increased productiv-
ity and learning, especially learning to read. At the same time, we coach students about
how to take charge of their negative reactions and, as a result, to improve their relationships with peers and adults. We also share with parents what we have learned about
temperament and coach them about creating a goodness of fit with their child's temperament.

   Creating a goodness of fit is a key factor in working with temperamental differences in children (Chess & Thomas, 1999; Thomas & Chess, 1977). The absence of a
goodness of fit creates a potential roadblock to learning to read. For example, creating a
goodness of fit for a student who has difficulty persisting and attending may mean providing frequent changes of activity, as we have built into our Beginning Word Detectives program (Gaskins, Cress, O'Hara, & Donnelly, 1996). Goodness of fit for a
distractible student may mean placing his or her desk facing a wall or enclosed in a
cubby. A third goodness of fit example relates to the "sensitivity" category of temperament. Students who need a great deal of stimulation to rouse a response often need
notification that in a specific amount of time, they will be expected to put away what
they are reading or writing and move on to the next activity. In such cases, Benchmark
teachers often implement a "countdown," providing the student with gentle, periodic
stimulation during the 2- to 3-minute countdown period.

   When goodness of fit is poor, the situation and the child's temperament may interact to produce negative emotions. In such cases, the child's emotional response may be
to refuse to cooperate, cry, withdraw, or become verbally abusive.

Emotion

Emotion is the other variable that teams with temperament to create affect. As the
example above and the following example suggest, emotion refers to a specific feeling
at a specific time. The emotions of frustration and anger initially are at work in the following scenario, which took place in Benchmark's after-school, guided-study program.
These are emotions that can interfere with a student's response to instruction.

T: (*kneeling beside 9-year-old Sarah's desk while other students are completing home-work*) Sarah, you look sad. Did something happen that upset you?

S: No. I just can't do this dumb math. I hate math, I hate being in math class, and I hate Mrs. S for making us do this stuff.

The next day, the conversation with Sarah took a different turn.

T: How did math go today?

S: Mrs. S saw me on the playground before school and let me come in early and work with her. She showed me how to do the math problems. I think I'm beginning to like Mrs. S.

These short scenarios illustrate that, whereas affect and temperament are quite stable, emotions are not. Emotions tend to change from situation to situation and can provide negative or positive energy for learning. For example, it is fairly common for students to carry emotions from home to school. Sometimes these are happy, productive emotions and sometimes they are not, such as when parents bicker over how accountable their child should be held for completing homework. The interaction between a student's emotional resiliency and emotionally laden home situations affects his or her availability for instruction.

At Benchmark, emotions are discussed openly with students, both in weekly class meetings led by the classroom consultant from support services and, when appropriate, in individual meetings with either the classroom teacher or a psychologist or social worker from support services. To be able to give full attention to learning, it is important for students to learn to manage their feelings. They also must be aware of how to manage the variables associated with conation, which means, in the jargon of Benchmark students, "taking charge."

CONATION

Occupying the middle position in our model of personality and intelligence variables is *conation* (Figure 3.1), the aspect of mental processing or behavior directed toward goal setting, will (Snow et al., 1996), and action; it is influenced by both personality and intelligence. Conative processes constitute a "crescendo of commitment" that runs "from wishing to wanting to intending to acting" (Cronbach, 2002, p. 87). *Motivation* and *volition* are components of conation. At Benchmark our struggling readers usually arrive wishing and wanting to read better. They seem to be motivated and to intend to put forth the effort to decode unknown words and understand what they read. However, they are easily torpedoed by self-defeating beliefs and styles, as illustrated in the student–teacher exchange below.

T: (*Stopping by John's desk, the teacher speaks quietly to him.*) I'm concerned about your not turning in your response to reading yesterday and today. Is there some way I can help you?

Frequent, usually brief, touch-base conferences allow teachers to learn about each student's strengths and challenges.

S: No, I just don't get fantasy. I can't make myself pay attention to what I'm reading when I don't get it and don't like it.

John's belief that he cannot understand fantasy, plus his passive style and sense of helplessness, undermine his conative processes. He seems to have neither the motivation nor the volition to accomplish the assigned task.

Even if John were motivated, he would not meet the criteria for conative behavior because conation suggests follow-through and conscientiousness in maintaining goal-orientated effort. Conative processes also include habitual ways of explaining success and failure (i.e., attributional styles) as well as learned industriousness and helplessness. Beliefs about personal capabilities, goal coordination, and control of attention and emotion are all conative processes. When affect interferes with cognition, conative processes can be marshaled to intervene to discipline, direct, and control mental functions, as in the example below.

S: I'm feeling really upset about a fight I had with my mother this morning. However, I'm not going to let it ruin my day. I'm going to do what Mrs. Munday taught me. I'm going to seal my upset feelings in an envelope and talk to myself about doing 10 note cards for my report on Alaska.

Examples such as this illustrate how affect, conation, and cognition are thoroughly intertwined and how children can be taught to be resilient and take charge of affect, conation, and cognition (Meltzer, 2004).

In the remainder of this chapter I discuss aspects of conation, including motivation and volition. Motivation is incentive or desire (the affective part) directed toward a particular action, whereas volition is the act of making a conscious choice or decision to take action (the cognitive part). Volition is the will or drive to achieve what one desires. *Interests* affect motivation, whereas volition is related to *cognitive style* and plays an important role in a person's realization of *purposes* and *goals*. Our experience at Benchmark suggests that students who once struggled in learning to read but do not act on their understanding of the role that conation plays in their success cannot successfully return to the mainstream, even if they read well and have an arsenal of learning, thinking, and problem-solving strategies. None of these count unless the student takes action to use them.

Motivation

Wishes, wants, needs, and goals are the province of motivation (Snow et al., 1996). Carl wishes he could decode and spell words with the automaticity exhibited by some of his Benchmark peers, but he has tried so conscientiously for so many years that he has about decided it is impossible. To both his mother and his teachers, he looks unmotivated. To his father, he seems discouraged. Is motivation one of the missing ingredients in Carl's learning to read?

Motivation is the emotional energy behind behavior and therefore affects persistence toward learning goals—that is, how much time a person is willing to devote to learning (Bransford, Brown, & Cocking, 2000). Motivation includes desiring to pursue a goal. If a student's goal orientation is directed toward performance (e.g., to earn a sticker or good grades), it is likely that the student will be motivated to persist just long enough to meet the minimum criteria for the goal, regardless of whether he or she learns or understands. On the other hand, if the student's goal orientation is to learn (e.g., to understand how to decode unknown words or how a constitutional government works), there is a high likelihood that the student will be motivated to persist until he or she feels satisfied that learning has taken place. In the past Carl has been motivated by award certificates and checks on goal cards, seemingly because this "evidence" was appreciated by his parents. His teacher wonders if, in fact, he really is motivated to *learn* the concepts that would help him decode and exactly how "deep" his understanding is of how our language works. Was Carl's real goal to take home award certificates?

Developing awareness of the value of setting goals as they relate to motivation is illustrated in the classroom scenarios below. The first scenario occurred during the first week of school as part of an introduction to goal setting in a fifth-grade class. The teacher placed a poster on the bulletin board at the front of the classroom, read it to her students, and initiated a discussion. The poster read: *A goal is the target for which a learner aims. When there is no goal, learning is aimless.*

> T: The poster I have placed on the bulletin board is a poster about motivation. Jot down on the scrap of paper I placed on your desk what you think is the point of the message on the poster as it relates to motivation. (*Gives students about 60 seconds to write.*) [We call this an every-pupil-response (EPR) technique because every pupil is actively involved.] Turn to your partner and compare what you wrote with what your partner wrote. Between the two of you decide

on an interpretation of the message on the poster and what it has to do with motivation. (*Teacher gives students 60 seconds to discuss the meaning of the poster.*) I'd like each partnership to take a turn sharing its interpretation of the message on the poster. Let's just move around the circle and when it is your turn, give your partnership's interpretation of the message on the poster. After we hear from a person, the next speaker for a partnership should either agree with the interpretation that was given, add to that interpretation, or give a different interpretation. Try not to repeat what someone has already said. George, would you like to begin? How did you and your partner interpret the poster?

S1: We think it means that if you have a goal, you'll be motivated to do it. (The teacher records on the chalkboard what each student says.)

S2: We think the same thing, plus coming up with a goal might make you want to do it more.

S3: We wondered if a purpose and a goal are the same thing. A purpose is also something that you aim to do.

S4: We agree with everything that has been said, plus we think that *aimless* means you really don't care. You have to have a goal to make yourself do stuff. If you don't have a goal, nothing will get done. That's being aimless.

S5: We think having a goal motivates you.

S6: Someone said what we were going to say.

T: Does any partnership have something more to add that hasn't been said? (*No one responds.*) Who would like to use the notes I have written on the chalkboard to sum up the class's interpretation of the message about motivation on the poster? (*A few hands are raised.*) B.J., you begin and others can add on when you finish.

S7: You learn more when you have a goal because you want to achieve your goal. That's motivation.

S8: All our teachers tell us we have to be actively involved in learning. It is easier to motivate yourself to be actively involved when you have a goal and know what you want to learn.

S9: If you know what you're aiming for, you will be motivated to go for it.

The teacher continued the discussion with an explanation of how to establish *meaningful* and relevant goals and the difference between performance and learning goals as they are related to motivation and learning. The discussion concluded with the realization among some students that, without the will or volition to achieve their goals, the goals are likely to remain unfulfilled wishes.

Goal-setting conferences are another format in which learning about goals and motivation takes place at Benchmark. In preparation for upcoming teacher–student conferences, Mrs. Arabia led a whole-class discussion with her fourth graders about "taking charge" (volition). She first asked students to write on their think pads (stapled-together pieces of scrap paper) what they think it means to be a "good student" and how they are "good students." Next, the class brainstormed a list describing what it means to "take charge." The list was posted on the classroom wall (see Figure 3.2).

Mrs. Arabia's class next brainstormed about how they would take charge in various segments of the school day. The lists developed by this class of students for taking charge of reading group, written responses, decoding, social studies, and writing can be found in Figure 3.3.

After school on the day the take-charge discussion was held, Mrs. Arabia planned for individual student conferences by thinking about each student's strengths, roadblocks, and one area in which she thought each student could begin to take charge. The next day Mrs. Arabia met individually with her students to set goals. She asked students how they would meet their goals and how they would keep track of the behaviors that helped them reach their goals. Note in the dialogue below that she begins by discussing what the student can already do well.

T: What makes you a good student?

S: I like to learn. I have a lot of background knowledge. I participate.

T: I appreciate the way you participate. You share great ideas and you are not afraid to share your opinions. You make great connections. For example, in social studies class, I liked the way you were thinking that William Clark's ability to draw maps would be useful on the expedition to explore the Louisiana Purchase. What is hard for you in school? What would you like to be able to do better?

S: When I read, I still get the little words wrong. I can figure out the big words.

T: What are you or we doing that can help with that?

FIGURE 3.2. "Take Charge" as defined by Mrs. Arabia's students.

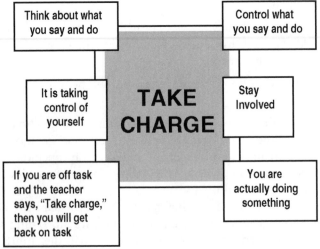

From *Success with Struggling Readers* by Irene Gaskins. Copyright 2005 by The Guilford Press. See copyright page for photocopying limitations.

FIGURE 3.3. "Take Charge" in all your classes.

READING GROUP	WRITTEN RESPONSES	DECODING	SOCIAL STUDIES	WRITING
Reread if sentence doesn't make sense	Read and reflect	Think about words and how they work	Connect what you're learning to what you know	Use big ideas to connect details
Chunk unknown words	Write something different	Try to decode	Think of big ideas	Stay involved, keep writing
Read and reflect	Challenge yourself	Chunk words	Write notes while listening/reading	Ask for clarification
Stay involved	Go back and check words	Read	Read and reflect	Remember, we are a team
Share ideas	Work without bothering someone	Make sure it makes sense	Be involved and pay attention	Talk to each other
Use strategies	Be independent sometimes		Think about what the teacher is saying	Write and reflect
Make connections	Use COPS (proofreading checklist)			Reread
Talk to other people	Underline words			Think, "How can I make it better?"
Ask about word meanings	Reread for understanding			Ask for feedback
				Make a plan

From *Success with Struggling Readers* by Irene Gaskins. Copyright 2005 by The Guilford Press. See copyright page for photocopying limitations.

S: Taped repeated reading? I think I am getting better at reading—I could read the book about Will Clark. I didn't want to stop reading. Spelling is hard, too.

T: What helps?

S: Stretching out the word, saying it first, using the 7 Steps to Good Spelling chart [Gaskins, 2000].

T: I am thinking that writing seems hard, too. You have a lot of ideas, but getting them down on paper is slow. Are you working on the computer using the word-processing program?

S: I am typing a play about Indiana Jones at home.

T: That's great. I hope you'll share it with us. When you are writing your
    response to reading, what helps you get the ideas down?

S: I'd like to keep working on saying my ideas out loud first, then writing them.
    Ms. R does that with me in after-school guided study. That helps.

T: Why don't we write that as your goal? How will you remind yourself and
    make sure you try this?

S: I can put a goal card on my desk and put a check whenever I tell my ideas out
    loud before writing.

As illustrated in this vignette, setting meaningful goals plays an important role in motivation (Harackiewicz & Sansone, 2002). We find that this principle is particularly useful
when working with struggling readers. Perhaps Carl has set an unrealistic goal for
himself in trying to read and spell at the same rate and level of automaticity as his
peers. It appears that a more reasonable goal would be to decode and spell five or six
words each day by applying what he has learned about how our language works.

Other important motivational factors include feeling competent and understanding the rationale for what is being learned. Most psychologists agree that people are
motivated to become competent (e.g., Deci, 1995; Maslow, 1968). However, for such
motivation to occur, the level of challenge must be at the appropriate level of difficulty
(Bransford et al., 2000). If the level of difficulty is too high, students become discouraged and unmotivated. They begin to feel that competence is unlikely. The need for
feeling competent is why we are so careful at Benchmark about giving students materials they are prepared to handle successfully. Motivation is also affected when students
know the reason for what they are learning or are expected to do. Students want what
they are asked to learn and do to be personally relevant (Brandt, 1998) and to benefit
them. Setting personally relevant goals to take charge of one's thinking and doing,
working at an appropriate level of difficulty, and understanding the rationale for learning and behavior tasks lead naturally to the second part of conation, *volition*. Setting
goals is a fine start, but carrying them out requires volition.

Volition/Self-Regulation

Volitional processes mediate the enactment of goals and intentions. Volition "includes
implementing and protecting goals, and managing resources to protect intentions"
(Cronbach, 2002, p. 175). Volition, or the will to take action, involves the self-regulation
of effort and action (Hofer, Yu, & Bintrich, 1998). Similar to the Stanford Aptitude Seminar (Cronbach, 2002), the Benchmark staff believes that volitional processes include
action orientation, action controls, mindful effort investment, and self-monitoring, and
we explicitly teach these metacognitive processes.

Action Orientation

Although action orientation is thought by some psychologists (Cronbach, 2002) to be a
relatively stable propensity, Benchmark teachers find they are able to influence students in this area. One way they do this is by thinking aloud as they model their own

authentic thought processes that are directed toward taking action in achieving a goal. Recently, I modeled my action orientation by sharing with a Benchmark class my thoughts about tackling a project I needed to complete. My discussion with them went something like this:

> "Twice a year I edit the Delaware Valley Reading Association newsletter. When it was time to work on the newsletter again this week, I said to myself: 'This job always seems overwhelming, so I'd better break it into manageable parts. I will edit all the articles that have been submitted on Saturday morning before I take my morning coffee break. Absolutely no coffee until I finish editing! After my coffee break, I will type all the articles into a three-column format. When that is finished, I will reward myself with a long walk. If I can just get all the articles into my computer in newspaper format, I know I can easily finish the newsletter on Sunday. That will leave me the rest of Saturday to do whatever I want.' Just having a plan of action makes me feel so much better, and I love checking off each item on my plan as I complete it. A realistic plan for completing the job led me to the realization: I'm going to be able to finish the newsletter with time to spare."

Students begin to gain insight into how an experienced thinker manages tasks each time teachers engage in mental modeling (Duffy, Roehler, & Herrmann, 1988). After teachers have modeled their thinking on several occasions, they can then ask students to think aloud as they work toward a goal or solve a problem, thereby helping students develop a habit or a general orientation to act.

Action Controls

The second part of self-regulation is action controls. Students maintain their intentions toward goals by taking charge of and controlling such factors as environment, attention, motivation, and emotion, some of which were modeled above. We explicitly teach students how to accomplish this control by guiding them, step by step, through a way of thinking and working that will establish habits conducive to perseverance. The Benchmark staff calls this procedure "Analyze the Task," but it is much more than just analyzing the task, it is a way to plan and carry out a task. This strategy is explained in Chapter 13.

Mindful Effort

A third aspect of self-regulation is mindful effort: the intentional use of nonautomatic, effort-demanding mental processes and strategies, and the flexible adaptation of mental effort. Mindful effort is frequently *not* expended by every student when approaching the many tasks that comprise a school day, from spelling to note taking. Students know basic strategies for accomplishing the tasks but sometimes do not use them because applying these strategies is a more effort-demanding mental process than the expected outcome seems to merit. Like Cronbach's (2002) group, we have learned that those students who put forth effort to specify how they plan to reach learning goals, often as a result of seeking help and self-regulation, are more likely to achieve their goals than those who do not plan. Once a student makes a plan, he or she is more likely to realize that the task is manageable—and therefore worth the effort. Planning is discussed in Chapter 13 as one kind of procedural knowledge.

Self-Monitoring

The fourth aspect of self-regulation is self-monitoring. Students who self-monitor deliberately apply learning strategies to promote deeper learning and are aware of personal limitations and situation/task/text difficulties that may impede progress. They take control of these variables, and they take control of their affective and cognitive responses. (Self-monitoring and control strategies are discussed in Chapters 12 and 13.)

In a nutshell, volition is the deliberate action to plan, control, put forth effort, and monitor a learning, thinking, or problem-solving process. Motivation alone is not sufficient for successful learning.

Teachers from our lower school through our middle school scaffold students' volitional processes. For example, in a class of second and third graders who are reading on first-reader level, lower school supervisor Colleen O'Hara had this discussion with a student who tends to understand what he reads, but who struggles to remember to apply all he knows about spelling and grammar in his written responses.

T: I see that your goal when you are completing seatwork is to proofread your written responses using your proofreading checklist.

S: Yes.

T: Why do you have that goal?

S: Well, if I want to earn a seatwork pass, I need to proofread my work more carefully.

T: So, what will you do?

S: I'll use my proofreading chart.

T: How will that help?

S: Well, it tells me each step I have to take to check my work. Like I need to check for capitals at the beginning of each sentence and for the spelling of each character's name. Here, see? (*Shows the teacher his proofreading checklist.*)

T: What will you do to check for accurate spelling?

S: I can underline a word if I don't know how to spell it and it's not in the book or on my spelling sheet. Even if I underline it, I still have to try to spell it using Key Words.

T: It sounds like a lot of work. Are you sure it's worth it?

S: Yes. Yesterday, when I used my checklist, my written response was much better. I know I'll get a day off from seatwork if I take time to follow the chart.

Although setting a performance goal and its accompanying extrinsic reward is not as ideal as intrinsic motivation, for many of our students it is the only way we have been able to get them "hooked" on the benefits of taking care of the mundane, mechanical aspects of written expression. The good news is that, with enough practice, paying attention to the mechanics of writing becomes habitual. Our students are genuinely interested in producing written work that meets the standard for sharing with others—and motivation and volition are enhanced when students are interested. The next section deals with personal and situational interests, which flow from the broader function of emotion.

Interest

Discovering what interests each struggling reader and meeting that interest with appropriate texts and projects usually enhance the chances for success with a student because of heightened attention, concentration, and positive affect (Renninger & Hidi, 2001). We define interest as feelings and attention focused toward a person, object, or activity. Interest is also the relatively enduring predisposition toward particular objects, events, or ideas (Alexander & Jetton, 2000; Renninger & Hidi, 2001). We focus on two categories of interest: personal and situational. Personal interests are comprised of a student's relatively enduring predispositions to pursue and stick with particular content over time (Renninger & Hidi, 2001). Personal interests are a deeply ingrained part of an individual's cognitive and affective nature and often serve as catalysts for the active pursuit of experiences, knowledge, and skills associated with those interests (Alexander & Jetton, 2000). Examples of personal interests might be reading science fiction, exploring the outdoors, building things, understanding how things work, and playing baseball. Situational interest is the interest that is triggered in the moment and is typically regarded as fleeting. Examples of situational interest in the classroom are interest in a novel science project or interest in text material that is particularly intriguing.

Benchmark teachers are well aware that they have more control over situational interest than over personal interest, and they endeavor to design lessons around situations students will find interesting. The factors that contribute to the development of particular interests are the knowledge and experiences students bring to the classroom plus what the classroom provides. Cultural factors also contribute to task interest and engagement. School culture that supports and empowers the development of some interests as opposed to others contributes to the development of interest, as in the case of drama club, chorus club, and the middle school musical at Benchmark. Benchmark teachers are eager to facilitate student interest in subject areas for which students have less-developed interest. Conditions that make tasks more attractive and enjoyable for students include student control and curiosity (Alderman, 2004). The goal is to transform situational interest into general curiosity that is sustainable across situations and does not require teacher intervention.

Students benefit when a teacher succeeds in eliciting interest; they experience increased attention to, and memory for, subject matter and an interest in effectively processing information (Renninger & Hidi, 2001). Interest, even when situational, enables students to focus on schoolwork. This focus is characterized by engagement and strong feelings. Not surprisingly, researchers have found that students understand and remember information better about topics of high interest than about topics of low interest (Alderman, 2004). Ron is a perfect example of this point. His interests are amazingly broad for a 10-year-old, perhaps as a result of being exposed to a wide variety of interesting experiences by his parents. Ron's interests and experiences provide anchors for understanding and remembering the concepts discussed in social studies and science, most of which he has not encountered previously in texts because reading most subject-matter texts is such a chore for him.

Edie Isaacson, Susan Audley's Benchmark support teacher, shared with me several examples of how Mrs. Audley used interest to motivate her third- and fourth-grade students for the class's explorer project. Mrs. Audley assigned an explorer to each student to research. She selected each explorer based on what she knew about each student's individual interests. For example, one student had just returned from Florida and was enthusiastic about his visit to St. Augustine, so this student was assigned to research Ponce de León, the Spanish explorer who "discovered" Florida. Another student was assigned to research the explorer who discovered Mexico, because he often shared stories with the class about a friend who had moved to the United States from Mexico. Because the selection of each explorer had been tailor-made for each student, based on a particular interest known by the teacher, all the students were eager to learn about their explorers.

Another way Mrs. Audley uses interest is to improve reading fluency is by capitalizing on students' love of performing with an activity called readers theater. The students in her class look forward each morning to spending a few minutes practicing readers theater. In visiting this classroom, you can see the very students who usually are reluctant to read come alive with interest and enjoyment. They give their full concentration to reading their lines with expression. Each student takes a turn reading a line of a poem or short story. As students practice their parts, one cannot help but notice that the result of their interest in performing is a desire to understand the poem or story. The students know that understanding what they read will lead to a better rendition of their lines. Because they enjoy entertaining their classmates, they are interested in reading well. If you listen to them when they are practicing readers theater, you would never guess that they are all struggling readers. They read with interest and enjoyment.

Cognitive Style

The concept of style, as used at Benchmark, expresses an individual's habitual use of cognitive abilities. Style is composed of consistencies in mental processing. When we refer to a student's cognitive style, we are describing a characteristic mode of attending, perceiving, or thinking. Styles are expressions of both personality and ability preferences (Snow et al., 1996). Although most psychologists and researchers agree on the existence of the constructs we at Benchmark identify as cognitive styles (e.g., reflectivity, adaptability, persistence), others have used these same terms to describe dispositions (e.g., Perkins, 1995; Shepard, 2000) and aspects of temperament (e.g., Carey, 1997; Thomas & Chess, 1977). When we talk about temperament at Benchmark, we are talking about a style of behavior, whereas cognitive style and dispositions concern mental processing. The confusion between cognitive style and temperament seems to occur because some terms, such as *adaptability*, are used to describe both cognitive style (mental processing) and temperament (behavior). This "double duty" adds to both the complexity and richness of this explanatory model.

A few cognitive style variables that are common to successful learners, and often not characteristic of the struggling readers we teach, are *attentiveness, active involvement, adaptability, reflectivity,* and *persistence*. Organization is another trait not common among our struggling readers, and we suspect may qualify as a cognitive style. Our reason for identifying these person variables is not to categorize students. Instead, our twofold goal is (1) to encourage teachers to recognize these styles and to make students aware of the role they play in becoming successful learners, and (2) to teach students how to take control of cognitive styles that may be roadblocks to successful learning, thinking, and problem solving. Identifying cognitive style variables has proved to be a powerful tool in understanding our students, precisely because these variables are central to a student's awareness and control of his or her usual pattern of mental processing. A student's pattern of mental processing determines how well he or she will succeed in learning to read and in learning to use what is read to gain knowledge and understanding.

It has been our experience that changing a student's unproductive mental processing style is easier than changing temperament (i.e., one's usual way of behaving or reacting). Perhaps this is the case in our context because our students really do care about performing well academically, and we have been successful in convincing many of them that efficient and effective styles of mental processing are keys to their success. In many of our classrooms, teachers have posters labeled "Keys to Success" upon which appear the thinking style characteristics we would like students to cultivate. (See Figure 3.4.) We call the Keys to Success ARAPA + O.

Teachers introduce each cognitive style characteristic individually, sharing the definition and relating the characteristic to people or fictional characters with whom students are familiar. For example, in discussing *attentive*, the teacher may relate the suc-

FIGURE 3.4. Keys to success.

ARAPA + O
Attentive
Reflective
Active
Persistent
Adaptable
+
Organized

From *Success with Struggling Readers* by Irene Gaskins. Copyright 2005 by The Guilford Press. See copyright page for photocopying limitations.

cess of a detective to his or her careful perusal of an area for clues. Benchmark teachers also reinforce the model for students by attributing their success to the use of the Keys to Success. For example, I have heard teachers say:

> "Some of you were very *attentive*. You never took your eyes off the board when I was modeling how to spell that word. I also observed *active* involvement. I heard you say the sounds with me for each letter pattern as I said them. I am not surprised that you were able to spell the new word correctly in your reading response."

Benchmark teachers have become masters at catching students in the act of using the Keys to Success. When I am in classrooms, I might observe a teacher whisper to a student:

> "Jill, you were the last one to put up your hand, yet you summarized the story beautifully. It is obvious that you took time to *reflect* and *organize* your thoughts. That is very impressive."

On another occasion I heard a teacher of beginning readers say:

> "I've just got to compliment one of you—you'll know who I'm talking about. This person wrote a story this morning that his partner thought didn't make sense. His partner gave him feedback about how he could improve his story, and this young man proved to be exceptionally *adaptable* and applied his partner's suggestions to make his story better."

The young children at Benchmark love being recognized in this way and beam from ear to ear when a teacher points out that they are using the Keys to Success.

A style issue that we encounter with some of our seventh- and eighth-grade students is that, despite the fact that they have learned well the tools and strategies we have taught them for achieving academic success, they lack the adaptability to use them on their own. These students can tell their teachers exactly how to complete a long-term project, study for a test, or satisfactorily complete a homework assignment. Furthermore, when it comes to reflecting on why they have been successful or unsuccessful, they are honest and accurate, stating exactly the difficulties or strengths that played into the final result. Ethan Pennington, a teacher in Benchmark's middle school, told me about a student to whom he taught English one year and social studies the following year. He found Suzie to be a puzzle. She seemed to work hard and want to do well, but she rarely followed his, or her own, advice. This is one debriefing session he had with Suzie after she failed, once again, to do well on a social studies test.

> T: What did you do while we were studying this chapter to help yourself understand the information?
>
> S: I surveyed the chapter, wrote down the purpose questions the class agreed on, took notes, and organized the notes.

T: Excellent! Did you take notes on all the information in the chapter, or just on the information related to our purpose questions?

S: Only the information that answered the purpose questions.

T: You seem to really know the strategy. You have pages and pages of notes. Were they helpful?

S: Not really. Studying them was like reading the chapter all over again.

T: Do you remember what we talked about when you handed in your first set of notes?

S: Yes, you said that I had lots of unnecessary notes about unimportant details.

T: How did you change your notes after I gave you that feedback?

S: I didn't, because I didn't want to leave anything out.

T: I know that feeling. Sometimes it takes more time to figure out what is important than it takes to just copy down everything. But in the end it will take you less time because you will have only what's important in your notes and studying will be easier.

Suzie's inability to let go of her old way of studying seemed to be due either to an ingrained style of inflexibility or to compulsiveness, and either of these characteristics might have been due to a fear of taking a risk to try a new way of taking notes. During scaffolded instruction she had demonstrated that she needed little support to successfully take brief and appropriate notes. However, on her own, she resorted to her old ways, despite the fact that she saw her classmates were successful when they used more efficient strategies. Throughout her 3 years in the middle school, Suzie continued to do it her way when she was working on her own. Such cases are rare for students who enter Benchmark when they are in the primary grades; however, Suzie began at Benchmark when she was in fifth grade. It has been our experience that the later a student enters Benchmark, the more ingrained are their ineffective coping mechanisms.

Benchmark teachers often share with their students information they learn about cognitive style variables from their professional reading. Such sharing is usually the result of concerns a teacher has about maladaptive cognitive styles exhibited by students in class. For example, on two different days a Benchmark teacher shared with students information she had learned from her professional reading related to persistence, adaptability, and reflectivity.

T: Yesterday I was looking for information about intelligence. I looked in two books in Benchmark's professional library. The books were by psychologists who conduct research about intelligent people. Both researchers commented that to be a successful learner, it is better to be persistent and moderately intelligent than to be very intelligent and not persistent [Howe, 1990; Simonton, 1994]. What do you think this means? [A discussion of the importance of persistence followed.]

A few days later the teacher shared this:

T: Another thing I learned from the book by Simonton [1994] is that people who are successful usually have failed more often than those who are less successful. Apparently people who take risks and occasionally fail are also people who are adaptable and learn from their failures. I know that Edison, the inventor we credit with inventing the electric light bulb, had many, many failures before he finally got the light bulb to work well. With each failure, Edison reflected about what he had learned from his previous failures and he tried a new approach to making the light bulb. Most successful inventors experience a lot of failures. Experiencing failures reminds me of the words of a teacher I once had. She used to say: "If you aren't making mistakes, you probably aren't learning anything new." (*As the teacher talks, she writes on the chalkboard*: failures, risks, adaptable, reflected, mistakes, learn.) I'd like each of you to write on your scrap paper a wise saying that uses at least two of the words that I just wrote on the chalkboard. (*Students write for about 2 minutes and then share their wise sayings.*)

S: If you aren't willing to risk failure and to be flexible, you won't learn much.

S: It's okay to make mistakes, especially if you learn from them.

S: When I take a risk and try doing my work a different way, I reflect on the results and figure out what worked for me.

These words of wisdom, based on an understanding of learner variables, research, and theory, are a small sampling of what Benchmark teachers share with students. In addition, students are encouraged to share personal instances of these principles so that they (the wise sayings) become really meaningful to students and part of their arsenal of heuristics.

SUMMARY

In this chapter I continued to explore the notion of person variables and presented classroom examples related to affect (temperament and emotion) and conation (motivation and volition) and the role each plays in the ultimate success of a struggling reader. It was noted that some person variables are more ingrained than others—

Just as children readily adjust to each other's differences, those who teach must adjust to children's learning differences and teach according to how each child learns best.

temperament, for example—in which case teachers must be especially attuned to creating a goodness of fit and to counseling parents to do the same. Affect is a relatively stable emotional state, whereas emotions are variable responses an individual makes to specific situations.

Motivation and volition are the two elements of conation (which is a combination of personality and intelligence) and supply the energy that allows students to respond to instruction. Interests and cognitive style can be positive or negative fuel for this energy and need to be part of the plan when teachers are designing instruction.

None of these person variables is independent. Each interacts with other person variables, as well as with situation, task, and text variables, to determine how well struggling readers respond to instruction. In Chapter 4 we continue to use the ILM to understand why learning to read is so difficult for some students.

CHAPTER 4

Exploring the Strengths and Challenges of Struggling Readers

Intelligence, Physical Development, and Health

In this chapter we continue to explore person variables that may provide insight into why learning to read is so difficult for a struggling reader. Specifically, we explore intelligence and its components, as well as physical development and health. These person variables interact with other variables to play a role in students' experience of learning to read and write. Clearly these interactions will be different for each student.

Intelligence, the second major mind category to be considered (personality was the first) involves the processing knowledge. It is often defined as the capacity to learn or scholastic aptitude (Harris & Hodges, 1995). Attempts to quantify intelligence include such individually administered tests as the Stanford–Binet and Wechsler Intelligence Scale for Children (WISC). As we observe students struggle with learning to read—many of whom have high-average or superior intelligence—we consider the variables that affect how they use their intelligence for thinking (cognition) and, more specifically, for learning to read. We consider the interactions of two kinds of knowledge—knowledge of *what* (declarative knowledge) and knowledge of *how* (procedural knowledge)—and two aspects of action orientation or conation—motivation and volition (discussed in Chapter 3). In exploring these areas, we ask: "Are any kinds of knowledge or aspects of action orientation areas of strength for a student, upon which we can build? Are there areas of challenge for which specific strategies or heuristics are needed?"

Figure 4.1 contains a schematic of the relationship of knowledge and action orientation to intelligent behavior. Several examples of intelligent behavior that we aim to guide our students to achieve are to read text fluently, understand what they read, and apply what they learn from reading. In explaining intelligence to Benchmark students, we simplify the concept to:

Intelligent behavior = Knowledge + Motivation + Control

FIGURE 4.1. How people put intelligence to work.

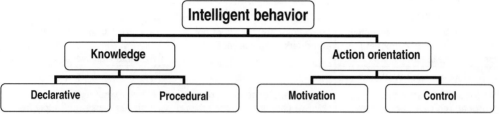

From *Success with Struggling Readers* by Irene Gaskins.   Copyright 2005 by The Guilford Press. See copyright page for photocopying limitations.

This formula for intelligent behavior is explained in Figure 4.2 which contains a sampling of the many variables that contribute to intelligent behavior. In this formula, knowledge is divided into two kinds: declarative and procedural. Declarative knowledge is the knowledge of *what*, including vocabulary knowledge, world/domain knowledge, linguistic knowledge, discourse knowledge, beliefs, and so on. Much of declarative knowledge is acquired from reading books. Therefore, the student for whom reading is a struggle may enter school with superior vocabulary and world knowledge, only to lose that standing to more competent readers a few years later. The best way to prevent this undesirable outcome is for parents regularly to read to their struggling readers from books that are age-appropriate, but which would be too difficulty for them to read and understand on their own.

Procedural knowledge—knowledge of how—includes knowledge of how to use cognitive and metacognitive strategies, how to read words fluently, how to integrate nonprint and text, how to use skills, as well as the how of countless tasks. Most of our struggling readers learn the strategies that are explicitly taught at Benchmark; however, for a few of them, learning to apply strategies, especially decoding strategies, can be a painstakingly slow process. Perhaps as a result, they often do not seem as motivated as their more successful peers.

As noted in Figure 4.2, motivation is affected by values, beliefs, goals, attributions, self-efficacy, competence, connectedness, autonomy/choice, and interests, to mention just a sampling of possible variables. Whether knowledge will be put to use or motivational desires achieved depends on whether or not a person applies strategies to take control of person, situation, task, and text variables. Taking control, the third category in our formula for intelligent behavior, includes being goal-directed, planful, and strategic. At Benchmark we believe (1) that few, if any, individuals perform as intelligently as they could, and (2) that intelligence can be taught (Gaskins, Rauch, et al., 1997). Intelligence plays its primary role in *cognitive processes*.

COGNITION

Cognition is thinking; it includes aspects of awareness, perception, reasoning, and judgment. Two major sources of input for cognition are declarative and procedural knowledge (described above). Cognition requires declarative knowledge, such as

FIGURE 4.2. Intelligent behavior = Knowledge + Motivation + Control.

KNOWLEDGE Knowledge of:	MOTIVATION Influenced by:	CONTROL Take charge of:
Content Knowledge of concepts, essential understandings, and supporting facts and /or experience.	Values and Beliefs The values and beliefs of home and peers influence motivation.	Task Analyze the task into parts and make a plan to complete the task. Be metacognitive.
How the Mind Works Knowledge that learning is intentional; requires attention and active processing; is enhanced by chunking (due to limited slots in working memory), by connecting new information to old, by periodic review, and by interaction with others.	Goals Goals shape experience by guiding how we channel attention; they provide standards for monitoring progress; specific goals increase motivation more than general goals; learning (mastery) goals foster deeper understanding than performance goals; self-improvement goals are more effective than competitive goals; individual competition is not as effective as group work.	Text Monitor what is read to make sure it makes sense and apply fix-up strategies as necessary.
Strategies Knowledge of strategies for monitoring, seeing patterns, and making inferences—see Benchmark's "Framework for Learning and Understanding," Figure 13.2.	Attributions How individuals explain success or failure is more important than whether they succeed or fail. Attribute success to goal-directed, planful, and strategic effort.	Person Take charge of personal characteristics that may hinder task completion. Take charge of actions. Actions should be goal-directed, planful, and strategic.
Self Knowledge of one's typical approach to learning tasks (e.g., attentive, reflective, adaptable, persistent, active). Knowledge of one's cognitive filters (e.g., emotions, beliefs, past understandings). Knowledge of how to be a self advocate.	Self-efficacy Learners' views of themselves are often closely connected to learning outcomes.	Situation Create the learning context that works best for you.
Situations Knowledge of situations that support and interfere with learning.	Competence/Progress Students need to see that they are making progress.	
Text Characteristics Knowledge of various genres and patterns of expository text structure.	Connectedness Learning is promoted when students feel connected to teachers and peers.	
	Autonomy/Choice Students feel personally committed to tasks they choose.	
	Interest Learners' interests influence their response to instruction.	

From *Success with Struggling Readers* by Irene Gaskins. Copyright 2005 by The Guilford Press. See copyright page for photocopying limitations.

knowing the meaning of words, and all those other bits of knowledge people learn in content courses such as social studies and science. Knowing how multiplication is like addition and that sounds heard in words map onto letters to spell those words are types of declarative knowledge. Cognition also requires procedural knowledge, such as knowing how to decode words, solve math problems, and use strategies to comprehend or complete a science project. One particular aspect of declarative knowledge, concepts, is discussed in Chapter 14. Procedural knowledge, the knowledge of *skills* and *strategies*, is discussed in Chapters 10–13.

Although Benchmark is a school for struggling readers, the primary emphasis at the school is not simply reading words; the primary emphasis is on cognition—thinking! The school's stated mission is: "To provide students with the tools and strategies they need to become lifelong learners, thinkers, and problem solvers." Teaching students to read well is only a part, albeit a vital part, of achieving that mission. In the next section I discuss general and special mental functions and abilities that psychologists delineate as playing a role in cognition.

General and Special Mental Functions and Components of Intelligence

General and special mental functions and abilities are sometimes referred to as processing abilities (e.g., working memory, attention, auditory processing, visual–spatial perception, abstract reasoning, organization). These mental functions might be thought of as the programs we run in a computer to process data. Declarative and procedural knowledge provide the data, and motivation and control provide the power and regulation. How these mental functions and abilities work can be translated into principles and practices that guide learning. These principles and practices are discussed in Chapters 7–9.

Opinions about the hierarchical relationships among, and clusterings of, these mental functions and abilities tend to vary among those who study them, although most focus on the same processes. Here I review a few of the processes found in several of these hierarchies and clusterings cited in the psychological and medical literature.

One presentation of mental functions, popular as a result of the national best seller *A Mind at a Time*, is postulated by pediatrician Mel Levine (2002). He refers to these mental functions as "systems of the mind." They include attention control, memory, language, motor skills, spatial ordering, sequential ordering, higher thinking, and social thinking. In his book Levine discusses differences in mental processing and relates these differences to learning issues—some of the same issues we see among our students, although we frame them differently, in terms of Benchmark's Interactive Learning Model (ILM). The exact delineation of categories is not foremost to us because we see the overlap of these categories as simply an example of the interaction of person variables. In another book, *The Myth of Laziness*, Levine (2003) further develops his concept of "output control," which he categorized as part of attention control in his earlier work. Output failure is an issue for many of our students, particularly with regard to written output, so this topic especially interests the Benchmark staff. However, as framed by Levine, output control (or failure) is too general a term to serve us well in constructing a model. Instead, it is a problem to be explored by studying the interaction of variables in the ILM.

Other organizational schemes for mental functions and abilities are the product of research whose purpose is to identify the underlying cognitive basis for performance on IQ tests (Stanovich, 2002). These researchers suggest such cognitive abilities as perceptual speed, discrimination accuracy, working memory capacity, and long-term memory retrieval efficiency. An example of this approach to conceptualizing mental functions and abilities is the use of the subtests of the WISC-III and WISC-IV to describe a child's processing abilities—in a sense, the computer hardware a student brings to the learning process. Awareness of a student's relative strengths and challenges with regard to mental functions and abilities provides helpful information for understanding a student (i.e., insights into which mental functions may be strengths and which may provide challenges), but the resulting profile does not tell the complete story about a student's mental functions and abilities. We need more than test-based knowledge about cognition; we also need an understanding of affect and conation (discussed earlier) and other outside-the-person variables.

Howard Gardner's *Frames of Mind* (1983) presents another way of looking at mental functions and abilities. In his original work, Gardner clustered mental functions and abilities into seven types of intelligence: linguistic, logical-mathematical, musical, bodily-kinesthetic, spatial, interpersonal, and intrapersonal . Gardner (1999) has added an eighth type of intelligence, naturalistic intelligence. He also has admitted to the "attractiveness" of adding a ninth type of intelligence, existential intelligence, but has decided that "the distance from the other intelligence is vast enough to dictate prudence—at least for now" (1999, p. 66). One of the very positive aspects of Gardner's framework is that it places value on two person variables (interpersonal and intrapersonal intelligence) that may be as important, if not more important, than the "intelligences" that are privileged in the world of school: linguistic and logical-mathematical intelligence. Particularly now in the 21st century, interpersonal intelligence is important to achieving success in the workplace, and intrapersonal intelligence, the ability to understand oneself, is a key to success both at school and at work. Another positive aspect of Gardner's framework is that it values such individual differences as musical, bodily-kinesthetic, spatial, and naturalistic abilities that are often strengths of our struggling readers, yet typically undervalued in the classroom.

Perhaps the most cited framework of mental functions and abilities is Carroll's (1993) model, which has been adapted by the Stanford Aptitude Seminar (Cronbach, 2002). Carroll's model includes the following eight categories derived from factor analytic studies:

1. Fluid–analytic reasoning (inductive, logical, and quantitative types of reasoning)
2. Crystallized–scholastic achievement (verbal comprehension, reading comprehension, phonetic coding)
3. Visual–spatial–mechanical (visualization, spatial relations, imagery)
4. Auditory discrimination (musical and speech discrimination, sound sensitivity)
5. Memory (memory span, associative memory, recall memory)
6. Idea production (originality of ideas, ideational fluency, flexibility)
7. Speediness (perceptual speed, numerical facility, test-taking speed)
8. Reaction time (choice reaction time, semantic-processing speed, comparison speed) (Cronbach, 2002).

Carroll's first two categories are sometimes classified as intellectual abilities (e.g., Ackerman & Beier, 2003), with one category designated as general (*g*) or fluid (*Gf*) intelligence. This category is closest to what is typically measured on individual intelligence tests. The second category, crystallized intelligence (*Gc*), is a measure of what students learn in school. Ackerman and Beier refer to *Gf* as "Intelligence-as-Process" and *Gc* as "Intelligence-as-Knowledge" (p. 5). These two categories are similar to Gardner's linguistic and logical-mathematical types of intelligence and to what is measured by the verbal portions of the Stanford–Binet and WISC. Visual–spatial intelligence is another category that is recognized by most authors of cognitive frameworks. For some of our struggling readers, it is a definite strength, at least as instantiated in their artistic creations and mechanical abilities evidenced in making sets for our drama and musical productions. Carroll's other five categories seem to hold more challenge for Benchmark students than for most successful students, yet each category is a strength for some of our students, again illustrating that struggling readers do not have the same mental-processing challenges.

The mental functions discussed by Levine, Stanovitch, Gardner, and Carroll may individually have explanatory power regarding a student's struggles in reading or lack of success as a student. However, explanatory power is increased when the ability or mental function is considered as part of an interactive complex (Ackerman & Beier, 2003). A trait complex may include abilities, interests, personality, self-concept, and knowledge. In the case of initial failure in learning to read words, as experienced by the majority of Benchmark's students, that failure may lead to decreased interest in reading and a decrease in supportive personality traits—which in turn may lead to a decrease in cognitive investment in acquiring and applying new knowledge about decoding and comprehension strategies. The role of educators is to interrupt this low-achievement spiral of abilities, interests, personality, self-concept, and knowledge. To do so, a multipronged intervention that addresses most or all of these factors is needed. At Benchmark we call this style of intervention a multidimensional approach.

A few of the perplexing mental functions and abilities that are frequently cited in Benchmark's lower school population are:

- Poor attention
- Poor listening
- Poor decoding
- Poor memory for sight vocabulary and math facts
- Poor orientation in space, including poor ability to match names of places to their location on a map
- Poor orientation in time, including poor ability to tell time; to identify the sequence of the alphabet, the days of the week, and the months of the year; and to orient events with respect to historical time

Lower school teachers help students improve mental functions and abilities, such as staying attentive and listening carefully, by addressing the trait complex. Some examples of how they may address trait complexes are described here.

1. Every-Pupil-Response (EPR) activities are used as an integral part of almost all instruction (e.g., "thumbs up" or "thumbs down" to indicate students' understanding;

a written response to a teacher's question, then a brief discussion with a partner before a question is discussed with the entire class). EPRs keep every student involved and feeling competent because he or she is successful.

2. "Word rings" are assigned as homework to improve memory for sight words. Word cards attached to the word ring exhibit a word in isolation on one side; on the reverse side is a sentence with a context clue and a decoding clue, such as a known word with the same spelling pattern as the word to be learned. Homework also includes practicing math facts by using flash cards and computer games. Providing students with a choice of methods allows them to learn in the way that works best for each of them.

3. Associating places with locations on a map is facilitated by mnemonic devices, such as

"California is the state that looks like a sack, and the capital is Sacramento."
"Put wheels on Nevada's straight, flat side and you have a car, and the capital of Nevada is Carson City."
"Oregon is by the Pacific Ocean where we can go sail'en, and Salem is the capital of Oregon."

Most students find mnemonic devices an interesting and fulfilling way to learn, but they need a great deal of explicit instruction and scaffolding to construct the necessary *meaningful* connections. Left on their own to construct mnemonics, our students often construct "stories" that are as hard to remember and associate with the to-be-remembered item as the item itself. Therefore, the constructed mnemonic that was intended to be helpful does not serve its purpose.

4. Time orientation with regard to history is aided by a timeline posted in every lower school classroom and used as a touchstone when discussing stories or novels students have read or when learning about history or science. This method of supporting orientation in time is rewarding for students because with daily practice, they become competent in their sequencing of events in history and science.

5. Math teachers work with students to help students learn to tell time and to identify the sequence of days of the week and months of the year. These activities address more than just the problematic mental function by increasing all aspects of the trait complex: interest, personality traits, self-concept, and relevant knowledge.

BELIEFS

Beliefs are variables not often recognized as knowledge, yet beliefs act as knowledge and influence thinking and understanding. For most people, if they believe something, they regard it as knowledge. Philosophers and psychologists have also noted that knowledge and belief are not always easily distinguishable (Calderhead, 1996). *Knowledge* refers to facts that are substantiated, whereas *beliefs* are accepted "without the need for immediate proof, or for any proof" (Damasio, 2000, p. 326). There is a failure of source monitoring in forming beliefs; that is, the facts surrounding the belief are not checked. Instead, emotions and feelings are often the regulators of beliefs.

Another contrast between knowledge and belief is related to change as a result of experience. Knowledge involves a disposition to behave that "is constantly subject to corrective modification and updating by experience, while belief is a disposition to behave in a manner that is resistant to correction by experience" (Eichenbaum & Bodkin, 2000, p. 177). That is not to say that because supporting data are not required for a belief, that a belief is not true. A belief may be true. It is just that to be considered knowledge, the belief must be justified or confirmed as factual.

A third contrast between knowledge and belief is the source of authority. Knowledge is comprised of all that is "taken as known" by society's disciplines and institutions; beliefs are personally held convictions (Olson, 2003). Olson suggests that teachers need to establish with learners

> the joint intention to understand the official knowledge of the society by relating it to the personal beliefs and intentions of the learners. What they cannot aspire to is to induce learners to adopt as personal beliefs the knowledge officially sanctioned by the society. There is somewhat more hope that they can share a metacognitive epistemology for evaluating and judging the validity of beliefs by appealing to the reasons behind those beliefs and the validity of those reasons themselves. Although both teacher and learner have some responsibility for achieving this understanding, each remains responsible for his or her own privately held beliefs and reasons for holding them. (p. 247)

Students have a right to their beliefs, but they must learn to validate them and to not deem them as fact until validated. There need to be reasons for beliefs.

Beliefs have both cognitive and volitional significance (Snow et al., 1996) by affecting students' understanding and their willingness to take control of their learning. For example, it is fairly well accepted that students construct meaning based on what they already know and believe (Bransford et al., 2000). Therefore, teachers need to be aware of the incomplete understandings, false beliefs, and naive explanations of concepts that students bring to the subject matter they are studying and guide them toward achieving a more mature understanding. It is well documented, however, that changing misconceptions can be a challenging task. On the other hand, ignoring these ideas and beliefs may lead to very different understandings than the teacher intends. Vosnaidou and Brewer (1989) tell of the challenge in changing children's belief that the earth is flat. When told the earth was round, some of the children in their study pictured the earth as a pancake rather than a sphere.

Examples of the volitional significance of beliefs are found in the motivation literature and apply to many of the struggling readers at Benchmark. Beliefs about one's competence or ability is a major component of motivation. A central issue related to self-perceptions of competence is beliefs about effort and ability. Beliefs about ability are closely related to the expectation students have for success. If students believe they can succeed at a task, they are more likely to undertake it and value it (Alderman, 2004). Self-motivational components (beliefs) include self-efficacy, outcome expectations, attributions, intrinsic interest or valuing, and goal orientation (Zimmerman & Campillo, 2003). Self-efficacy involves personal beliefs about being able to learn or perform effectively in a specific area. For example, if a student believes that the spelling part of his or her brain is either damaged or different from that of other students, he or she may put little effort into trying to correctly spell even simple, phonetically regular words when he or she is writing. Among Benchmark students we have found that attributions of success regarding the use of strategies leads to improved self-efficacy.

Students are eager to come to school each day when they know that their social, emotional, and academic needs will be met.

Faulty beliefs about learning can be very damaging and are fairly common among our students. Because of faulty beliefs, these students may make attributional errors such as: "I got an A on that test, so the test must have been easy." (A more accurate reason may be that the student put into practice the study techniques he or she had been taught.) "The teacher gave me a D on my science project—that just proves I am dumb." (In actuality, the primary issue was that the student did not follow the teacher's rubric and timetable for completing the project.)

Struggling readers tend to make skewed attributions that arise from faulty beliefs. For this reason, Benchmark's middle school teachers require students to complete a two-part self-assessment for most of their assignments. The first part is completed before students hand in an assignment or test. They explain what they did to prepare for and complete the assignment or test and what grade they believe they will earn. The second part is completed when the assignment or test is returned to the students with written feedback and a grade. Students study the feedback and then write an assessment of what they did that worked and what they will do differently next time. The goal is to help students more accurately align their beliefs about how their brains work and the result of that brain work. By the time our students graduate from Benchmark, their beliefs have usually become more accurate regarding their strengths and challenges as readers and learners as well as the efforts that lead to success. Interestingly, if these new beliefs (that replaced faulty beliefs) are too tenuous, as many are, the old beliefs reappear. Benchmark supervisor Eleanor Gensemer tells this story about Adam, one of our recent graduates who dropped in to visit.

T: How is school going?

S: The work is easy.

T: How do you know?

S: I'm getting really good grades.

T: Do the other students in your class believe the work is easy?

S: No, they think it's hard, and some of them aren't doing very well.

T: So what's a more logical explanation for why you are doing well?

S: That I'm really smart? (*Mrs. Gensemer gives him a quizzical look.*) That Benchmark prepared me well for what they are asking me to do?

T: So you're giving Benchmark credit for preparing you well—is that all there is to it?

S: That I'm not just working hard, but I'm working *smart*. I'm using the strategies I learned at Benchmark?

T: Of course!

Although Adam was able, with coaching, to somewhat recover his confidence and his belief in himself as a learner, at least for the moment, it was clear that in a new situation his suspicion that his success was not due to his strategic effort returned quickly to a foremost position in his mind. Mrs. Gensemer, his former trusted teacher and mentor, touches base with Adam periodically to refocus him on what he learned at Benchmark, especially his self-advocacy skills that he implemented so successfully during his final year at Benchmark. Adam is doing well in his new school, but his faulty belief system is just below the surface, waiting for an opportunity to raise its head and undermine Adam's confidence. Long-held beliefs are tough to overcome and can seem as real as the facts.

In summary, many variables such as temperament, emotion, motivation, volition, knowledge, attitudes, interests, cognitive style, and beliefs interact with each other and with situation, task, and text variables to determine learning. I have divided person variables into two categories, those that involve the mind and those that involve the body. In the previous chapter and the section above, mind variables were discussed. In the next section, I discuss two categories of body variables that are particularly relevant to school success: physical development and health.

PHYSICAL DEVELOPMENT

A primary developmental milestone that affects many of our students is a delay in the development of fine-motor coordination. As a result, students with this developmental difference find it difficult to keep pace with the writing demands of the classroom. We help students cope with their difficulties in writing in several ways, including providing cursive handwriting instruction and keyboarding instruction and assigning a temporary scribe to a student, as is explained below.

Accommodations for Writing Difficulties

Cursive Handwriting

Benchmark's handwriting program was initially developed by one of our teachers, Joan Davidson, during the early years of the school. With modifications, the program continues to be taught by a designated handwriting teacher for 20 minutes twice a week to all of our students in grades 3–6.

In the Benchmark handwriting program, each change in the direction of a stroke is named (e.g., rocker curve, slant line), and students are taught to talk their way through forming each cursive letter. By using a handwriting specialist for this program, students receive the consistency of method and expectations that we have learned increases their chances of improving their cursive writing. Students also have weekly cursive homework to gain additional practice for what they were taught. Once all the uppercase and lowercase letters have been introduced, students are expected to complete their written assignments in cursive writing.

Students tell us that, when handwriting was taught in their previous schools, they often felt frustrated and gave up on learning conventional ways to form letters. As a result, they now seem to appreciate the opportunity for a fresh start, especially the opportunity to learn cursive instead of manuscript. Furthermore, the flow of connected lines in cursive seems to make writing easier for our students than making the several strokes that are necessary for most manuscript letters.

Keyboard Skills

A second way we help students cope with writing difficulties is by teaching them keyboarding skills. Beginning as early as second grade, we use a systematic computer program (Type to Learn) to teach students the standard hand position and location of keys. Every other day, students are assigned to a 10-minute practice period on one of the classroom computers. As soon as students can type 15 words per minute, they are allowed to use an Alpha Smart (an electronic keyboard) or computer to complete their classwork. This provides great incentive for mastering keyboard skills. We use 15 words per minute as our criterion because keyboarding at a rate slower than 15 words per minute has not proved to outweigh the inefficiencies of hand writing. As a result of emphasizing keyboard skills from an early age, most of our students in fifth grade and above, who have been at the school for several years, have become fairly competent with word processing. In fact, some are more proficient computer users than some of the adults in the school. The added benefits of using an Alpha Smart or computer for word processing are written assignments that are legible and that have been spell-checked.

Temporary Scribe

A third way we assist students for whom fine-motor coordination is suspected to be at least part of the reason for difficulty in completing written assignments is by assigning a temporary scribe. It is not uncommon for a teacher or support teacher to scribe for students who experience difficulty when they must think about what they want to write, remember how to form the letters and spell words, and get something written

Learning to use an electronic keyboard can help struggling readers overcome such roadblocks to writing as the need to think about how letters are formed and words are spelled.

before they forget what they want to say. Using a scribe releases students from the mechanical problems associated with writing so that they can concentrate on what they want to say. It also allows them to discover that they can be good thinkers with important things to say. When a scribe begins working with a student, the scribe does all the writing and the student does the thinking. However, with each interaction, the scribe does less of the writing. Instead of doing all the writing, the scribe helps the student think through what he or she wants to write, then coaches the student as he or she writes what was just discussed. Over time, these students who once needed a scribe find that they can initiate their own rehearsal prior to writing, sometimes by talking with a partner, sometimes by thinking and jotting brief notes on their own. Interestingly, some of our students who exhibit fine-motor difficulties are the same students who perform well, or even exceptionally well, on the soccer or football field.

HEALTH

The second category of body variables that is salient for Benchmark students is health status. Allergies, vision or hearing problems, susceptibility to the common cold and stomach viruses, asthma, and inadequate sleep are common variables that may significantly impact the course of learning.

Accommodations for Absences

Frequent absences due to illness, for example, put students at a disadvantage with respect to learning, despite the fact that assignments are sent home via e-mail or with a friend. While absent, students miss content instruction and explanations of strategies they might use to understand concepts and complete make-up assignments. They also miss learning concepts and strategies that will provide the foundation for understanding future concepts and assignments. To help students compensate for missed instruction, teachers are available during the lunch period and after school to reteach concepts and processes that students missed when they were absent. This catch-up process is initiated by teachers. However, the expectation is that, during their stay at Benchmark, and with diminishing cues from teachers, students will initiate the catch-up process on their own.

SUMMARY

In this chapter we continued the discussion of person variables begun in Chapter 3, specifically considering the components of intelligence, as well as physical development and health, and how each is related to learning to read and success in school.

Intelligent behavior is composed of knowledge, motivation, and control. Several well-known theories of general and special mental functions and components of intelligence were discussed, with the conclusion that students have different strengths and challenges in relation to these mental functions, and that it is the responsibility of educators to provide instruction that allows students to build on their strengths and compensate for their challenges. The goal is to interrupt the low-achievement spiral of abilities, interests, personality, self-concept, and knowledge by employing multidimensional approaches to instruction.

As can be seen in the ILM (Figure 2.1), many person variables have the potential to interact to determine how a student responds to instruction. Not only do these inside-the-person variables interact with one another, but they also interact with the outside-the-person variables of situation, task, and text (which we begin to explore in the next chapter). In view of all the possible interactions that can affect a student's success in school, it seems logical that those of us who teach struggling readers must see it as our responsibility to do more than just teach students how to read. As part of the empowerment process, we need to make students aware of the possible interactions among variables that may affect how well they learn to read, understand, and convey their understanding in writing. Then, with heightened awareness, students will be more likely to profit from instruction in how to take control of these variables to self-regulate their learning. The result will be students who orchestrate both academic and real-life success—that is our goal for all struggling readers.

PART II

CONTEXT AND THEORIES OF LEARNING

Confidence that they can do anything, even learn to read, is greatly increased for those who ascend the ropes course to a platform high in the air, then jump off and fly down the zip wire.

CHAPTER 5

The Context for Learning

Teacher Knowledge, Classroom Culture,
and Instruction

A productive learning context is one that engenders and reinforces students wanting to learn, and then wanting to learn some more. When wanting to learn is absent, the learning context is unproductive or counterproductive (Sarason, 2004). Orchestrating a productive learning context in schools, homes, and communities is a monumental task—a task that has been made particularly challenging in recent years by the pace of change in our country. The information explosion of the past decade and our nation's shift from an industrial focus to one of service and technology are evidence that our way of life is changing and raise questions about the instruction that will best prepare students for the future. Have contexts for learning kept pace with these changes? Do we know what we should teach young people today that will still have value 10–15 years from now, when they are adults?

The answer to the first question is that, in most cases, contexts for learning have had difficulty keeping pace with change. However, in answer to the second question, we do have a good idea about the attitudes and understandings that will be valued in this, the 21st century, and we need to act on that knowledge. We need to create elementary and secondary schools that aim to do more than prepare young people to succeed in a static curriculum or to secure a job. We need schools that see their mission as preparing young people for a fulfilling adulthood—an adulthood that necessitates their being lifelong learners, thinkers, and problem solvers.

In the recent past, preparing young people for a productive adulthood meant teaching them to read, write, and do math, as well as teaching the content of the subject-matter disciplines. These elements of 20th-century curriculum and instruction, however, are insufficient to prepare young people well for today's society, in which jobs are performed collaboratively and information is voluminous and ever changing. Csikszentmihalyi and Schneider (2000), who recently completed a national longitudinal study of how adolescents develop attitudes and acquire skills to achieve their career goals and expectations, argue that today's society is operating with an outdated understanding of what it takes for a child to become a productive adult. They recommend that schools focus on two essential areas of learning. First, instead of memorizing bits and pieces of information from the traditional disciplines, students should learn the fundamental *principles* and *processes* that underlie these disciplines and upon which a scientifically based society rests. This focus is echoed by curriculum specialists, for example Erickson (2001) and Tomlinson (1998), as well as by educational philosophers, including Noddings (1992, 1998).

Second, teachers need to collaborate with families and communities to help young people develop the *values* and *attitudes* they need to meet the challenges of the future. For example, teachers need to value and encourage discipline, internal locus of control, responsibility, persistence, and the skillful use of minds and bodies. Instruction needs to be skillfully planned so that students find that hard work and concentrated involvement are rewarding. Additional characteristics that teachers must foster are an optimistic disposition, curiosity, enjoyment of a challenge, and the ability to work with others. To achieve these goals, educators will need to enlist the support of family and community; however, much of this education will fall to teachers. Their challenge is to recognize the qualities each student brings to a situation, then adjust the situation to improve the fit (Snow et al., 1996).

In this chapter I discuss one segment of the outside-the-person variables that interacts with inside-the-person variables to affect the principles, processes, values, and attitudes students learn. As diagrammed in the Benchmark Interactive Learning Model (ILM; Figure 2.1), the outside-the-person, or learning context, variables are situation, task, and text. I have divided situation variables into *cognitive* (based on cognitive psychology) and *sociocultural* factors. Cognitive variables considered here are *teacher knowledge*, *classroom culture*, and *instruction*. Within the sociocultural category are social variables that include *family* and *friends* and their characteristics, such as *socioeconomic status*, *religion*, and *support for the school*. Also included in the sociocultural category are cultural variables such as those related to *language*, *customs*, and *values*. The sociocultural variables, their impact on learning, and how teachers can support learners of diverse cultural backgrounds are discussed in Chapter 6, along with a discussion of task and text variables.

This chapter and the next are devoted to the context variables that are related to productive learning. In this chapter I present the variables in the cognitive group (Figure 5.1)—the variables over which educators have the most control. I begin by discussing teacher knowledge, which I believe is the glue that holds together the context for learning.

TEACHER KNOWLEDGE

The history of Benchmark School can be told in terms of teachers becoming knowledgeable. It is the secret to our success. Benchmark was founded in 1970 as I began my third year teaching reading courses at the University of Pennsylvania. In addition to my desire to better understand how to meet the needs of struggling readers, I also wanted to form a group of colleagues who would join me in discovering how we could become the most effective teachers we could be.

FIGURE 5.1. Cognitive group.

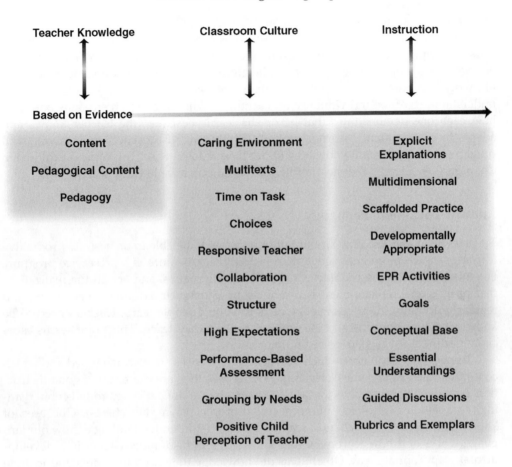

From *Success with Struggling Readers* by Irene Gaskins. Copyright 2005 by The Guilford Press. See copyright page for photocopying limitations.

The group I initially assembled was composed of some of Penn's best students, some of whom were, or eventually became, Benchmark teachers. We subscribed to and read journals about reading, special education, and educational research; then we shared with one another what we learned and how it applied to teaching struggling readers. In addition, Ralph Preston (Director of the Reading Clinic at the University of Pennsylvania at the time) formed the Benchmark Curriculum Advisory Board, composed of well-known experts in the Philadelphia area upon whom we could call for advice on issues that puzzled us about working with our students. We made frequent use of the advice of Morton Botel, William Carey, Rachel Cox, Roy Kress, Laura Murphy, Ralph Preston, and Margaret Rawson, among others. We also brought in psychologists, psychiatrists, and clinical social workers as consultants to guide us in understanding and dealing with the emotional overlay that accompanied our students' failure to learn to read despite average or above-average potential.

Understand Principles of Learning

Everything about teaching at Benchmark was about teachers learning—and this attitude of continuous learning still thrives today. We learned that teacher knowledge, classroom culture, and instruction rest on the assumption that *the nature of human learning should determine pedagogical practice*. Therefore, teachers must understand how learning works. In addition, we came to realize that one way teachers demonstrate their understanding of the individuality of learning is when they teach students based on how each one demonstrates that he or she learns best (i.e., the teacher knows and adapts to each student's learner profile). In other words, teachers must understand principles of learning and know how to put them into practice. This topic is explored in Chapters 7–9. Clearly, the most influential situation variable is the teacher.

Know a Lot about Pedagogy

Teachers need an incredible amount of knowledge to be able to orchestrate productive learning—much more knowledge than is possible to acquire in a preservice program. For this reason, successful teachers are those who realize, and act on the realization, that professional development is a career-long pursuit. In addition to acquiring and regularly updating their knowledge of how young people learn, teachers need to be knowledgeable about the specific areas of content they teach. This point seems especially pertinent to teachers of beginning reading.

Teachers need to know which instructional practices are research based and which continue to persist in some classrooms not because they are examples of good instruction, but solely because "it is the way we have always done it" (e.g., round-robin reading, completion of isolated phonics and comprehension skill sheets). One area of knowledge needed by teachers of reading is an in-depth understanding of how our language works and how to convey that knowledge to beginning readers in a developmentally appropriate way. Other areas of knowledge they need to understand include how to explain comprehension strategies to students and how to teach young readers ways to be metacognitive. (These topics are discussed in Chapters 12 and 13.) Not only is it important that teachers be well versed in the content they teach, but they must also know pedagogically sound ways to convey that content. Teachers also need to be knowledgeable about general pedagogical principles, such as organization of the classroom, management of behavior, and planning.

A second area of expertise that teachers need to develop is how to establish a productive learning environment or culture. Words often used in describing a productive classroom culture include *caring, collaborative, responsive,* and *structured.* Other words and phrases that relate to a productive classroom culture are *multitext, time on task, choices, application, expectations,* and *performance-based assessment. Academic press* and *social support* (Lee & Smith, 1999) are key phrases used in the research literature to describe productive learning cultures. By these terms we mean that academics are serious business, that time in the classroom is used well to meet appropriate academic goals, and that students feel supported by teachers and other students in a collaborative pursuit of these academic goals. Establishing a productive classroom culture that incites students to want to learn and to keep on learning is one of a teacher's highest achievements (discussed in more depth in the next section of this chapter).

Another area about which teachers need to be knowledgeable is instruction: the methods teachers use to convey declarative and procedural knowledge. One instructional model used at Benchmark is *explicit explanation* (Duffy et al., 1987). In this model teachers explicitly explain to students how to accomplish the tasks they assign. (See Chapters 10–13 for examples.) Explicit explanation as a teaching method contrasts with *assigning* and *mentioning*, the common practices revealed in Durkin's (1978–1979) study of fourth-grade classrooms.

Yet another instructional technique featured at Benchmark is a multidimensional approach (Gaskins, 1999) that is the opposite of a one-method-fits-all approach. Our teachers are flexible in their use of methods, often combining methods that are verified by research in relation to what works for individual students. For example, in our class of youngest students, Sherry Cress has combined techniques from Reading Recovery, whole language, balanced reading, guided reading, writing workshop, partner reading, and other programs to design a curriculum that works for the beginning readers she teaches. Each lesson is scaffolded to meet the needs of her students, and expectations and instruction are developmentally appropriate. Knowing that academically engaged time correlates with achievement, Benchmark teachers make frequent use of the Every-Pupil-Response (EPR) technique. When EPR techniques are used, all students respond at the same time and often work with a partner; therefore, there is less opportunity for a student to be passive or inattentive (see Chapter 3 for examples). The techniques mentioned here are just a few of the instructional tools from which teachers can choose as they respond to the individual strengths and challenges exhibited by their students. Of course, to make effective selections, teachers must know a great deal about many different instructional possibilities and the research base for each. Research-based knowledge is crucial to a teacher's success.

In the next section I discuss in more depth a key influence in determining if and what students will learn and whether students want to learn. This very influential variable is the classroom culture—a culture based on a teacher's knowledge of classroom research and child development. The discussion of classroom culture is followed by a discussion of instruction.

CLASSROOM CULTURE

Few would disagree that teachers need to emphasize both the principles and processes that undergird success in each content area as well as the values and attitudes necessary for successful learning and application. Yet, as necessary and as important as these are, it is a culture of caring (Noddings, 1992, 1998) that makes the learning of principles and processes possible. *Caring* is the cornerstone of socially mediated learning. The staff of Benchmark School, along with Goldstein (1999), among others, believe that because learning is about interpersonal connections and the co-construction of knowledge, educators must connect the affective and the intellectual. As one example of this connection, Ryan and Deci (2000) recommend that instruction be organized so that each student's basic psychological needs for autonomy, competence, and relatedness are met. When school experiences fit students' needs, motivation to learn usually follows; when school experiences do not, problems ensue, and the potential of students is not fulfilled.

In this section about creating a context for learning, I discuss the issues that the staff of Benchmark School, in collaboration with our students' parents, think about each day as we endeavor to create a caring, motivating learning context. We strive to create a context in which students' beliefs (including values and attitudes) about learning are addressed, processes for learning are explicitly taught, and understanding—particularly understanding of principles that provide the foundation for learning, thinking, and problem solving—is co-constructed. To achieve success in these areas, we must pay attention to the affective context for learning.

Caring: The Affective Context for Learning

There are many contexts for learning: home, school, cultural community, social group, and place of worship. And within each of these there are smaller contexts for learning. For example, within the school there are classrooms, small groups, and dyads. These are all places where caring dialogues are held between adults and students, as well as between students. They are places where the affective tone determines what is learned. In this section *dialogue in the zone of promixal development* (Vygotsky, 1978) is the focus of attention. A student's zone of promixal development includes the range of tasks that the student cannot yet handle alone but can do with the help of a more skilled partner. By being available to support students in meeting challenges and to guide them to see

Collaboration fosters a sense of belonging and competence that increases the likelihood that students will take the risks that learning entails.

purpose or value in classroom activities, adults create a positive affective context in which a more skillful partner helps students feel cared for and safe. Such conditions, especially in the case of adolescents, influence students' decisions to engage, or not to engage, in learning (Roeser, Recycles, & Saner, 2000). The positive affect in the learning context is the crucial factor.

The Power of Caring

Whatever the context for learning, it must first and foremost be a caring one. Because caring relationships require continuity to develop (Noddings, 1992), such a context provides young people with continuity of place, people, purpose, and curriculum. Most young people like the security of routine. By creating caring relations with students, teachers show them how to care. In their book about adolescence, Knowles and Brown (2000) reported that showing care and respect for students has the power to promote learning to a greater degree than instructional methodologies. Caring, of course, is not a substitute for instruction, but caring does establish the culture for learning. Bosworth's (1995) research, reported by Knowles and Brown (2000), identifies possible ways teachers demonstrate that they care: They walk around the room talking to students to see how they are doing and to answer questions; they help students with work, notice and inquire about changes in behavior, recognize different learning styles, seek to know students as unique human beings, and explain lesson content well, making sure that all students understand. In addition, at Benchmark a class culture of caring is fostered by teachers who encourage acts of kindness, charitable projects, and sharing time at lunch.

The Importance of Dialogue

Caring is more than the characteristic attitudes associated with providing care; it also requires knowledge and skill to be able to respond effectively to students and to understand what they need, as well as the history of that need. A caring relationship is fostered by open-ended dialogue (Noddings, 1992, 1998). Ideally there should be a time in each student's day for sustained conversation and mutual exploration with an adult—a time when an adult talks with a student about academic matters, personal problems, short- and long-term goals, who the young person wants to become, and the importance of performing well in school.

In Benchmark's middle school, there is an opportunity for collaborative dialogue with a teacher and peers during the mentor period (called advisory sessions in some schools), which occurs mid-morning each day for 30 minutes. As the year progresses, students begin to develop trusting relationships with their mentors and close social bonds with the five to seven classmates who are part of their mentor group. These trusting relationships, which develop gradually over the 3 years a mentor works with the same students, allow mentors to influence attitudes and beliefs as well as behavior. At Benchmark, much of the personal talk concerns the student's individual cognitive style (usual manner of thinking), as the mentor coaches him or her about what to do to be successful, given a particular cognitive style. Sometimes mentors set limits for students until they can develop greater self-discipline. During mentor time, dialogue with students allows teachers to build the knowledge they need to guide both their responses to students' needs and to formulate comments for affirming and encouraging the best in students. Dialogue also fosters the life skills of interpersonal reasoning. Students learn how to communicate, share decision making, arrive at compromises, and support one another in solving academic and everyday problems. This time of dialogue with adults and peers helps students to learn how to sympathize and empathize with other people; it is also a time to discuss everyday happenings, giving the adult opportunities to provide practical guidance (e.g., how to watch television intelligently, how to schedule homework). The heart of a successful mentor program is the development of a trusting, caring community in which students perceive their mentors as demonstrating unconditional support for their growth (Knowles & Brown, 2000).

Dilemmas of Evaluation, Resistance, and Grouping

Establishing a caring context for learning, however, carries with it certain dilemmas. For example, how does one evaluate learning and measure progress without endangering the caring relationships that are being built? At Benchmark teachers assess students' learning by measuring progress from where each student began (or against a rubric or standard), rather than by comparison to other students. Ideally, the methods used to foster and measure progress should not include rewards, grades, and penalties, which tend to separate teacher and student. However, confirmation of a student's best possible motives and attributes, consistent with reality, allows caregivers to remain in connection with the student and sows the seeds for a positive self-talk in him or her.

Another dilemma we face in fostering a caring environment is resistance to involvement in learning activities. Resistance often appears to be a kind of communication, a way of signaling adults that a discourse needs to be built around a particular problem or problems (Abowitz, 2000). In response to students who resist or assert that they do not care, Benchmark teachers try to give sufficient attention to their felt needs and interests to bring them back into the learning community. In such situations teachers often learn that students will take risks to please adults whom they like and trust but previously resisted.

In the past we also struggled with where, and even if, ability grouping fits into a caring environment, and suspected that the arguments against tracking were "political and economic, not educational" (Noddings, 1992, p. 41). It stands to reason that in a caring environment, each student should be taught at his or her appropriate level, with instruction matched to specific needs, interests, and talents; and that there should be different objectives for students with different capacities and interests. Ability grouping is one way to match students and curriculum. Another way is to *facilitate* students' success. Noddings (1992) reports that

> some teachers interpreted the facilitative function of the teacher to mean that the teacher should only respond to students' requests for help. These teachers never intervened and actually let students sit idle for days, even weeks. Nothing could be further from the spirit we are discussing here. Of course teachers should initiate! They should suggest, persuade, inspire, encourage, negotiate compromises, offer concrete help. Above all they should engage students in dialogue so that decisions are well informed. We do not respect students when we leave them alone to make decisions on whim. (p. 157)

At Benchmark we scaffold instruction to facilitate students' success when they are unable to complete a learning task successfully on their own (Gaskins, Rauch, et al., 1997).

Safety to Risk

Another aspect of a caring culture is creating a sense of safety that promotes risk taking. From the day they enter Benchmark, we teach our students to ask questions when they are confused or when they do not know the meaning of words. It is one of the most important strategies they will learn. The courage to ask questions can only be mustered if the classroom culture feels safe. Karen Berry, a Benchmark teacher, shared this example from her classroom.

> "In my classroom of new-to-Benchmark students I work hard to create a culture where questioning is valued, accepted, and, in fact, *expected*. I constantly point out that 'smart people ask questions,' which is a new belief that I want students to accept. This stance asks students to examine their emotional variables (values and attitudes); motivational variables (they must do something about misunderstandings); and social variables (friends—will they laugh?). Students are expected to monitor their understanding and then take *action* if something does not make sense. A 'safe signal' for letting the teacher know that something does not make sense is for the student to put his or her thumb down. The teacher then is aware that the student is confused. I let the thumbs-down student call on a classmate to explain the word or phrase or direction as long as that student does not also have his or her thumb down. This encourages other students to then 'check out their brain' to see if they are understanding or are in need of further clarification. I'll give an example of one scenario."

T: Let's read this sentence to see if there's an example of an adaptation to help fish survive. "Fish eat plankton." (*Mandy puts thumb down.*) Good! Mandy is monitoring for sense and noticed she does not understand something. What isn't clear?

S1:   What is *plankton*?

T: Okay, Mandy needs to check out the meaning of *plankton*. That's smart because it might be important to our notes since eating plankton helps fish survive. Mandy, using the sentence clues, can you guess what plankton is?

S1:   Is it a kind of food?

T: That would make sense. Who can add on to what kind of food plankton is? Mandy, call on someone with their thumb up. (*Mandy calls on a student, who defines "plankton" correctly.*)

S2:   Do all fish eat plankton?

T: That's a good question. I'm not sure about that. Let's check that out with our science teacher, Mrs. DiCocco.

> "Because of the classroom culture, Mandy was able to feel comfortable questioning. She was complimented for monitoring for sense. Other students collaborated by

helping Mandy. This productive and accepting atmosphere will motivate Mandy (and others) to question again. Also, the teacher modeled questioning, saying that she would question the science teacher for further information. Because the teacher is a person of authority, her willingness to seek information from another person reinforces the belief and expectation that smart people ask questions, especially about things they do not understand."

Classroom culture has a significant impact on students' levels of motivation, as is discussed in the next section.

Fostering Motivation

As discussed in Chapter 3, all humans have a basic psychological need for autonomy, competence, and relatedness (Deci, 1995; Maslow, 1968). Whether students are motivated is affected by how well the classroom culture provides for the fulfillment of these needs. Events that negatively affect a person's feelings of personal control, competence, or sense of belonging tend to diminish motivation. Events that support perceived control, competence, and belonging enhance motivation.

Enhancing Competency, Belonging, and Autonomy

Changing maladaptive patterns of motivation is a challenge teachers confront in all contexts but particularly in middle schools. The desired change is to move students from being motivated to protect themselves from situations they perceive as either meaningless or threatening to being motivated to engage in meaningful intellectual activities. Teachers can enhance competency-related motivation in many ways: They can (1) guide students to successful achievement through scaffolded strategy development and feedback, (2) frame the value and purposes of activities for students, and (3) provide emotional support and encouragement during the learning process, especially when difficulties are encountered. Motivation grounded in relatedness or a sense of belonging can be enhanced through collaborative problem solving and carefully designed group work (Roeser et al., 2000). Adolescents like to participate in practical problem solving and activities that reflect real issues, especially social issues, such as how to fit in, how to get along, and how to interact with peers and adults (Knowles & Brown, 2000). Autonomy-related motivation can be addressed by allowing students to make more choices and thereby gain a sense of control over their lives.

Deciding about Extrinsic versus Intrinsic Rewards

The use of extrinsic rewards to motivate learning is a perpetual topic of debate among educators. Some educators and researchers, including Noddings (1992), have expressed concern about the seeming inconsistency between practicing caregiving in schools while, at the same time, emphasizing rewards and penalties. Purkey (2000) believes that it should *not* be a primary task of parents, teachers, counselors, and others to provide students with a constant diet of praise, rewards, compliments, and affirmations. Rather, their major job is to reduce or eliminate faulty, illogical, negative, and counterproductive student self-talk that results in low self-efficacy, high self-doubt, and persistent self-hatred. Ryan and Deci (2000) also are concerned about attempts to control or regulate students by rewards. They fear that rewards may supplant students' intrinsic need to be in control, "leading to an atrophy of self-regulation strategies and capacities" (p. 47). Other researchers suggest that using extrinsic rewards to motivate students to do something they would have done anyway has detrimental effects on performance and, more importantly, on their subsequent motivation to perform the activity. This phenomenon is more likely to occur if students initially found the activity interesting (Sansone & Harackiewicz, 2000).

On the other hand, as a result of their research and theoretical analysis, Harackiewicz and Sansome (2000) concluded that performance-contingent rewards can potentially support intrinsic motivation when rewards convince students of their competence and lead them to become more involved in learning activities. It is important to note that the success of such interventions depends on students attaining competence and *feeling* competent. At Benchmark, particularly with our new-to-Benchmark students, we have had success motivating students by giving them award certificates at the end of the school day for progress they have made on a specific goal, such as writing complete and reasonable reading responses or participating a specific number of times during reading group discussion.

Supporting Learning-Oriented Goals

Another issue affecting motivation and over which teachers have some influence is whether a student's goal orientation is learning oriented or performance oriented. The crux of this matter for teachers is that a student's goal orientation usually determines how he or she values information and teacher guidance. Students who have learning-related goals tend to be eager to seek and apply relevant information and guidance from the teacher or peers. However, performance-oriented students are usually more interested in what they have to do to get the grade they want. An example of a performance-oriented student is the student who notices and cares about only the grade on his or her paper and does not use the teacher's written comments to learn how to improve his or her understanding or competence. The work of Butler (2000) suggests that having learning goals is particularly beneficial for less able students whose present capacities are inadequate to meet task demands. Learning goals orient students to seek and apply the information and guidance they need in order to learn. Regardless of goal orientation (learning or performance), keeping students motivated requires that teachers provide information (e.g., worked-out solutions, constructive help, task-specific feedback) and opportunities for students to learn from peers; these measures orient students at all ability levels to learn to evaluate how well they are doing and to seek continuing opportunities to learn. Butler's work also suggests that if teachers want students to be learning oriented rather than performance oriented, they must emphasize that understanding and application are more important than memorizing information for the sole purpose of earning a good grade.

In approaching goal orientation of students, teachers need to consider the meaning that students assign to an achievement situation and clarify for students that ability is *acquirable*. The meaning students assign to achievement situations affects their motivation. The work of Molden and Dweck (2000) suggests that "concerns with failure and attempts to avoid appearing incompetent grow directly out of the belief that an achievement task measures one's fixed intelligence—and therefore that task performance has implications for self-worth" (p. 138). That is, when students perceive a task as measuring an enduring quality of the self, they are more likely to regard failure as unchangeable and stigmatizing. On the other hand, when students believe that a task simply identifies a current level of an acquirable ability, such as strategy use, there is usually not the same concern about possible failure and its avoidance, and students are more likely to attribute failure to lack of effort or to a poor choice of strategies. They usually see these problems as changeable (Molden & Dweck, 2000). When students perceive that a task is a measure of fixed intelligence, they feel vulnerable and concerned about investing in success. The result is a tendency to pursue avoidance-oriented goals. For these students, performance goals that are challenging create motivational vulnerability. The key issue is the meaning a student gives to experiences of success or failure. Is the success due to intelligence or to specific strategies and effort? Teachers can influence the meaning that students assign to success and failure, just as they can influence self-talk and beliefs about self, the topic discussed next.

Influencing Beliefs and Self-Talk

How parents, educators, and peers think and act toward students influences what students say to themselves—and what students say to themselves about themselves affects their motivation. We know that "everybody and everything in and around a school affects what students say to themselves, [thus] altering what students say to themselves involves altering the total school environment and culture. The task of educators is to structure experiences that reduce negative, counterproductive, faulty self-talk, while inviting students to define themselves in essentially positive and realistic ways" (Purkey, 2000, p. 3).

Positive self-talk has the greatest likelihood of developing in a caring environment. Purkey (2000) speaks of the *whispering self*, the "part of consciousness that constantly speaks internally, often in innuendo and half-truths. *It is the current self with a voice*" (p. 4). Self-talk, based on Vygotsky's (1978) theory of the internalization of dialogue as inner speech, is thought itself. It regulates how students feel and act, interprets what they experience, guides and controls academic achievement, and determines the quality of students' lives. The self develops as a result of repeated everyday events and interactions with parents, teachers, and peers. The self is the mediating variable in human behavior, the filter through which all new phenomena are interpreted.

How students feel about themselves depends on how their minds filter and interpret everyday experiences. How students define themselves depends on how they think others define them. Students who experience consistent difficulty and disapproval in school typically talk to themselves in derogatory terms: "I'm dumb, worthless, irresponsible, and incapable of doing the work that is assigned." Often this negative self-talk becomes "learned helplessness" (Seligman, 1975). Our goal at Benchmark is to interact with students in such a way that they create and maintain inner voices that proclaim, "I am able, valuable, responsible, and capable of handling the work my teachers assign." With such an optimistic belief system, better classroom performances will follow (Seligman, 1990). Benchmark teachers give specific praise for the actions students take to meet their goals; they point out that it is not by luck that a student achieved his or her goal but by the specific actions that the student employed.

Positive self-talk is fostered when individual differences are appreciated, rules are fair, mistakes are accepted, and nurturance is pervasive. Caring teachers structure situations that provide authentic, successful experiences, and they avoid placing students in situations in which repeated failure is likely. They point out areas of accomplishment rather than focus on mistakes. They find something special that each student can do or is interested in, and invite students to see themselves as able, valuable, and responsible. Even in our youngest classes the teachers have experts—someone good at drawing, others with good background knowledge about animals, sports, planets, etc. A caring teacher also helps young people develop a positive, yet realistic, image of what he or she can become or do, because the "possible self" is the essential link between self-concept and motivation. In a caring environment young people experience respect, trust, and confidence from caregivers and, as a result, develop self-respect, self-trust, and self-confidence. As students come to define themselves in positive ways, they face each day with greater confidence and assurance, accepting their limitations and recognizing their potential.

It is axiomatic that teachers' perceptions of their students influence how students perceive themselves. Thus, teachers who want to change their students' negative self-talk know that change begins with how *they* think about their students. To begin the change process, teachers make a conscious effort to monitor their own self-talk about students; whenever they recognize negative self-talk, they replace it with positive, realistic self-talk.

Teachers who have been successful in changing their own self-talk realize that the self is malleable and can be changed; therefore, each of us possesses an infinite capacity for development. Benchmark teachers are intentional in their efforts to influence students' self-talk. They model positive self-talk and encourage students to listen to their own self-talk. They coach students to challenge and modify their self-talk when it is self-defeating, faulty, or irrational. In addition, teachers and students discuss how the words they choose to say to themselves can either enhance or interfere with classroom learning. Caring about students in these ways is a teacher's number-one priority, because it is the first step to helping students determine who they will become. Part of caring about students is orchestrating a context in which students can talk to themselves in ways that lead to productive learning, thinking, and problem solving. "A teacher cannot escape the fact that the self-talk of students is within his or her influence" (Purkey, 2000, p. 57). The following material provides an overview of some of the aspects of a multidimensional approach to working with struggling readers that a knowledgeable Benchmark teacher needs to know.

INSTRUCTION

Multidimensional Curriculum, Instruction, and Activities

No one curriculum or method of instruction provides the best fit for all students. Indeed, teaching all students in the class using one favored approach almost guarantees that some students will not be successful. For example, most people use at least four different strategies to read words (Gaskins, 2004). Some will have difficulty distinguishing visual differences in words and therefore have trouble learning sight words; others may have difficulty making closure after identifying the individual sounds in words (a cue that they will not learn easily using a sounding and blending approach). At Benchmark there is a multiplicity of instructional methods available to accommodate the capacities and interests of all students. Teachers need to know what these methods are, how to use them, and be willing to use them based on the needs of their students.

Our program is multidimensional in the sense that we are on the lookout for what students need to know and assess whether it appears in the curriculum. In view of our students' difficulties in the pencil-and-paper world of the classroom, we do not want to make the mistake of presenting a curriculum that draws on only a few of the multiple aspects of intelligence. On the other hand, we also do not want to make the decision to have a diverse curriculum that tries to do too much. Our goal is a balanced curriculum that aims to help all students find their special talents and abilities, as well as develop respect for the talents of others. As Noddings (1992) states, "Forcing all students through a curriculum designed for the capacities of a few cannot be done in the service of equality" (p. 31). We do not want children to believe that only one form of education is acceptable and that there is only one set of occupations for which it is worth the effort to strive. We need to value talents and abilities that lead to such technical jobs and trades as tailoring, plumbing, computer programming, repairing cars, and building with stone. It seems to make sense to use whatever subject matter that is mandated in the curriculum as a launching pad for learning major concepts, processes, and attitudes that will have applicability for life. This is what we have chosen to do at Benchmark. In addition, care theorists suggest, along with Socrates, that "an education worthy of the name must help students to examine their own lives and explore the great questions human beings have always asked" (Noddings, 1998, p. 191). Now *this* is a challenge no middle school student can resist!

Discovering Strengths

Searching for abilities, talents, and character strengths (Seligman, 2003) in our students is one of the staff's favorite pursuits and affects how our struggling readers feel about themselves. In addition to the classroom, this search goes on particularly during after-school activities. Each trimester students have the opportunity to participate in activities of their choice, including soccer, the ropes course challenge club, girls' club, board games, knitting club, chorus, art club, drama club, sports club, set construction, readers theater, golf, basketball, yearbook, chess, and many more. In each of these areas students discover talents, abilities, and character strengths they never knew they had.

The lower school drama club is an example of an activity where students grow in confidence as they discover their strengths. Approximately 35 students participate. They practice their parts, make costumes, and design and build sets from November until the end of March each year. They then put on two grand productions in our performing arts center. Middle school students who are experienced with Benchmark productions coach the lower school drama club participants during rehearsals and work as set crew for the performances. Our lower school students gain poise as actors, and the middle school coaches, who take their jobs very seriously, learn from the experience and are a tremendous help to the staff. In watching the middle school students work with the lower school students, we see leadership abilities and strengths of character that may not be as easy to detect in the day-to-day routine of classrooms.

Each year our middle school produces a Broadway musical. The entire middle school takes part—approximately 80 students—some as actors, others working with wardrobe and sets. Over the 12 years that this activity has taken place, we have discovered that the experience of producing a musical bonds the student body and staff in a way no other activity ever has. In addition, the musical provides an opportunity for

Successfully producing a Broadway musical requires a caring community, a diversity of talents, and much reading of both the script and books with background information about the setting and characters in the show. Pictured is Benchmark's 2003 production of *Fiddler on the Roof.*

many of our students to find new talents. Jay, for example, struggles in the classroom and is probably the least self-confident student in the middle school—that is, until you put a hammer in his hand. He is definitely the most talented member of the set crew and becomes an entirely different person during the 4 months he works on the set. In that time he becomes a confident leader; he knows what he is doing, and he knows that he excels at it. There are many similar stories to be told about many of our students: the discouraged first-year middle school student who became wardrobe mistress and sews so well that students prefer that she make alterations in their costumes rather than the moms who help out; the shy third-year student who became student director and discovered that he really understood how to develop the talent in his fellow classmates. All middle school students must audition for the musical, and some students also apply for key jobs such as set crew, sound technician, lighting technician, wardrobe mistress, makeup artist, hair stylist, and the like.

Relating Strengths to Curriculum and Instruction

The time period in which the script is set becomes the focus for a unit of study. For example, when they performed *Camelot*, students studied King Arthur and his Knights of the Round Table and the history of the associated time period. *Fiddler on the Roof* led to the study of the Russian Revolution. *Guys and Dolls* brought a focus not only to the history of the early 1900s but to math. Students actually requested that math teachers present lessons that would help them understand odds and probability related to the gambling scenes. Not too surprisingly, students are more interested in, and learn more about, a historical time period when it relates to something personal, such as their part in the musical, and they are able to perform better when they understand the time period in which the musical is set. Whoever thought that young adolescents would love studying the Russian Revolution—but they did.

As part of a multidimensional approach, the Benchmark staff teaches students the processes they need to accomplish their academic goals. The ability to take charge of the mental processes involved in learning determines, in large part, a young person's success in becoming a lifelong learner, thinker, and problem solver. For this ability to become a reality for students, teachers must have a deep understanding about three mental systems—the self-system, the metacognitive system, and the cognitive system—plus a fourth element, knowledge.

Understanding Mental Processing

One model that is helpful for understanding mental processing is the one presented by Marzano (2001). Marzano describes the workings of the mental systems in this way: When a new task (or an opportunity to change whatever one is doing or attending to at a particular time) presents itself, the self-system makes a decision about whether or not to engage; if the self-system decides to engage, the metacognitive system sets goals and strategies, followed by the cognitive system's processing of relevant information.

The self-system is composed of a network of beliefs and goals that are used to make decisions about whether a student will engage in the new task. As such, it is the prime determiner of the motivation a student brings to a task. Once a student makes the decision to engage in a task, the metacognitive system is engaged. This system sets goals relative to the new task and is responsible for designing strategies for accomplishing the goals. Once engaged, the metacognitive system is continually interacting with the cognitive system, which takes responsibility for the effective processing of the information that is essential to complete the task. The cognitive system is responsible for such operations as making inferences, comparing, classifying, and summarizing. According to Marzano's (2001) model, the three systems of thought are hierarchically arranged: "the self-system exerts more influence over learning than does the metacognitive system, which, in turn, exerts more influence over learning than does the cognitive system" (p. 14).

One of the major differences between Marzano's (2001) "new taxonomy" (described above) and Bloom's "taxonomy" (Bloom, Engelhart, Furst, Hill, & Karthwohl, 1956) is that the new taxonomy separates various types of knowledge from the mental processes that operate on them. If a student does not possess the requisite knowledge for a task, the effects of mental processes will be minimal. Marzano (2001) organizes knowledge into three general categories—information (often referred to as declarative knowledge), mental procedures (procedural knowledge), and psychomotor procedures—and describes areas of the curriculum in terms of how much of these three types of knowledge each comprises. He views these types of knowledge as domains that are acted upon by the cognitive, metacognitive, and self-systems. Marzano (2001) also sees the domain of information as hierarchical, with vocabulary and facts at the bottom of the hierarchy and general structures (e.g., concepts and principles) at the top. The domain of mental procedures includes strategic processes and skills, whereas the domain of psychomotor procedures is composed of the physical procedures needed to negotiate daily life and to engage in complex physical activities for work and recreation.

Putting all this together, we can see the interrelationship of mental processing.

1. The *self-system* evaluates importance relative to needs or goals, efficacy beliefs, emotional response, and overall motivation to increase competence in view of the other three types of self-system thinking. In this way, the self-system determines the extent to which a student is motivated to learn a given knowledge component.

2. If the self-system determines that the knowledge is important enough to learn, the *metacognitive system* establishes clear learning goals relative to the knowledge. Then through its four functions—goal specification and monitoring for process, clarity, and accuracy—it oversees the planning and carrying out of those goals.

3. Under the direction of the metacognitive system, the elements of the *cognitive system* (including retrieval, comprehension, analysis, and knowledge utilization) are then employed. The cognitive system is responsible for processes as simple as retrieval and as complex as using the knowledge in a new context.

Explaining Thinking and Self-Regulation Explicitly

In addition to understanding mental processing, it is important that teachers provide students with explicit explanations about how to take charge of their cognitive systems—what Zimmerman (1990) calls *self-regulation*. Self-regulation "pertains to students' self-generated thoughts, feelings, and actions used to achieve academic goals" (Dembo & Eaton, 2000, p. 474). It is the ability to control factors in the cognitive and affective systems that affect learning. At Benchmark we begin teaching self-regulation by sharing, with even our youngest students, basic information about how the brain works. For example, we teach students that they must actively do something with the information that is passing before them or they will lose it. We even conduct mini-experiments with them to make the point. We discuss "hooking" what they are learning to what they already know and teach ways of organizing new information so that it will be remembered. We share with students that, when given a task, successful learners monitor and control their behavior by setting goals, using their prior knowledge, considering alternative strategies, developing a plan, and considering fix-up strategies when they run into trouble. We teach students how to take charge of variables that affect learning, such as their motivation, methods of learning, use of time, physical environment, social environment, and performance (Gaskins & Elliot, 1991).

Researchers who examine the thinking of proficient readers find that there are between five and eight thinking strategies that proficient readers use consistently (Pressley, 2002). Keene and Zimmermann (1997), in their popular book *Mosaic of Thought*, recommend teaching eight strategies: be metacognitive, connect the known to the new, determine importance, question, use sensory images, infer, synthesize, and solve reading problems. Benchmark's framework for learning and understanding (Figure 13.2) posits three major categories of thinking strategies: monitor for sense, make inferences, and look for patterns. All eight of the Keene and Zimmerman (1997) strategies and the cognitive and metacognitive categories suggested by Marzano (2001) fit into the three Benchmark categories. Basically, as illustrated above, researchers have come to agree on the basic strategies that proficient readers most often employ.

There is growing consensus among practitioners and researchers (e.g., Gaskins & Elliot, 1991; Keene & Zimmerman, 1997; Pressley, 1998, 2002) that each of the five to eight major thinking strategies should be taught initially with singular focus to students from kindergarten through 12th grade and then gradually combined with other strategies to complete real-world tasks. Teachers should model the strategies and then have students practice them with a variety of texts, and the emphasis on orchestrating strategies should be consistently encouraged and scaffolded over many years. To create students who are metacognitive (i.e., think about their own thinking), teachers need to make them aware of the components of metacognition. For example, when students are reading, they need to know what and when they are comprehending, when comprehension is not taking place, and how to implement fix-up strategies when meaning-making processes break down. Students should be taught to set goals or purposes for reading and to plan how to meet the demands of text.

Another process that benefits from explicit explanation and teacher guidance is time management, a major problem (especially procrastination) for our young people. To help students plan their time, some of our teachers ask them to come to school each day with a list of after-school activities and plans for that day. Sometime during the day, an adult supervises each student as he or she completes a homework plan that takes into consideration his or her plans for the evening's activities. In discussing the previous day's plan, teachers guide students to see how they can have more control and autonomy by planning exactly how they will use their out-of-school time so that they will have free time, as well as accomplish their school work and take part in regularly scheduled activities. After several months of planning with students, they begin to realize that improved time management can help them complete necessary tasks more efficiently. Benchmark's process for guiding students to manage their time is very much like that described by Dembo and Eaton (2000). Like these researchers, we believe that it is the school's job to help students realize that when it comes to success, "no one has more control over a student's success than the student himself or herself" (p. 487).

Another area in which teachers guide students' development is that of learning declarative knowledge, our next topic.

Teaching Big Ideas

Contrary to schooling in the 20th century, when students were rewarded with good grades for memorizing facts, the focus in today's multidimensional classroom must be on teaching students overarching principles and concepts and essential understandings in each area of the curriculum. These have more lasting and generative value than, say, the myriad facts and details of the past decade, many of which will likely be different in the next decade. As a result Benchmark teachers are not as interested in students memorizing facts and details as they are in their generating, demonstrating, and applying principles, concepts, and essential understandings. Benchmark students are not told what they should learn. Instead, they are given opportunities to make sense of information and look for major ideas. The teacher acts as a guide who facilitates students' search for meaning. The teacher sets up conditions for students' explorations, points students in the right direction, and provides frequent feedback to assure accurate understanding and application. Students are encouraged to discuss their thinking aloud, to bounce ideas off of their peers, and to produce collaborative work. Prior to collaborative work, teachers facilitate discussions about key strategies for working successfully with others. One of many advantages to working in teams or small groups is that students are more likely to take risks associated with learning new concepts when they have the opportunity to collaborate with someone before joining a large-group discussion.

SUMMARY

As discussed in this chapter, part of orchestrating a productive learning context requires that we understand and modulate the outside-the-person variables that affect what students learn. Teacher knowledge, classroom culture, and multidimensional instruction are all important cognitive variables that will affect learners, but more importantly, they are the variables over which teachers can exert the most control. The context for optimum learning is an environment in which the student feels cared for and safe, where instruction is scaffolded, and where positive self-talk is nurtured. It is an environment in which maladaptive patterns of motivation are changed to competency-related ones, and in which instruction and curriculum are multidimensional and allow for abilities, talents, and character strengths to be discovered and valued. To create this atmosphere, teachers must have a deep understanding of the interrelationship of mental processes (the self-system, the metacognitive system, and the cognitive system) and knowledge, and they must understand and apply principles of learning.

In the next chapter I discuss the outside-the-person (situation) variables that affect what students learn and over which teachers have the least control: sociocultural variables of family and friends, including their socioeconomic status, religious preference, support for the school, language, customs, and values. In Chapter 6, I discuss task and text variables, those situation variables that the teacher can control by employing research-based classroom practices.

The Context for Learning

Sociocultural, Task, and Text Variables

When one thinks of a context for learning, thoughts usually turn first to the classroom. However, learning takes place within a context that extends far beyond the classroom to the various sociocultural environments in which children live. Sociocultural factors have to be considered in explaining learning because learning is cultural (see Figure 6.1). Learning represents "how a specific cultural group or discourse community interprets the world and transmits information" (RAND, 2002, p. xvi). Those who teach students from a variety of sociocultural environments serve children best when they understand the sociocultural differences in communicational practices and lifestyles. Some of the context factors that affect learning are economic resources, class membership, ethnicity, neighborhood, and school culture. All are reflected in oral language and in students' self-concepts. In this chapter I continue the discussion of the context for learning and focus on the sociocultural group, followed by a discussion of task and text variables.

SOCIOCULTURAL GROUP VARIABLES

Congruence between Home and School Regarding Literacy

The struggle to learn to read may be the result of school-based definitions of literacy that are not congruent with those learned at home. For example, in some homes, literacy is defined as being able to speak, read, and write several languages. In fact, during most school years at Benchmark, at least one or two students come from homes where maintaining the parents' native language and learning English are both primary values. Parents of these children believe it is important that their children learn to speak, read, and write English, plus learn the language of their homeland; and, often as a result, only the homeland language is spoken in the home. These parents feel that teaching their child to speak, read, and write in English is the job of the school.

Interestingly, learning to speak, read, and write speak two languages often is not a problem for the Benchmark student's siblings, but for a student with a propensity for

FIGURE 6.1. Sociocultural group.

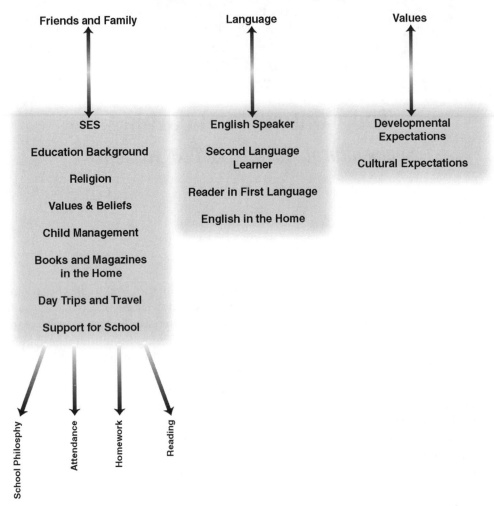

From *Success with Struggling Readers* by Irene Gaskins. Copyright 2005 by The Guilford Press. See copyright page for photocopying limitations.

language problems, the panoply of languages is one of confusion. We believe a child needs to learn to speak English before it is reasonable to expect that he or she read in English. Sometimes parents do not agree. This is a case of the school's definition of literacy not being congruent with that of the home. Another case of incongruence occurs when the school believes that struggling readers should spend several hours an evening reading and completing homework, but home life is too chaotic or parents do not value time spent on what they consider nonutilitarian course work. Parents, in such cases, may not realize the underlying message their child may pick up from his or her parents' attitude. Their child could be thinking:

> "My parents don't agree with the school policy on nightly reading. They don't think reading each night will make that much difference in how well I do in reading. I wonder if they think the school doesn't know how to teach me to read.

Resources in the School

For other children who are struggling readers, their difficulties may be related to attending schools with fewer resources, fewer experienced teachers, less focus on academics, and lower performance expectations from teachers than found in schools in middle-class neighborhoods. Despite their school's lack of resources, most of these children blossom when given the opportunity for a second chance at learning to read under the guidance of a knowledgeable teacher. Many barriers can be overcome in a caring school culture that provides good instruction, as is illustrated in the beating the odds studies (Taylor, Pearson, Clark, & Walpole, 2000).

At Benchmark lack of resources in their previous schools has often played a role in these students' struggle to read, especially in the case of our tuition-assistance students. Because these prior schools tend to have limited materials, all students are given the same text for reading instruction, regardless of their reading levels. In addition, once students are identified as struggling readers, they are often pulled out of class for additional reading instruction and taught by untrained aides or volunteers—despite the fact that these are the very students who need instruction in text at their specific reading level and from the most knowledgeable reading teachers.

Second-Language Learners

Another sociocultural variable that adds a burden to learning is being a second-language learner. Second-language learners are particularly challenged in the later grades, when they must venture beyond the primary-grade English texts. These later texts often incorporate sophisticated vocabulary and complex linguistic and discourse structures that are unfamiliar to a second-language speaker. This situation is exacerbated by the greater amount of cognitive effort required when reading in a second language. From a sociocultural perspective, the way in which the instruction is delivered and the social interactions that contextualize the learning experience can be a considerable challenge for children who are second-language learners. The identities and capacities of learners, the texts that are available and valued, and the tasks in which learners are engaged are all influenced by being second-language learners (RAND, 2002).

Benchmark's second-language learners are often easily identified by a visitor to their classrooms when whole-class instruction, such as social studies or science, is in progress. Either these second-language learners look bewildered or inattentive or, as is usually the case, they have a support teacher sitting beside them as an academic coach. Even social interactions are difficult; thus our teachers often assign a kind and empathic "buddy" to help the second-language learner navigate in social situations.

Differences in Discourse Communities

Within one classroom, the sociocultural context of home and community can vary greatly for some learners and minimally for others. The greater the difference, the more difficult the task of learning. Because students who are not European American and middle class usually do not belong to their teacher's primary discourse community, they may have more new norms and mores to learn than other children. They will also be faced with the challenge of "understanding text in ways that satisfy U.S. teachers and the demands of U.S. test writers" (RAND, 2002, p. 21). Benchmark teachers and students tend to enjoy other cultures and different perspectives, thus "other under-standings" are encouraged, valued, and accepted. This acceptance also helps students from different discourse communities become aware of these differences.

Match between Sociocultural Factors and Classroom Culture

Learning and understanding are comprised of cognitive, linguistic, and cultural activities that can put a learner at risk if sociocultural factors and the classroom culture are a poor match. In analyzing the match, a teacher needs to consider community and schoolwide variables, the culture of the classroom, the specific curriculum and instructional activities, and the nature of the interaction between teacher and students, as well as among students. A student who might be regarded as at risk due to sociocultural factors may be very successful in an instructional setting where the teacher attends to this student's needs when selecting texts, designing tasks for him or her, and deciding how to structure the context to best support the student's participation and learning. Making these instructional accommodations is a given in classrooms with a low teacher–student ratio such as exists at Benchmark; it is much more difficult to achieve when there is not an extra pair of hands to assist the teacher.

Expectations of the Teacher

Social group membership may have a negative effect on the performance of learners whose teachers have varying expectations for children from low- versus middle-income families and for those who are second-language learners. Beliefs about appropriate social interaction among some groups may conflict with the teachers' beliefs and put some children at a disadvantage. Teachers also need to be aware that, in the past, students from low-income families tended to receive a different set of reading tasks than higher-performing students as a result of being disproportionately placed in the

By regularly being read to at their conceptual level, struggling readers can keep pace intellectually with their peers who read on, or above, grade level.

lowest reading groups or lowest tracks where isolated skills instruction dominated (Allington, 1983). Such practices have not had beneficial consequences for these students.

Benchmark teachers believe that they must address the skill and strategy deficits that our students exhibit, while at the same time teaching and expecting the use of higher-level thinking strategies. The latter often is accomplished via read-aloud and taped readings of texts at students' conceptual levels.

THE ROLE OF EDUCATORS

The question for educators, then, becomes: "What are some general principles to guide what we do in school?" One principle is to reach out to families and communities to develop a shared sense of purpose between adults and young people. Teachers, parents, and those in the community can guide young people to understand the rationale for, and value of, what they are asked to do or learn, whether it is classwork, homework, long-term projects, or routine chores. Educators can collaborate with parents and community leaders to model the beliefs, expectations, values, and attitudes that are needed for success in school and in life.

Foster Support from the Adults in Students' Lives

In Bempechat's (1998) 6-year study of high-achieving poor minority students, she found that high achievers, no matter what their ethnic, cultural, or socioeconomic background, had similar stories to tell about the role support, values, and the expectations of their parents played in their success. These results reinforce the notion that young people, no matter what their reading level, ability level, or socioeconomic status, have the best chance for success if they have a caring adult supporting them who models the beliefs, expectations, values, and attitudes that are necessary for success in life. Ideally, of course, this support would come from a parent or guardian. Schools need to nurture a sense of efficacy and empowerment in family members, because what is said in homes becomes the self-talk that guides what young people think and do.

Nurture Parent Understandings

One way to foster positive home support is by reinforcing parents' productive beliefs about learning and achievement. In addition, schools should be sensitive to the variety of perspectives parents and children from different cultures and social groups bring to their experiences with schooling and the beliefs that develop as a result. For example, we can help parents understand that intelligence is not fixed and that effortful application of skills and strategies can compensate for any perceived lack of ability. We also want to help parents understand that learning is a process, that mistakes are part of the process and can be a springboard for learning, and that strategic persistence is an important key to success. If parents believe these principles, then it is likely their children will too. Parents also can help their children accept that even if school sometimes seems boring, they must persist. It is little surprise that, according to Bempechat's

(1998) research, the best form of parent support is encouragement—not pressure—for their child to do well in school.

Begin with What Is Known

There is no doubt that factors such as social class, ethnicity, and native language can have a significant effect on early reading development and continue to affect children well into adolescence. As just one example, Reynolds, Taylor, Steffensen, Shirey, and Anderson (1982) found that when students read culturally familiar material for which they already had a schema, they read it faster, recalled it more accurately, and made fewer comprehension errors. Although many researchers have documented that children from low-income homes are less prepared to engage in formal literacy learning than those from higher-income homes, we also have evidence that effective school programs can help children achieve, regardless of their economic class (Goldenberg, 2001; Taylor et al., 2000). In the case of second-language learners, research suggests that learning to read a second language is impeded if a child has limited proficiency in speaking that language. On the other hand, learning to read one's native language may facilitate a child's ability to learn to read a second language. Research also suggests that disruption of first-language learning by virtue of total immersion in second-language learning may impede language and literacy development in both languages (RAND, 2002). One conclusion to be drawn from this research is that children may be well served if they learn to speak English before being expected to learn to read English. Another possible conclusion is that learning to read in one's native language prior to learning to read English is an advantage when a child begins to learn to read in English.

Conclusions about Sociocultural Variables

Researchers have convincingly demonstrated that contextual factors such as economic resources, class membership, ethnicity, and neighborhood do not have to be the factors that determine success or failure in school. Where there is dynamic instructional leadership and dedicated, knowledgeable teachers, students are beating the odds (Bempechat, 1998; Meier, 1995; Taylor et al., 2000). Next we explore task variables and their interaction with other variables.

TASK VARIABLES

The tasks that teachers assign at Benchmark are intended to provide students with practice applying the skills, strategies, and knowledge that have been the focus of classroom instruction. An *academic task* is something a student needs or wants to learn or accomplish, based on what a teacher has already explained, modeled, and scaffolded. Tasks, as we use the term at Benchmark, are the short- and long-term assignments given by teachers. A meaningful task may be as simple as reading an unknown word or making an inference based on a story that was just completed. The task may also be learning specific multiplication facts or understanding how a simple machine works. Examples of more complex tasks that are assigned in our classrooms include writing a summary of a book, making an oral presentation about the adaptation of a specific animal to an ecosystem, or researching and developing a brochure about Alaska. At Benchmark, tasks are not assigned to be completed independent of the teacher until all the components of the task have been explicitly explained, modeled, and scaffolded over days, weeks, months, and sometimes over years. Anything less leads to the unproductive activities that Durkin (1978–1979) described in her classroom research.

Task variables are the elements involved in accomplishing the task. For example, in reading an unknown word, the task variables include the student's knowledge of, and ability to apply, sound–symbol relationships, as well as the appropriate background knowledge to recognize the word when it is decoded. The task variables for researching and developing a brochure would include management of time, space, and materials (probably the most difficult aspects of a project for our students); appropriate research skills and strategies; background knowledge about the topic; knowledge of the writing process; and much more. To facilitate our students' management of tasks, we teach them a strategy we call *analyzing the task*—that is, figuring out what is involved in accomplishing the task (see Figure 13.7). Our goal is that students use the process of analyzing the task to approach academic tasks systematically and strategically and as a way to recognize when they need to seek assistance. We have learned from experience that when a student is unclear about what the task variables are, the task is not likely to be completed satisfactorily.

As with all new strategies when they are introduced, Benchmark students are given explicit explanations, modeling, and scaffolding regarding how to analyze a task. They are taught that the first step is to restate the expectations of the task in their own words, then have their restatement checked for accuracy by a classmate or the teacher. Once students are sure they understand what the expectations are, they divide the task into manageable parts, consider possible roadblocks to completing the task, make a plan, and determine strategies to manage the roadblocks and the task itself. As students complete the task, they are guided to evaluate the effectiveness of their progress and to modify their approach, as needed.

Analyzing the task includes not only analyzing task variables but also the person, situation, and text variables that influence accomplishing the task. Our students become well aware of how task variables interact with person, situation, and text variables to influence what is learned and how successful they are in completing projects or tests. For example, students think about personal characteristics that may be roadblocks to completing their brochure project and they make a plan for how they will take charge of those characteristics (e.g., procrastination, disorganization, impulsivity). They also think of situation variables that may prove to be roadblocks, such as extracurricular activities or the lack of a quiet place to work. Students think about the texts that are available as resources and determine whether they are too dense, outdated, or just generally inappropriate and make plans to search for new texts at the library or on the Internet.

It is the teacher's job to make the task clear and to teach students the skills and strategies necessary to complete the task. The teacher must also make sure that the student possesses the conceptual knowledge upon which the task is to build. As the student completes the task, the teacher must step in to scaffold success. The teacher may help a student make a day-to-day schedule of work and hold him or her accountable for following it, or the teacher may monitor a student's daily note taking for relevance to the topic.

What follows is one example of how we teach students to analyze the task. This particular adaptation of the strategy has been named "A-NOW" by our students. (*A* = analyze, *N* = notes, *O* = organize, *W* = write). The need for the strategy arose in response to our students' frequently completing only part of an assignment or test question, therefore earning only partial credit (which some deemed unfair). To make the point that it is important to read directions carefully and put them in their own words, we require students to write directions in their own words—and the rewrite *is* graded. Much to our students' amazement, the simple task of rewriting the directions results in improved grades because they complete the assignments according to the directions.

When given essay tests (in the older classes of the lower school and in the middle school), students are asked to follow the A-NOW procedure. This means that on the test paper the students must rewrite the essay question in their own words: (A)nalyze, jot (N)otes for answering the question, (O)rganize the notes, and only then, (W)rite the essay. Initially, students complain that they will not have time to write all that they know if they have to use the A-NOW strategy. As a concession, we tell them that if they are unable to complete the essay, we will grade their notes instead of the essay. They think this is a good deal, and teachers have the pleasure of reading an organized outline or essay. Our students continue to apply the A-NOW strategy with much success when they move on to high school and college.

School tasks interact with text variables so often that the characteristics of texts play a significant role in determining how successful students will be in completing a task. Therefore, text variables must be considered in our discussion of variables that affect learning.

TEXT VARIABLES

Text variables are comprised of the elements of any printed or electronic materials, such as the hard copy of a book and electronic text such as hypertext. These texts may include graphs, maps, and charts. If the text variables are a good fit with the learner, task, and situation variables, the likelihood is increased that learning will occur. If the fit is poor, learning may be impaired. Text variables that may affect learning include level of vocabulary, proposed audience for the text, characteristics of text genre, clarity of text structure, and the nature of illustrations and graphics. Some of the specific matches between text and person variables that need to be considered when a student appears to be having difficulty with a text are (1) number of sight words known by students compared to the expectations of the text; (2) students' ability to decode unknown words found in the text; (3) students' familiarity with content and characters in the text; (4) level of meaning vocabulary in the text compared to the student's meaning vocabulary; (5) students' knowledge of the text structure and study techniques needed for learning from the text; (6) amount of white space on each page; (7) font style and size; (8) sentence length, book length, and book size; (9) support from illustrations; (10) familiarity with the genre; and (11) even popularity of the book among peers.

In addition, we need to realize that "particular features of the text create difficulty for particular readers engaged in particular activities; texts are not difficult or easy in and of themselves, but they become difficult or easy at the interface with readers and the purpose of the activity" (RAND, 2002, p. 94). One feature that we have found to be routinely difficult for our struggling readers is length of sentences. Sentences with complex syntax tend to present comprehension problems or a high load on working memory. Another text variable of which we make our students aware is the category to which a text belongs and how it is organized. Examples of text categories are narration, exposition, persuasion, and description. An example of organization is that of narrative texts, which include story grammar and the construction of the point/moral/themes of stories. Clearly some texts are better suited to a particular task than others.

The RAND Reading Study Group (2002) suggested that one place to start in understanding variability in texts is to look at all the categories of texts and the dimensions on which they vary. These categories and dimensions, as described by the Study Group, are summarized below.

1. Discourse genre, such as narration, description, exposition, and persuasion.
2. Discourse structure, including rhetorical composition and coherence.
3. Media forms, such as textbooks, multimedia, advertisements, hypertext, and the Internet.
4. Sentence difficulty, including vocabulary, syntax, and the propositional text base (the explicit meaning of the text's content drawn from propositions in the text, i.e., statements or idea units, but without more-subtle details about verb tense and deictic references (here, there, now, then, this, that).
5. Content, including different types of mental models, cultures, socioeconomic strata; age-appropriate selection of subject matter; and the practices that are prominent in the culture.
6. Texts with varying degrees of engagement for particular classes of readers. (p. 25)

Once students have learned to decode, two areas of text difficulty that can be troublesome are the *density of concepts in a text* and the *type of text* (Gaskins, 2003). Concept density refers to the number of concepts a reader encounters per unit of text. Narrative text tends to be easier for most students to read as compared to expository text, because expository text presents many more concepts per page. At Benchmark, we explicitly teach students about the differences between narrative and expository text, explaining and modeling the different processes required for the optimal reading of each. Teachers explain that the two genres have different purposes and therefore the pace of reading and depth of analysis will probably be different.

There is another type of density associated with expository text, the density of unknown words, which tends to be higher in expository than in narrative text. Benchmark teachers have systems in place to help students acknowledge their awareness of words for which they do not know the meaning. One system is to have students jot down unfamiliar words, the phrases in which they appear, and the page numbers. During discussion students share with peers their questions and hunches about word meanings and request clarification from members of the group. Vocabulary is not taught in isolation, nor are students expected to look up lists of words in the dictionary. Instead students are encouraged to extract the meaning of words from context clues or through collaboration with peers. Of course, it is fine to use a dictionary as a last resort.

It is not uncommon for struggling readers to attempt to read all types of text (e.g., textbook, novel, advertisement, hypertext) at the same pace and with the same level of (or lack of) reflectivity. As new types of texts are introduced, Benchmark teachers teach the learning strategies that each type of text necessitates. For example, as students begin to use the Internet to research topics, teachers provide them with explicit explanations about how to determine the appropriateness of hypertext information for a topic and how to corroborate the accuracy of the information. Search strategies are also taught.

In view of the variability in texts and the increased number of texts available, how does one assign texts so that each student will be reading in an appropriate text? The RAND Reading Study Group (2002) advises:

> The assignment of texts should strategically balance a student's interest in the subject matter, the student's level of development, the particular challenges faced by the student, the pedagogical goals in the curriculum, and the availability of texts. Teachers will need an enhanced knowledge of the texts that are available and access to computer technologies to help them manage the complex task of text assignment that will be expected in schools of the future. (p. 25)

Texts selected for students need to be sufficiently challenging and engaging, in addition to appropriately expanding their comprehension at a deep level.

Finally, there is no doubt that situation variables influence discrepancies in access to texts and in the perceived difficulty and appropriateness of texts. It is well documented that children who attend schools in poor districts have far fewer texts available than do children who attend schools in more prosperous areas; the availability of texts in homes and libraries varies similarly. Texts that deal with certain social issues or that require an interpretation and appreciation of alternative perspectives may be considered inappropriate by parents from some cultural or religious groups. Furthermore, texts at an appropriate instructional level may be rejected as too babyish by older learners, yet texts that seem too difficult may be read successfully if the topic is sufficiently interesting and relevant to the learner. Text factors interact with reader, task, and situation to determine what and how much students learn from texts (RAND, 2002).

SUMMARY

In this chapter I reviewed school, home, and community variables, as well as task and text variables, that affect what students learn. To provide students with the best possible chance to learn, especially if sociocultural factors suggest that a student is at risk for failure, the learning environment should be based on research-determined maxims, five of which are listed below (see also Figure 6.2).

1. A knowledgeable teacher is the key variable in determining what a student learns.
2. Despite unfavorable sociocultural variables, children learn when those who are in charge of their learning environment care deeply about them and establish a caring learning culture (see Chapter 5).
3. Knowledgeable teachers apply research-based principles of learning and, as a result, are able to beat the odds when they teach children who are at risk for failure due to sociocultural variables (Taylor et al., 2000).

FIGURE 6.2. The context for learning: Five maxims.

1. **Effective teachers are knowledgeable.** Teachers need to know a lot about the content they teach, the pedagogy for teaching that content, and general pedagogical knowledge. They need to become lifelong learners about teaching.

2. **A caring learning culture fosters student learning.** Students learn best when those who are in charge of their learning environment care deeply about them and can establish a caring learning culture. Teachers should study the characteristics of caring learning environments and become experts at creating them.

3. **Research-based teaching practices.**
   a. A multidimensional approach: Teachers must know a great deal about many possible approaches and use those that match the needs of students.
   b. Clear explanations and modeling of thinking processes for completing tasks: Teachers must understand how the mind works and teach the skills and strategies that will enhance students' mental functioning.
   c. An emphasis on principles, concepts, and essential understandings instead of facts and details: Teachers need to understand the big ideas of the content and learn how to lead students to discover these principles, concepts, and essential understandings.

4. **Understanding of, and respect for, sociocultural factors fosters effective teaching.** Sociocultural factors should be understood and respected, while providing instruction that meets students where they are and moves them forward.

5. **Selection of appropriate tasks and texts fosters effective teaching.** Teachers should vary tasks and texts according to the needs and interests of students and be selected with regard to the skills and strategies that have been taught.

From *Success with Struggling Readers* by Irene Gaskins. Copyright 2005 by The Guilford Press. See copyright page for photocopying limitations.

4. Sociocultural factors should be understood and respected, while providing students with instruction that meets them where they are and moves them forward.
5. Selection of tasks and texts should depend on the skills and strategies that have been taught and reflect the needs and interests of each student.

This discussion of sociocultural, task, and text variables concludes our exploration of the four categories of variables (person, situation, task, text) that interact when students are engaged in the process of learning. These variables, which comprise the ILM, provide us with our first learning principle, discussed in Chapter 7: Learning is an interactive process.

Learning Principles about the Interaction of Variables, Explicit Instruction, and Social Activity

What could be a better guide for how to teach struggling readers than using what we know about how humans learn? At least, that is the thinking of the Benchmark staff. Throughout the school's existence, we have combed the research literature for scientifically based principles about how children learn, then turned these principles into practices for teaching struggling readers. Currently, six principles of learning undergird the design and assessment of Benchmark instruction (see Figure 7.1). In determining interventions for struggling readers, we identify the interactions of variables in the Interactive Learning Model (ILM; Figure 2.1) that result in roadblocks to learning; then, based on the six learning principles, we design instruction that teaches students how to use their strengths to take charge of, compensate for, or cope with their roadblocks. Once a lesson is taught, Benchmark teachers use the same learning principles to assess their teaching, plan future lessons, and determine ways they might better meet the needs of their students. Three learning principles are discussed in this chapter, and three are discussed in the chapter that follows. Research citations, explanations, and classroom examples are provided for each principle.

LEARNING PRINCIPLE 1:
LEARNING IS AN INTERACTIVE PROCESS

As discussed in previous chapters, it is well documented that learning is an interactive process (Matlin, 2003; Pressley, 1995; Snow et al., 1996; Zimmerman, 1998). Every day in our work with students at Benchmark we are witnesses to the fact that what a person learns is the result of an interaction between person, situation, task, and text variables.

FIGURE 7.1. Six principles of learning:
Understanding and teaching struggling readers.

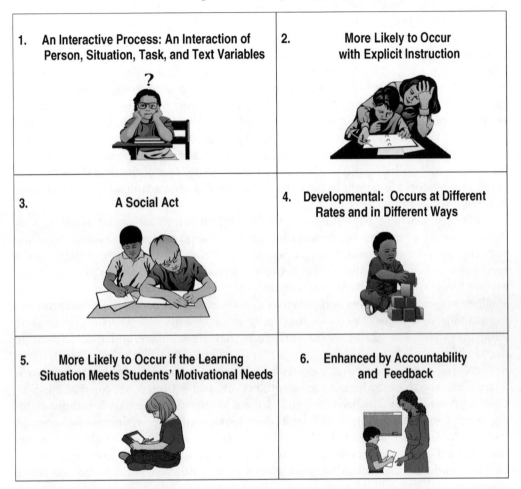

From *Success with Struggling Readers* by Irene Gaskins. Copyright 2005 by The Guilford Press. See copyright page for photocopying limitations.

The ILM reminds us that neither the struggles nor the successes of learners can be explained by one or a few variables; it is the interaction of many variables that creates the filter through which a student's learning is processed. As an example, just three among the many variables of which this filter is composed are cultural and social expectations, the self-perceptions that the learner brings to the learning situation (Silverman & Casazza, 2000), and emotion, which influences learning by affecting attention and priorities (Bereiter, 2002; R. Gaskins, 1996). Other person, situation, task, and text variables that affect a student's success in learning to read are outlined in Figure 2.1. The following classroom examples are illustrations of learning as an interactive process. In these examples, a few of the variables that interact to determine how a student learns are labeled.

An Example from the Lower School

Melinda Rahm, a Benchmark teacher who has taught second- and third-grade students who enter the school as nonreaders, commented that many of the new-to-Benchmark beginning readers do not seem to realize that what they read must make sense (the task). In previous schools, the texts these students read tended to be at least a grade level above their reading levels (text variable). As a result, students arrive at Benchmark feeling incompetent (person variable) and do not demonstrate the awareness or persistence (person variables) to demand meaning from text. They seem to believe reading is nothing more than reciting decoded words and, as a result, are undaunted when what they say is pure nonsense. Accepting nonsense should not strike us as too surprising, for much of what these struggling readers attempted to read before attending Benchmark probably did not make sense. Therefore, one of the first strategies our beginning readers are taught is "monitor for sense and take action when reading does not make sense."

Whether teaching beginning readers or slightly more advanced readers, Mrs. Rahm carefully structures her lessons (situation variable) so that all students have the opportunity to be successful. She places students in texts that are at their instructional levels. (We use 95–98% word-reading accuracy in text as our criterion.) The words are neither too easy, nor too hard (text variable). Mrs. Rahm breaks the reading task into small, manageable segments and provides explicit instruction, modeling, and scaffolding (situation variables) to ensure that students meet with success in understanding what they read. For example, she introduces new vocabulary and models how to decode new words before students encounter them in the text. She also guides students in surveying the story title and pictures and in accessing relevant background knowledge. Next, she asks students to make predictions and set purposes for reading. Students then read several pages as she guides them to the clues necessary for understanding what they are reading. When a student looks confused or uninvolved (person variables), Mrs. Rahm intercedes to model or cue how the student might take action (reread, read on for more clues, or ask for help). Because Mrs. Rahm constantly monitors her students' understanding and guides them (situation variable) to use active reader strategies to achieve success, they come to reading group each day feeling safe to risk sharing both their understanding of the text and their confusion.

Learning to read depends on many variables. Therefore, when students struggle in reading, many variables must be considered as targets for adjustment. Perhaps the text is too difficult, the learning situation is a poor match for the way a child learns, the reading task is presented in segments that are too long, or the child is feeling discouraged by past failures. These variables, in combination with others, interact to make learning to read a struggle. As the classroom illustrations in this book suggest, many factors must be considered when student learning is the issue, whether it is learning to read or learning math concepts, as illustrated below.

An Example from Lower School Math

Students in Janice Sands' second-level math class occasionally have teamwork-challenge problems that are completed at home. A teamwork-challenge problem is a hands-on investigation into a mathematical concept that involves parents, the Benchmark student, siblings, and others. The investigations involve challenging problems that students would not be able to complete independently. However, students are motivated by the challenge. They feel safe when working with a parent or sibling and enjoy having ample time to investigate the concepts, so they feel successful. One of the investigations recently completed involved fractions. Students were given a problem to complete with their families that required them to measure the ingredients to make hot chocolate. Through this activity, students constructed knowledge about equivalent fractions, part–whole relationships, and the addition of fractions. Successfully completing this activity did not depend on just one variable, such as each student's ability to understand fractions (person variable). It also depended upon the family valuing the worth of the activity and supporting the student (situation variables), the complexity of the activity (task variable), and the difficulty of the words in the recipe (text variable). All these factors interacted to determine whether learning the intended concept about fractions would take place. Should a child come to school the next day having not completed the activity (or having completed the activity, but not having grasped the concept the activity was intended to reinforce), the teacher would consider more than one variable as the possible culprit underlying the child's difficulty. Successfully learning the fraction concept is the result of an interaction of many variables.

As illustrated above, four variables that can affect learning are (1) amount of time to complete a task, (2) novelty of the task, (3) complexity of the task, and (4) whether the learner regards it as safe or a risk. For struggling readers learning is often enhanced when the interaction is between ample time, low novelty, low complexity, and low risk. When any of these variables is present in the opposite direction (i.e., little time, high novelty, high complexity, high risk), a student may feel anxious and, as a result, learn very little. On the other hand, these same possibly anxiety-producing variables may interact with a student's persistent disposition and love of a challenge to produce amazing learning for the time allowed. With so many possible interactions, it is often unclear specifically which variables are interfering with learning.

The following scenario illustrates how two middle school teachers deal with the task variables of time, novelty, complexity, and risk as these variables interact with person, situation, and text variables.

An Example from the Middle School

To prepare first-year middle school students to write a brochure about Alaska (task variable), Alexandra Cummin and Marianne Smith explicitly teach, model, and scaffold (situation variables) note taking and the organization of nonfiction information. For each step of the process, the teachers guide students to put in their own words the big ideas of the nonfiction reading (text variable) before taking notes on their own. When reading and note taking are completed, students come together as a whole group (situation variable that meets students' motivational need for relatedness) to discuss their understanding of the information about Alaska. Peers support or challenge one another's ideas before the group comes to a consensus about the best way to convey the information in their brochures. At this point, the teacher is guiding students to listen to, and interact with, each other in the acquisition and organization of the information. Students monitor (person variable) their own and their peers' understanding of the material and decide how to use it as a group. Providing ample time for discussion and

Learning is an interactive process.

paying particular attention to helping (situation variable) students organize the information reduces the complexity (task variable) of the assignment, helps students realize the similarity of this novel task (writing a brochure) to other writing tasks they have completed, and lessens anxiety (person variable).

Further information about learning as an interactive process can be found in Chapters 2–6, which discuss the many person, situation, task, and text variables that interact to affect if and what a student learns. The next learning principle elaborates on the benefits of explicit explanations that teach students how to accomplish the tasks assigned.

LEARNING PRINCIPLE 2: LEARNING IS MORE LIKELY TO OCCUR IF INSTRUCTION IS EXPLICIT

Providing struggling readers with explicit explanations about how to put into practice the strategies they need to accomplish assigned tasks increases the likelihood that reading and learning will improve (Bransford et al., 2000; Joyce & Weil, 2004; Pressley, 1995; Shepard, 2000). When I heard Dolores Durkin's presentation at the International Reading Association conference in 1977 and then read the report of her research (1977–1978), I was convinced that, as a staff, we could do a better job of teaching our students how to complete the tasks we assigned. Other researchers were also thinking about the issues of explicit teaching. In the 1980s I attended conference sessions about explicit explanation conducted by Duffy and Roehler, Paris, Pearson, and Lipson. Later I read the research report by Duffy, Roehler, and colleagues (1987) about the success of their program, in which teachers explicitly explained to students how to employ strategies for understanding what they read. I shared these findings with my staff. Explicit instruction made a lot of sense to all of us. Our experience teaching struggling readers suggested that, unlike students who achieve well in school because they have the ability to self-teach, our students tend to learn what they are taught and often do not figure out what is not taught. Students who achieve well in school tend to see patterns in their learning environment and use those patterns to generate additional knowledge about the "what and how" of learning. However, for some reason, self-teaching is not an intuitive matter for our struggling readers. We wanted our students to develop these same self-teaching abilities, and to do so, we felt they needed explicit explanations about what is to be learned, why it is important, when it can be used, and how to learn it, followed by teacher modeling and scaffolding of the task to be learned (Gaskins, 1994; Gaskins, Anderson, Pressley, Cunicelli, & Satlow, 1993). In fact, there are those who contend (e.g., Gee, 2003) that most people do not learn well when left on their own to learn in complex contexts about which they know very little. It seems likely that all students would benefit from explicit explanations.

In the late 1980s, as a result of a James S. McDonnell Foundation research and development grant and in collaboration with Richard Anderson and Michael Pressley, the Benchmark staff studied the research on explicit explanation of strategies for learning, thinking, and problem solving and developed an across-the-curriculum model of explicit instruction (Gaskins & Elliot, 1991). The study of this research led us to significant changes in our teaching practices. Benchmark teachers learned about setting realistic learning goals for their students and about explicitly explaining to students how to execute the strategies they might use to accomplish these goals. Here are some classroom examples of explicit explanations of how to summarize, how to complete a math activity, and how a middle school teacher draws from her students the explicit steps for a project.

Examples of Explicit Explanation from the Lower School

An example of explicit explanation comes from Sherry Cress's class, in the spring of the school year, when students are reading at the primer and second-half-of-first-grade levels. The goal was for her students to summarize the stories they read in literature basals. To accomplish this goal, she taught students to summarize by using the story elements they had learned earlier in the school year. Her explanation of the strategy went something like this:

> "Our *goal* today is to begin learning how to summarize the stories we read. A summary is a brief retelling of the important ideas in a story. Would someone like to predict *why* knowing how to summarize is important? [Mrs. Cress listens to a few student hypotheses.]
>
> "You all shared some good reasons. One *reason* I summarize is to check my understanding of what I read. Another *reason* I summarize is to share with others what the story is about. I also summarize as a way to help me remember what I have read.
>
> "*When* do you think you might use the summarizing strategy? [Mrs. Cress listens to a few student hypotheses.] Yes, we can summarize when we are reading as a way to check our understanding. We can also summarize when someone asks us to tell about a book or story we have read.

"I bet you are wondering '*How* are we going to decide what to include in our summaries?' We certainly don't want to go on and on and tell every detail of the story. The secret to summarizing is to use story elements. Would each of you write on the card I gave you the story elements you can remember? [Mrs. Cress gives students time to write.]

"Who would like to share one of the story elements you wrote? [She calls on students, who share that the story elements are the setting (composed of *when* and *where*), the characters, the central story problem, and the resolution of the problem.] I am pleased that all of you are so involved and that you remembered what the story elements are. I have made a chart for you illustrating how to summarize a story. [Mrs. Cress posts a chart that reads:

> The characters in the story were (give names of main characters) .
> The story took place at (tell place) during (tell time) .
> The problem was that _____ .
> The problem was solved when _____ .]

"Listen as I summarize a story I read. [Mrs. Cress points to each part of the chart as she summarizes]:

> "The characters in the story were Zeke and Zach.
> "The story took place in the boys' treehouse during the present time.
> "The problem was that while the boys were in the treehouse, someone took the ladder the boys used to get up to the treehouse.
> "The problem was solved when Dad remembered where the ladder had been when he borrowed it.

"Does anyone have any questions about how you will summarize the story that we are going to read today? On the back of the card I gave you, I would like you to write notes that you will use in telling your summary. [Mrs. Cress shares the notes she wrote for her summary.] You will want to write on your card just the information that goes in the blanks on the chart: the names of the main characters, the place and time, the problem, and how the problem was solved. Don't write in sentences. Just write a few words that will help you remember the four main points on the chart."

After this explicit explanation of how to summarize, Mrs. Cress introduced the story to be read and asked students to survey, access background knowledge, and set purposes for reading. After everyone finished reading and writing notes, the teacher scaffolded the telling of summaries by a few volunteers.

Explicit Writing Instruction

An example of explicit writing instruction comes from Susan North's class. A common genre of writing in lower school classrooms is the personal experience story. This is a story based on a past event experienced by the student. Before beginning the task, students brainstorm past experiences that would be interesting as a story. Mrs. North then reads several personal experience stories written by her former students. During the lesson, Mrs. North also reads a story she wrote about her first experience rock climbing.

Next, she leads her class in reviewing the steps of the writing process: plan, draft, reflect, request and apply feedback, revise, edit, publish. As students work on their stories over several days, explicit explanation is provided for each step of the process. Students are guided by a wall chart that reads:

- What: Plan—before we begin to write about a personal experience, we plan what we are going to write.
- Why: Planning helps us write a piece that is clear and interesting.
- When: We can use the planning strategy any time we are going to write something that someone else is going to read.
- How: Identify the purpose of the piece.
    Identify the audience.
    Gather information.
    Select and organize ideas.

Mrs. North provides students with a planning sheet that includes a bubble for the main ideas of the piece and three smaller bubbles for details to be included in the story. On the sheet a blank line is provided for students to use in planning their first sentence. Next, she gives the students copies of the story she had written about rock climbing and directs them to work in pairs to figure out what the plan for the rock climbing story may have looked like. Finally, students share ideas as a whole class. Mrs. North points out the topic sentence and the concluding sentence of her story and how all the details in the story relate to the main idea. At this point, she gives students time to begin planning their personal experience stories. Mrs. North responds to each of the student's plans individually, asking him or her to verbalize the plan and to add or alter details.

Explicit, step-by-step explanations and support turned what might have seemed like an overwhelming task into bite-sized pieces. Benchmark math teacher Janice Sands

Learning is more likely if instruction is explicit.

also explicitly explains to her students how to accomplish tasks they view as difficult, for example, learning math facts.

An Example from Lower School Math

Many of our struggling readers have difficulty memorizing basic facts. As a result, Mrs. Sands explicitly teaches students in her second-level class strategies for learning basic addition and subtraction facts. Not knowing these facts, they tend to rely on counting their fingers or objects to find answers to math problems. Such practices do not promote mathematical or algebraic thinking. Once students have learned the basic addition facts for 10, they have the tools needed to solve the facts to 18. We find that students need explicit instruction about how to use these tools. Students are given a 10-frame tool and two colors of chips. The +9 facts are worked with first. The teacher models for the students how to solve the problem on the 10-frame. For example, they work with the math problem of 9 + 6. Students are explicitly taught to place 9 chips on the 10-frame and then place the 6 chips under the 10-frame. Mrs. Sands asks the students:

> "How many more spaces do we need to fill to complete the 10-frame?" (1)
> "Where can we get that 1 from?" (Students are guided to move one chip from under the 10-frame onto the 10-frame.)
> "We were trying to solve the problem 9 + 6. Do we still have 9 + 6? (Yes)
> "How does it look different?" (We have filled the 10-frame.)
> "What problem do we now have?" (10 + 5)
> "Which is easier to solve, 10 + 5 or 9 + 6? Why?" (10 + 5, because 9 + 6 can be changed into 10 + 5 by moving a chip)

Several of these problems are solved before moving into adding with 8, 7, or 6. The same questions are asked each time to help students understand what questions they need to ask themselves to use the strategy effectively. Once students seem proficient with the 10-frames, they shift to solving problems mentally, with the teacher asking the questions. Next, students begin to ask themselves the questions, and they require less and less teacher support both with the 10-frames and with the mental computation.

Strategy instruction gradually becomes more complex and includes teaching students how to orchestrate many strategies to complete long-term assignments. Such instruction might include how to choose sources, how to budget time, how to take notes, and how to organize the notes to write a report, as shown in the next example.

An Example from the Middle School

This example involves the continuation of the brochure project. Earlier in the trimester students wrote a brochure about Alaska and the Arctic tundra. The next task students were asked to complete was a brochure on the rainforest ecosystem. Mrs. Smith began the class with a discussion about the process the class used to produce the Alaska brochure.

T: Can you recount the steps we used to gain an understanding about the Arctic tundra?

S: First, we read some books.

T: What kind of books?

S: Nonfiction.

S: You gave us packets, and we took notes.

T: Were these sources hard or easy to read?

S: They were easy to understand, but there wasn't enough information so we had to look at other books.

T: So what is the first part of the process?

S: To do some easy reading to build background knowledge.

T: What else did we do early on to build background knowledge?

S: We watched videos and played the biome game on the Internet.

T: How did that help you?

S: Watching the video gave us a good picture of the Arctic.

T: Once we brainstormed and built some background, what was the next step?

S: You gave us sources, and we took notes at home. When we came into class, we discussed and asked questions about what we didn't understand.

S: Then you reread parts to us, and we transferred our notes to cards and organized them into categories for our brochure.

S: Sometimes we took notes in a flowchart, but we didn't put them onto cards because they were too big.

T: So why did we take the step of transferring notes to cards?

S: Because you made us?

T: Any other comments?

S: So we could organize the information better.

This conversation continued through a review of the process of completing the first brochure. Students had already spent 2 nights completing easy reading about the rainforest to build background knowledge and to prepare for discussion. They were also required to bring to class source books from local libraries. Mrs. Smith next reintroduced the process:

T: How do you think the rainforest brochure will be similar to, or different from, the Arctic brochure?

S: The rainforest is more complicated. There are a lot more plants and animals.

T: So we have a more complicated job of figuring out what we want to include or leave out of the brochure. You have already done some easy reading. What should our next step be?

S: There's not enough information on our nonliving categories in what we have read so far.

S: Maybe we need different categories because there are so many plant and animal relationships.

S: I think landforms are really like the layers of the rainforest.

T: Good thinking. So maybe we should survey the books you brought in to see how different authors organize their information.

Students surveyed the books they brought to class and brainstormed categories, as Mrs. Smith listed them on the chalkboard. Next she led a discussion of the common sections found in their sources and asked what would be most important to include in a 2-page brochure. Mrs. Smith and the class also reviewed the roadblocks students experienced in producing the first brochure. In addition, they set personal goals on which each student would focus and discussed strategies they might use during the researching and writing of the new brochures. Their individual goals varied from improving sentence structure in their writing to vowing to hand in all drafts on time. Others wanted to improve their note taking, whereas still others said they planned to ask questions along the way to gain better understanding.

While researching in nonfiction texts, students also read fiction that was set in the ecosystem under study. This daily reading of fiction helped build background knowledge and vocabulary and developed the concepts of cultural and physical conservation of the regions. In this second brochure of the year, more responsibility was released to the students in managing the process and their time. Students were also given the freedom to choose which rainforest region to research. The final product of this ecosystem unit was to write a children's story set in the Arctic or in the rainforest. In preparation for these stories, students chose two animals to research from one of the ecosystems.

Explicit explanations provide students with the tools and strategies they need to successfully complete the tasks assigned. Anything less does not qualify as teaching. In addition, teachers can facilitate learning by encouraging students to co-construct declarative and procedural knowledge. This process enhances learning because learning is a social act, a topic discussed in the next section.

LEARNING PRINCIPLE 3: LEARNING IS A SOCIAL ACT

Today few would disagree that learning is social (Alexander, 2000; Anderson et al., 2000; Bransford et al., 2000; Gollub, Bertenthal, Labov, & Curtis, 2002; Lampert & McCombs, 1998; Shepard, 2000). However, 25 years ago the realization that learning is social was not commonplace. This thinking began to change in the 1980s, a time that proved to be an exciting one in education. The understanding that learning is social was just beginning to be taken seriously among researchers and academicians. The Center for the Study of Reading, under the direction of Richard Anderson, was churning out yellow-covered technical reports at a rate with which Benchmark's research seminar could barely keep pace. Conferences, journals, and books were full of new ideas about instruction. Some of these new ideas were inspired by the writings of Russian psychologist Lev Vygotsky and featured suggestions for how teachers could help students develop experience with, and be inducted into, the ways of thinking used by a community of learners. The reciprocal teaching work of Brown and Palincsar (e.g., 1982) captured our attention because it illustrated how individual learning is a social process. We learned about the *zone of proximal development* and how social interactions can supply both a model of expertise and the opportunity for guided practice, as students internalize desired skills and strategies learned from the teacher, or a more knowledgeable student, to eventually perform them independently. Books by Rogoff (1990), Tharp and Gallimore (1988), and Wertsch (1991) temporarily satisfied our thirst for inspiration about learning in a social context. These books inspired us to "rouse minds to life" by mediated learning interactions and adaptations of the apprenticeship model.

We were convinced that what and how well each of our struggling readers would learn would be the result of socially supported interactions. We believed that student learning and understanding were enhanced by dialogue with teachers and peers, and that shared understandings, as well as idiosyncratic understandings, arise from the social nature of learning. Our experience since those early days of developing communities of learners has taught us that it is crucial to create a social learning environment for struggling readers that is of a high quality and that can be sustained over many years (Pressley, 1995). Because what is taken into the mind is socially and culturally determined (Shepard, 2000), the staff believes that the quality of social support is critical.

Learning is a social act.

Unfortunately, putting into practice the principle that learning is a social act has been slow in coming to modern-day classrooms. Several generations ago educators plied their trade as if learning were totally an individual act and collaborating with a peer or peer group was, at best, off task and, at worst, cheating. Today, educators realize that it is during the give and take of collaboration and discussion that real learning takes place and that sophisticated thought develops through interaction with others. Not only is social learning more productive, it serves as a precursor of the modern work model and therefore prepares students for life after school.

While working collaboratively or discussing with others, learners are often asked to defend, elaborate, and clarify their thinking, a process that requires a deeper level of thinking and understanding than they might push themselves to achieve individually. In addition, others bring information and ways of accomplishing learning that an individual might not consider or know. Peers also encourage reflection by challenging the thinking of others. A further advantage of interacting with others is that in a community that is learning together, participants are more likely to take on the identity of learners—for example, exhibit individual motivation to achieve goals (Gee, 2003).

With the increasing realization that what they learn individually is rarely of the quality they can achieve within a network of relationships, our students begin to take the initiative to create their own enriching social environments. Successful learners seem to know intuitively that learning is an act influenced by social interactions, interpersonal relationships, and communication (Gee, 2003; Lampert & McCombs, 1998). Because not all students seek out peers as collaborators, Benchmark teachers provide explicit explanations about how to collaborate, and they organize learning tasks and collaborative groups to facilitate structured and scaffolded collaboration. With the help of student volunteers, teachers also model how to collaborate. By these processes, teachers socialize students into the discourse and practices of learning together. A few examples of that process follow.

An Example from the Lower School

Examples of learning as a social act can be seen everywhere at Benchmark. Teachers mediate student learning and encourage peer collaboration throughout the day. Often, before expecting a response to a question or statement in a reading group, science, or social studies lesson, the teacher tells the class: "Turn to your partner and spend 30 seconds discussing your response to our purpose question. See if you and your partner can agree on a joint response." This simple 30-second social activity primes the pump for a learning experience in which each student feels prepared to respond and to critique the responses of others. We found that before we used this Every-Pupil-Response (EPR) procedure, participation was left to a few students; however, the passivity among the rest of the students meant less learning for everyone.

An Example from Middle School Math

Another example of learning as a social act occurs frequently in math classrooms. During one pre-algebra lesson in Mrs. Sands's class, students were asked to make different types of comparison statements about data. After practice using the five types of comparisons (differences, ratios, fractions, scaling, and percents), students were given an assignment to write a short newspaper article about camping data. The article had to contain at least one sentence that used each of the comparison types. Each student worked with a partner to analyze data about camping in the United States, create headlines, and write articles. As they worked, students used a variety of means to clarify their understanding about each type of comparison. These included talking with their partners, asking for clarification from their teachers and from other students in the class, and explaining their ideas to others.

The next examples of social learning also come from Benchmark's middle school. Middle school students are the most social of our students, and they tend to prefer learning in small groups to working on their own.

Examples from the Middle School

Our middle school students collaborate throughout the school day to complete assignments in all areas of the curriculum and to discuss the literature and content-area texts they are reading. They are given short- and long-term assignments that require small groups to collaborate to accomplish tasks such as solving a problem, completing a project, or giving a presentation. In addition, students are taught to be self-advocates and to aggressively seek the social support they need. A period in the daily middle school schedule is designed precisely to facilitate collaboration: It is the 30-minute mentor-group period, a time when groups of three or four students meet with their mentors. Another time when collaboration takes place is during after-school guided study. Each of these meeting times provides opportunities for students to work with staff and other students to fill in background knowledge and to model strategies for one another. Collaboration also takes place when students are absent or do not understand an assignment. In such cases, it is their responsibility to call or e-mail a classmate to find out what they need to know to complete the next day's assignment. Using the excuse "I didn't know what the assignment was" or "I didn't understand the assignment" is not acceptable at Benchmark. Instead, students are expected to use social interaction to solve their problems.

Social support is one of the key characteristics of schools that produce successful students (Roeser et al., 2000). We think this is true because learning is a social act. Small groups also provide an opportunity for students who learn at different rates and in different ways, as described in the next chapter.

SUMMARY

In this chapter three principles of learning were discussed that researchers suggest should guide instruction in all classrooms, but particularly classrooms with struggling readers. Explanations and classroom examples were provided for each principle. The principles discussed were:

1. Learning is an interactive process that includes an interaction of person, situation, task, and text variables.
2. Learning is more likely to occur if teachers provide explicit explanations about strategies for accomplishing the tasks they assign.
3. Learning is a social act, and student learning is increased when students are encouraged to collaborate with peers and teachers for such reasons as to ask questions about and discuss text, to produce written products, and to complete projects.

In the next chapter three additional research-based principles are introduced, discussed, and illustrated with examples from Benchmark classrooms.

CHAPTER 8

Learning Principles That Guide Classroom Instruction

Developmental, Motivational, and Accountability Issues

I am absolutely convinced that everyone who is an educator has witnessed, and believes, that children learn at different rates and in different ways. So, if it is a known fact, why do some teach as if everyone in their classes learns at the same rate and in the same way? As long as this practice continues, some students will struggle and fail in learning to read. This issue, as well as motivational and accountability issues, are discussed in this chapter. Three other principles of learning that undergird instruction at Benchmark were discussed in Chapter 7. Our experience at Benchmark suggests that struggling readers learn best in classrooms that employ all six principles of learning.

LEARNING PRINCIPLE 4: LEARNING IS DEVELOPMENTAL AND THEREFORE OCCURS AT DIFFERENT RATES AND IN DIFFERENT WAYS

It is axiomatic that people learn differently (Fischer & Tose, 2001; Lambert & McCombs, 1998). My early work with children labeled dyslexic taught me just how different poor readers can be. During the mid-1960s, as discussed earlier, I was a research assistant for the University of Pennsylvania's Reading Clinic dyslexia study. At that time, I was gathering data for my own dissertation research about students who were virtually nonreaders in fourth grade. The goal of both studies was to discover the discriminating characteristics of bright children who had extreme difficulty learning to read, despite adequate instruction and without any contributing difficulties such as emotional, obvious neurological, visual, or auditory problems. I discovered in the Reading Clinic study and in my own research that struggling readers are more different than alike and are not easily discriminated, based on tests of mental functioning or abilities, from students who read better than they do (except on tests of reading and writing, and, in the case of my research, time and space orientation). In both studies the struggling readers differed from one another. They learned to read at different rates and in different ways. The most valuable lesson I learned was to *not* look at the student as the problem, but rather to look for the problem in the match between the student and the teaching method. All of us, not just struggling readers, learn at different rates and in different ways. It is the educator's job to adjust teaching to those varying rates and ways. When a teacher does not do so, some students will struggle and fail.

I have become a firm believer that each characteristic of each person has a unique developmental timetable and a unique pathway of development. As a result, students vary in what they are able to learn with and without scaffolding. The challenge for the teacher is to match instruction to student competence, providing just enough input so that educational progress occurs for every student (Pressley, 1995). Individuals have different strategies, different abilities, different interests, different learning preferences, and different patterns of interaction as a result of their heredity and their prior experiences; therefore, they need a range of opportunities to demonstrate their knowledge and skills (Gollub et al., 2002) as well as to learn to compensate for any challenges. The potential of each learner will develop to differing degrees, on varying timetables, calling for assorted kinds of support (Tomlinson et al., 2002). There will never be just one best method, or even a few best methods, for teaching all children to read. This is espe-

Learning occurs at different rates and in different ways.

cially true for children who struggle in learning to read. Certainly there are better methods, however, and those better methods are based on solid research and theory and on the individual differences exhibited by each student.

The challenge for teachers is to generate goals and processes that are within reach of students but not beyond their grasp. If we teach only within the parameters of what students know and can do, they will not learn more or develop more powerful strategies for learning. On the other hand, if we work too far outside their present knowledge and capacity, they will struggle too much to be able to learn optimally (Joyce & Weil, 2004,), and motivation and self-efficacy will be reduced. We must generate learning environments (including the cognitive tasks and the social demands of the environment) so that they pull the students forward toward growth without overwhelming them.

Research about how experts perform has informed our practice. With that research in mind, we design the curriculum to model how experts operate. We set high expectations, pulling our students to the best levels of performance we know. We teach the skills possessed by experts, although not in the same way for all students. We try to be flexible enough to provide students with both appropriate challenge and appropriate support at all points in their evolution as learners.

Because we track students' strengths and challenges, as well as achievements, we are especially aware of the differences in students' development. An example of these differences follows.

An Example from the Lower School

Each year for over 10 years, lower school supervisor Colleen O'Hara and I have paid particular attention to the progress of our youngest class of students who begin in Sherry Cress's class and the next year move, as an intact unit, to Theresa Scott's class. It never fails but that about half the class makes exciting progress in one or more areas (phonemic awareness, word reading, or comprehension) during the first year, whereas the other half seems to lag behind. By the end of the year in Ms. Scott's class, however, students are very similar in the progress they have made over their 2 years at Benchmark, particularly with regard to phonemic awareness and word reading. Those who made a jump-start the first year tend to level off and consolidate their gains, whereas those who lagged behind the first year often catch on and catch up to their same-age Benchmark peers. We interpret this trend to mean that some needed more repetition and individual support to make similar gains. These first-, second-, and third-grade beginning readers entered the school learning at different rates and in different ways. By teaching at a pace that met each student where he or she was, and in ways that worked for each, all students were allowed to learn at their own rates and in their own ways, and as a result make similar progress in reading over a 2-year period, despite their differences. We notice comparable patterns in math classes.

An Example from Lower School Math

Students in Mrs. Sands's second-level math class complete an activity called "Daily Number." This activity involves having students write equations that equal the date. The activity is structured so that each student works at a level that is comfortable but challenging. For example, several students use patterns to help them write their equations. They are challenged to change their patterns after four or five equations. Some students must use three or four numbers in their equations with mixed operations, whereas others may use only two numbers. Mrs. Sands revises her expectations based on each student's readiness for a greater challenge.

An Example from the Middle School

Mrs. Cummin commented that one of the best reasons for the middle school mentor-group period is that students learn at varying rates and in different ways. Mentor group is a time when students receive the individual support they need to create success. The daily 30-minute period is used to analyze and plan tasks with teacher support, discuss individual strengths and roadblocks, and generate goals and processes to complete tasks. Mentor group is critical in planning long-term tasks and breaking them down into manageable chunks, especially for students who experience difficulty managing their time. Mentors have high expectations and support students in working to their highest potential, while helping them understand and compensate for the roadblocks that get in their way.

No matter what the content area, we can be sure that students will not all learn at the same rate and in the same way; consequently, teachers must adjust the rate and way they teach according to where students are functioning. Teachers must also meet students' motivational needs, particularly for competence, affiliation, and autonomy. These needs are discussed in the next section.

LEARNING PRINCIPLE 5: LEARNING IS MORE LIKELY TO OCCUR IF THE LEARNING SITUATION MEETS STUDENTS' MOTIVATIONAL NEEDS

Motivation is a key ingredient for learning (Alexander, 2000; Goslin, 2003; Pressley, 1995). Indeed, learning is not "coldly" cognitive, "but encompasses motivational dimensions" (Alexander, 2000, p. 30). In fact, some researchers believe that motivation is "the indispensable element needed for school success" (Sternberg, 1998, p. 17). Without it, students may never try to learn. As discussed by some educators, motivation includes volition: the emotional energy behind what we do, including a personal decision to pursue a goal. Motivation affects what is learned, how much is learned, and how much effort will be put into the learning process (Gollub et al., 2002). It can be extrinsic/performance oriented (e.g., to get a good grade) or intrinsic/learning oriented (e.g., to satisfy curiosity). Whether extrinsic or intrinsic, the learner's level of motivation strongly affects his or her willingness to persist in the face of real or perceived difficulty—a phenomenon familiar to struggling readers—making motivation one of the crucial ingredients of our program at Benchmark. The value a student places on academic tasks also influences his or her motivation, as does the learner's beliefs about the relative importance of effort versus ability and whether or not he or she believes that the rewards for engagement are worth the effort (Goslin, 2003). Motivation is part emotion and part desire, and, as such, it has many facets.

Our views about motivation have been greatly influenced by the hierarchy of needs identified by Maslow (1968) and Deci (1995). Their perspective of motivation is that people behave to satisfy needs. Some psychologists group these needs into two categories: deficiency needs and growth needs. According to Maslow's theory, deficiency needs, the lowest four needs of the hierarchy (physiological needs and needs for safety, love and belonging, and self-esteem) are no longer motivators once they are satisfied. Those that follow on the hierarchy are growth needs for knowledge, aesthetic satisfaction, and self-actualization). These become motivators when basic needs are met.

As an extension of Maslow's theory, Deci (1995) notes that once basic physiological and safety needs are met, needs for autonomy, competence, and relatedness become primary. Autonomy is the feeling of having some control over situations rather than being controlled by the situation. In Benchmark classrooms, the need for autonomy is usually satisfied when students are given choices. Another need in Deci's (1995) model is for competence. We have learned that if we want students to take academic risks, we must be sure that the tasks we ask them to complete independently are tasks for which they have the strategies and capacities to be successful. When they do not have the strategies and capacities, teachers employ an apprenticeship model (Rogoff, 1990): They work side by side with students, giving them just the right amount of support, but not too much. Next in Deci's (1995) model is the need for affiliation or relatedness, the sense of being connected to, and involved with, others. We have been successful in fulfilling this need for many of our students by allowing them to collaborate in responding to text they have read or in completing projects.

Since the inception of Benchmark, many sessions of our research seminar have been devoted to discussing the teacher's role in motivating students. We have combed the literature for insights into how to get school-battered, struggling readers to *want* to read and learn. Our review of the research literature and our experience teaching struggling readers suggest that motivation is fostered when teachers make the most of the 10 basic tenets listed in Figure 8.1.

I conclude this section on motivation with examples of how we foster motivation at Benchmark and with a case study of the effect of faulty beliefs on motivation. The majority of the examples take place in the middle school where motivation is always an issue for someone.

Examples from Benchmark's Early Days

One key to motivation that we discovered during the first months of the school's existence was the necessity of supplying students who were reading well below their interest level with materials on topics they deemed sophisticated and found engaging, yet were written at a first- or second-grade reading level. In 1970 I designed a nuclear submarine unit to coincide with students reading the *Sailor Jack* series. This series (published in the 1960s and now out of print) is about the antics of a sailor and his pet parrot who live on a nuclear submarine. My husband (who, fortunately for me, assisted in writing the operating manual for the first nuclear submarine) served as my consultant as I researched atomic power and nuclear submarines. With this knowledge, I wrote supplementary readings for my intermediate-grade students that taught them the

FIGURE 8.1. Ten tenets for motivation.

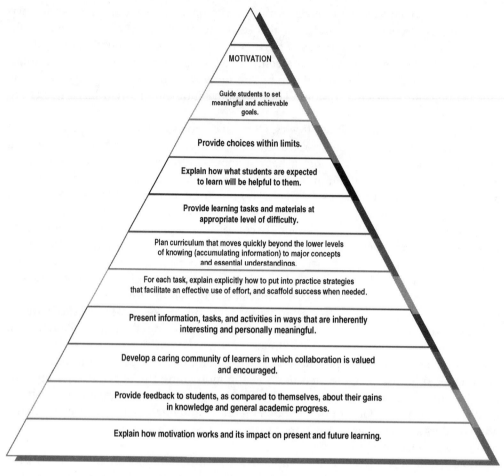

From *Success with Struggling Readers* by Irene Gaskins. Copyright 2005 by The Guilford Press. See copyright page for photocopying limitations.

basics of nuclear power and nuclear submarine design. My struggling readers liked learning about a topic that their peers, siblings, and even parents did not understand. Teaching to my students' interest and reading level was key to engaging their motivation to read.

Another important discovery about motivation was the result of a study conducted with Jonathan Baron (Gaskins & Baron, 1985). What we learned was the power of affiliation as it played itself out in our roles as mentors (i.e., being the adult friend and collaborator of a student). For the study, Bonnie Barnes, a member of the support services department, and I were mentors to lower-school students in the experimental group. Meeting individually with students for approximately 15 minutes, once a week, we coached them to recognize how their strengths and idiosyncrasies in cognitive style either enabled or prevented them from attaining their personal goals.

One of my mentees in the study was Paul. His strength, like so many Benchmark students, was that he was bright and verbal. His challenge was to overcome his incredible inflexibility, which was an impediment to his progress in all areas of the curriculum, but particularly in writing. I established that Paul's goal was to be flexible about receiving feedback concerning his written responses—not a very motivating goal for Paul because it was my goal, not his. The goal was written on a goal card. Paul was told to ask his teacher to place a mark on the card at the end of each day's language arts period, if he had been flexible in responding to the teacher's suggestions about how to improve his written response to what he read. Once a week Paul met with me to review his goal card and to discuss occasions when he had been flexible and when he had not. Paul's goal card rarely had checks on it. His teacher told me that Paul's most frequent answer to suggestions about how to improve a written response or composition was "I like it the way it is."

One day I shared with Paul that his teacher was becoming frustrated with him because she did not know how to help him improve his written expression. Paul said that he noticed that lately, when he put up his hand to ask his teacher to check his written work, she seemed to move away from him. I asked Paul why he thought that might be happening. He said it was probably because she did not like him. I explained that I thought it was because it was frustrating to work with someone who always says that he is right and does not want to change. Paul shared that he really wanted the teacher to like him and wondered what he could do so that she would like him. I asked if he would be able to say, "Thank you very much, I'll consider it," each time the teacher gave him suggestions, assuring him that the teacher would like him a lot better if he at least seemed to be more flexible. I changed Paul's goal card to read: My goal is to say, "Thank you very much, I'll consider it." This was to be Paul's response whenever his teacher gave him suggestions for improving his written work.

The next time we met, Paul's card was almost filled with checks. Paul was thrilled that the teacher seemed to like him better. Being liked by the adults in the school was important to Paul—so important that he took control of his tendency to be inflexible and gradually became more pleasant to teach. By the time Paul moved on to a regular school setting, some Benchmark teachers even considered him flexible! One key to motivation is discovering each student's goals and helping him or her achieve them. Paul's goal was for his teacher to like him; my goal was for Paul to become more flexible in accepting feedback. It was a win–win situation.

Our year-long cognitive style experiment, which included weekly mentor meetings, revealed the importance of these meetings to our mentees, perhaps because of the caring relationships that developed. In addition, the classroom teachers of these students felt that the mentoring and coaching motivated the students to change their maladaptive styles. As a result, mentor meetings became an essential part of our regular program. Mentoring continues to this day at Benchmark, and we witness daily how influential these special staff–student relationships are to students' motivation to succeed academically.

The next example takes place in a present-day lower school classroom. Motivation in this classroom is enhanced by the provision of choice, challenge, and appropriate level of text, as well as feedback about progress solely in relation to each student him- or herself.

An Example from the Lower School

Some lower school teachers ask their students to keep three leisure reading books in their desks: one that they regard as a challenging book that they hope someday to be able to read easily (many choose a *Harry Potter* book); one that is just right, usually a book in which approximately 98% of the words are sight words; and one that is a very easy read. Students like being in charge of choosing how hard or easy a book to read on any particular day. Reading at three different difficulty levels also allows students to get a sense of the progress they are making. Students are also given several choices about how they respond to the literature they read each day in class. For example, one day's choice may be to write a summary, make a concept map, or write a character sketch.

Examples from the Middle School

The middle school examples that follow remind us that many factors play an important role in fostering motivation: a sense of love and belonging, interest, collaboration, explicit explanations of processes, choice, clear goals, explanations about motivation, competence based on ample knowledge, and scaffolded success.

In a discussion with middle school teacher Ruth Kelemen, I was reminded that we must be careful not to assume that a struggling reader's needs for love, belonging, and self-esteem have been met just because parents took the initiative to see that their child receives the specialized instruction presented at Benchmark. As pointed out by Mrs. Kelemen, in some cases, the meeting of these needs for love, belonging, and self-esteem may be genuinely questioned by a student. Mrs. Kelemen feels she must help satisfy/ resatisfy these needs almost daily with some students—sometimes because they are teased for attending a special school and sometimes because things have not gone smoothly at home. Home life, while appearing to be loving and supportive, sometimes can erode self-esteem and feelings of being loved. Each day, middle school teachers quickly assess each student's status with regard to having his or her needs met. At the start of each school day, teachers consider, "Is this a day to totally nurture or a day to set the next goal to move a particular student forward?" Staff members help each other by passing the word that, for example, "Johnny is so overwhelmed by a problem at home that this is not the day to add a new challenge. Instead let's build up his self-esteem by reviewing last week's successes."

Another middle school teacher, Marianne Smith, has discovered that stimulating interest is important for helping students become more aware of the available life choices. She has been able to engage students' interest in topics that they would never choose themselves. She accomplishes this by presenting topics in interesting and challenging ways. For example, she teaches the study of physical and chemical properties by involving students in a fascinating unit about fibers. The various chemical and physical tests that the students conduct with fibers hold their attention and create new interests. Students experiment with the fibers: burning them to note their characteristic odors, dying them with natural dyes, examining them under the microscope, and diagramming the results of their investigations. Working in pairs, where it is easier to risk being wrong, their end tasks are to identify a mystery fiber and to create something out of fibers.

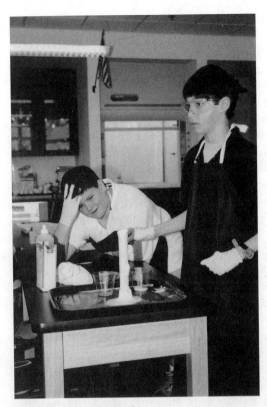

Learning is more likely if learning experiences are designed to meet students' motivational needs.

Motivation is high during this unit. Students feel they are doing real science that is challenging. They like the fact that the unit is focused, with a clear process for completing each investigation. Students know what they are supposed to accomplish within a framework that leaves room for discovery and creativity. Guided by Mrs. Smith, students have a choice in setting a goal for the unit. Because of having a choice, they "own" the goal, feel they can achieve it, and are motivated to work toward it. Mrs. Smith discusses with students what will get in the way of achieving their goals and what strategies will help them.

In mini-moments, Mrs. Smith shares her own struggles with motivation and the strategies she uses when a task seems overwhelming or boring. She has noticed that inadequate background knowledge about a topic is often a barrier to motivation. Conversely, the more knowledge students have about a topic, the more motivated they are. For example, before Mrs. Smith's class writes children's books set in the Arctic or rainforest, they are immersed in research to build background knowledge. The deeper their knowledge, the more motivated students seem to be to write their children's books, because they have ideas and understanding.

Mrs. Smith also shared examples of motivation in her language arts class and mentor group. She found that middle school students love the social aspect of a small reading group and are motivated to complete their nightly reading so that they can be part of group discussions. Daily mentor group also fosters a sense of belonging and provides students with a time when they can clarify assignments or their understanding of topics, as well as collaborate to complete assignments. In addition, there is a social aspect to mentor group that includes celebrations and food.

Middle school head Linda Six shared the following example, illustrating the importance of a student feeling competent to his or her level of motivation. This is an example of how Benchmark teachers coach students to become more competent, not only in the teacher's eyes, but, even more importantly, in their own eyes. The example also illustrates how Benchmark teachers scaffold instruction.

Scaffold to Build Competence

During class discussions, Norman appeared to possess a clear understanding of the literature he read each night (in this case, *The Old Man and the Sea*), yet Norman performed poorly on daily written responses to what he had read. To help diagnose where the breakdown was occurring, Mrs. Six invited Norman to be her apprentice, working one on one with her, as he answered questions about the reading. This process provided a window into his thinking and clues as to where things were going wrong for him. Once Mrs. Six had discovered the root of the problem, she could make these causes transparent to Norman, so together they could plan a strategy that would work for him and put him in charge of his learning. Most importantly, scaffolded success would boost Norman's self-confidence so he would take the risk of trying a variety of strategies until he found the right match for his cognitive style and the task at hand.

Mrs. Six began by discussing with Norman the discrepancy between the understanding he demonstrated during their discussions and what he wrote each day about the novel. Mrs. Six shared that she believed that Norman was doing everything he knew how to do, but there was surely something else that could be done, and they could discover it as they worked together. This conversation assured Norman that the teacher believed his comprehension was good, that he was a conscientious student, that there was a way for him to express his understanding in writing as well as orally, and that they could find this way by working together. At first Norman was resistant because he wanted to tackle the issue on his own. When asked why, he explained that it was hard for him to ask for help because it meant he was less than competent. After several conversations in which Mrs. Six explained that his perception was not accurate, that smart, competent people often seemed that way because they know when they need help, know where to go to get the help, and what to do with it once they get it, Norman agreed to try the notion of being an apprentice to Mrs. Six.

At first Mrs. Six read each question to Norman, they discussed the possible answers, and when Norman was sure he knew what he wanted to say, she scribed the answer for him. Norman was afraid this process was "cheating," but Mrs. Six assured him that it was far more important for them to figure out what was interfering with his ability to get what was in his head on paper than his becoming an expert on *The Old Man and the Sea*. After several successes, it was time for Norman and the teacher to reflect on what they were learning about his written expression. Norman remarked that he realized that without her coaching, he would often leave out part of the answer, even though he knew it. He said that Mrs. Six was helping by making sure he understood the question before he began thinking about the answer. At this point, Norman felt ready to assume more responsibility for the daily reading response. He and Mrs. Six agreed the next step would be for them to discuss each response, and she would write notes as they talked. After the notes were completed, Norman would return to his desk and, using the notes, write each response himself.

After several successes, it was time again to reflect. Norman was eager to share a personal discovery. When he became anxious, he was more dependent on Mrs. Six to pull the information from him. However, as he became more confident in his own abilities, he was better able to write clear, complete responses to questions. With this discovery, Norman felt he was ready to tackle the next written response on his own. Although the results were better than they had been before working with Mrs. Six, his written responses still did not accurately reflect his understanding. Norman and Mrs. Six talked again and decided that perhaps they had skipped a few steps in the apprenticeship model. They decided that they would discuss the responses before he wrote them, but the written part would be totally Norman's responsibility. The next step was that

Norman would write the responses independently, and Mrs. Six would check them for completeness before Normal handed in his final draft. Eventually Norman felt ready to handle the process independently. The scaffolding had been withdrawn gradually.

Norman and his teacher talked about all they had learned about his approach to this particular written task. They learned that Norman needed to read questions carefully and think about what each one was asking before starting to write his response. They learned that jotting notes before writing often ensured that all the information in Norman's head would find its way to the paper. They learned that when Norman became anxious, his anxiety interfered with his ability to express himself. Most importantly, Norman learned something Mrs. Six already knew—that he was a smart and capable young man and that there is always a way to meet a challenge, if he is willing to take some risks in the process. A more competent Norman was a more motivated Norman.

As has been illustrated, each teacher's ultimate goal, whether in teaching class or in a mentor group, is to create the conditions within which students feel connected and motivated. These conditions include providing choice, supporting relatedness, and providing the scaffolding needed to build competence.

The Toll Taken by Faulty Beliefs

Beliefs also affect motivation—beliefs about strengths and weaknesses as a learner and about self-efficacy for academic tasks. Faulty belief systems are probably the most powerful roadblock a teacher has to surmount and address when teaching students with learning issues. Mrs. Six tells the following story about a middle school student with whom she worked.

Ethan entered Benchmark as a fourth grader with superior intelligence, a sight vocabulary of less than 50 words, and serious decoding issues. Although he was pleasant to his teachers and popular with his peers, Ethan suffered with the misperception that he was a failure and always would be. When he reached Benchmark's middle school, he continued to take a pleasant but helpless/hopeless stance about taking control of his learning. His beliefs about himself interfered with his progress, because they prevented him from getting involved in learning. During his first 2 years of middle school, Ethan was unable to envision an accurate picture of himself. Although he had learned to read and write adequately, and he participated intelligently in class discussions, his belief system prevented him from taking the risks he needed to grapple with his learning issues and to become successful in the written-output world of school, where one's competence is judged based on what one writes about his or her learning, thinking, and problem solving.

After many frustrating attempts by both parents and teachers to get Ethan to believe in his fine abilities and put them to work, several things happened during his final year at Benchmark that changed his approach to learning. One was that Ethan's physician placed him on a trial dose of medication for attention-related difficulties. Ethan discovered that when on the medication, he had to exert much less effort to stay focused in his classes, resulting in an increased motivation to learn.

The second event that changed Ethan's approach to learning occurred when Benchmark's placement counselor suggested that Ethan would need a high school environment that was as supportive as Benchmark's. Ethan was very disappointed by this news and informed his parents and the Benchmark staff that he wanted the intellectual challenge provided by a more competitive academic environment.

The third event that helped turn Ethan around was a discussion about his intellectual abilities. After reviewing Ethan's WISC-III scores with a psychologist from Benchmark's support services department, one of Ethan's teachers shared with Ethan his WISC-III profile. The teacher drew a bell curve and asked Ethan to make an X at the place that he thought represented the average of his scores on the 10 subtests of the WISC-III. Ethan made an X a bit to the right of the center of the bell curve, indicating that he thought that he was at about the 60th percentile. He was told that his placement of the X was too low. On subsequent tries, he edged the X up until it was at an accurate spot—the 96th percentile. Ethan and his teacher talked about the meaning of *percentile*: that for every 100 students his age, Ethan's IQ was higher than 96 of those students.

The conversation then turned to what Ethan was willing to do as a result of getting the medication he needed to be more attentive, being dissatisfied with possible high school placements, and being convinced (finally) that he had the native intelligence to do just about anything he wanted with his life. This was the turning point for Ethan. He finally began to share the roots of his faulty belief system. The memories of being humiliated when having to read aloud in his third-grade class were so vivid that he could describe the room, the other students, even the teacher's dress! As an 8-year-old, seeing that others could read words and he could not, others could spell and he could not, led to the logical, if inaccurate, conclusion that he was stupid. It was confusing to him because he knew he could listen to the discussion of a text which he could not read and draw more insightful conclusions than the classmates who were better readers and spellers. He wrongly concluded that it was impossible for him to trust what parents and teachers had told him all his life—that he was smart. He had far more powerful proof of the opposite. (Here is where his intelligence worked against him!) It was safer to coast through school telling everyone, including himself, that no one should expect too much of him. After all, he was Ethan, the one who could not read or spell; what could they expect?

Ethan was not a young man who wore his heart on his sleeve. He was very private, and this conversation with his teacher in which his turnaround began provided a precious and rare insight into Ethan's struggles. The teacher asked if Ethan was ready to have her push him to the limit academically. He said he thought he was up to the challenge. The rest of the school year was spent in many intense, reflective conversations between Ethan and his teachers. Such conversations were still difficult for him, and he still avoided them when he could. Even after many hours spent in one-on-one conversations, in which Mrs. Six shared specific proof of Ethan's intelligence and her investment in him, Ethan still doubted the strength of her support. He worried that she would give up on him because his responses to instruction were not consistent.

Ethan had a very successful final year at Benchmark. His grades were better than they had ever been, although they still did not reflect his potential. He was stage manager, student director, and a supporting character for the Benchmark spring musical, and was accepted at a prestigious boarding school. However, that is not the end of the belief-system influence on his learning. Often, when our students experience a change in teacher or school, they revert back to their original faulty belief system. Ethan went off to boarding school and put back on his original facade of pretending that he did not have any special needs. Fortunately, when he got into deep academic trouble, he called Mrs. Six, and she was able to get him back on track—where he has stayed. Ethan had very good 11th- and 12th-grade years at school and attended a fine college. (See one of his college application essays in Figure 8.2.) Long-held faulty beliefs play havoc with motivation. The antidote for faulty beliefs is many successes over many years and personal relationships that foster success.

Arranging instruction so that all students can feel competent, accepted, and autonomous is a key to motivating students to dare to risk learning. We have not been successful in teaching students if we have not motivated them to *want* to learn (Sarason, 2004).

LEARNING PRINCIPLE 6: LEARNING IS ENHANCED BY IMMEDIATE FEEDBACK AND ACCOUNTABILITY

Requiring accountability and providing immediate feedback in a positive, nonjudgmental learning environment make it more likely that learning will occur (Lambert & McCombs, 1998; Shepard, 2000). Donald Graves's (1975) work in the mid-1970s, then his visits to Benchmark at the end of that decade, taught those on the Benchmark staff a great deal about the kind of feedback that enhances learning (Gaskins, 1982). Graves taught us how to motivate our lower school students to write by allowing them to write about things about which they knew the most and to provide feedback initially based only on the content of their compositions. Usually this meant expressing to a student how impressed we were with how much he or she knew about a topic, followed by asking questions to elicit more information and to clarify the information that was included. There were no red marks on students' papers. In fact, there were no marks at all. Teachers wrote comments and questions for clarification on yellow stickies (usually after the student read his or her piece to the class) and attached them to each student's

Learning is enhanced by accountability and feedback.

FIGURE 8.2. Ethan's college application essay.

The word teacher has always been one of those words that leaves a bad taste in my mouth after I say it. The traditional idea of a teacher has always seemed to be the enemy, the force that I fought with to try to get through life. In general teaching seemed to hold me back from who I was and what I could have been. There have been very few teachers in my life that I view in a positive way. The best positive teachers that I have had are ones who let me learn on my own. They pointed me in a direction and let me get there my own way. But my most effective teacher has been failure.

Another teacher who acted much like my martial arts instructor was a teacher who I had during middle school. She is the reason that I ended up at G School. The things that she has done for me in the way of guidance are too numerous to fit into three pages. I am dyslexic and have attention deficit disorder. I could not read until I was in 5th grade. The effects of not being able to read and therefore learn as a child were devastating. I just remember how every day (before Benchmark School) I would come home from school and cry in my room by myself. I got kicked out of my first school because I could not read and I ended up at a school for kids with learning disabilities. It was a good place for me because the school helped me learn to read in the way that I needed—the same way that I learned karate. The teaches there gave me the tools and it was up to me to go at my own pace and create my own way by adapting strategies and different approaches to match my learning style. When I got to 8th grade, I was faced with the biggest roadblock in my life. It needed to be moved so I would succeed in being a happy person. (What was the roadblock?) I had the tools to do well in life but I would not use them. My life revolved around school and therefore I had never really felt what success was like. So I developed this deep depression and hate for myself. I don't think a day went by when I didn't think about killing myself. But then this teacher took me by the hand and forced me to really try. She made me take on my life and stop floating around. She made me do my schoolwork to the full potential that I could. She forced me to try out for the school musical, which is something that I would never have thought to try. And surprise! I got one of the lead parts. This was a major risk for me because my stage fright was so bad there were practices where I actually felt physically ill. However, I played the part, and was student director and stage manager for the play. All three roles were successes for me. I started to experience some successes in school. Because of this, I gained confidence and was able to move onward in life. I decided to move on to G School to try to leave the person that I was behind. I left the room that I would cry in when I was a child and I left my parents who never really knew who I was or what I was going through. This middle school teacher still helps me to this day and I have never really thanked her. She reads all of my papers and essays for spelling and grammar. And she will have read this before you get it. So I guess she knows now.

But my most effective teacher in life has been failure. It is my biggest fear and my closest enemy. In life I can link everything that I hate about myself to the fact that I could not read. Everyone's definition of failure is different. I'm a pessimist. My whole life, the glass has been half empty and this is because of everything I struggled with as a child in school and was never good enough for my parents. I could never seem to meet the standard so I learned to expect very little from myself.

But now that I find myself in this paradoxical transition between self-loathing and finding the confidence to get through a day without hate, failure has become my strongest catalyst for change. Failures in my past taught me what not to do in the future and that is the best way for me to learn. But now that I am developing hope for life, failure is more powerful. When I fail now it takes a large chunk out of the confidence that I am starting to develop. However, what constitutes as failure is tied to much higher expectations. So no matter what I do, failure and with it depression are right behind me and all I can do is run from them.

From *Success with Struggling Readers* by Irene Gaskins. Copyright 2005 by The Guilford Press. See copyright page for photocopying limitations.

paper. It was the author's choice to decide which comments and questions he or she addressed when revising the text. Once the content seemed satisfactory, organization of the paper was critiqued by each student sharing his or her piece with a partner. The same process was used to address choice of words and suggestions about "juicy" words. Only when a student elected to publish a paper was attention paid to the mechanics of writing, and even then, without the help of a red pen. The process used in correcting the mechanics was the apprenticeship model. The teacher sat side by side with the student as she or he demonstrated and taught.

We discovered that when students receive feedback in the manner just described, they are usually not resistant to making changes. In fact, we were surprised to discover that they loved filling the walls of their classrooms with their writing (Gaskins, 1991). We held students accountable for always getting feedback from a peer before reading their composition to the class or asking the teacher for feedback. Feedback was immediate and addressed to a specific aspect of writing. The consequence for not accepting accurate and helpful feedback was that the piece was usually judged not ready for publication and subsequent placement in the Benchmark library. One of the bonuses of our early work with Graves was that we discovered that the students who wrote the most and shared the most also became the best readers: Becoming a good writer involves a lot of reading and rereading. We were delighted to discover that this model of supportive feedback works in all areas of the curriculum.

The goal of feedback is to help students take the next steps in learning. Students profit from ample feedback and opportunities to revise their work while a work is in progress. Giving students feedback after they deem a project finished is usually not as beneficial in moving students forward. Students appreciate exemplars of work that they can use as models, as well as rubrics. Rubrics make expectations transparent and put students in charge of evaluating their own work. We know that when learners are provided with feedback about what they are doing well and what needs improvement, learning is enhanced (Pressley, 1995).

To convince students to put effort into their assignments, they need to be in on the "secret" of what the teacher is expecting. They want a clear understanding of the accountability demands they face and the criteria by which their assignments will be assessed. In possession of these understandings, they are able to evaluate their own work in the same way that their teacher does (Shepard, 2000). Teachers have found that students who self-evaluate become more interested in the criteria used in evaluation and in substantive feedback. Students involved in analyzing their own work assume ownership of the evaluation process, especially if criteria are clear and reasonable. Benchmark teachers provide rubrics and exemplars and encourage students to seek feedback and critique their own work. After students have given a task their best effort and compared their work to the exemplars and rubrics that teachers provide, they seek feedback from their peers and their teachers. Seeking feedback is especially important on projects that span several days, weeks, or months. Students are encouraged to touch base with peers and teachers to make sure they are on the right track. In addition, students share drafts of projects, such as reports or essays, with the teacher to receive comments before a final draft is due.

Ongoing feedback during Every-Pupil-Response (EPR) periods and same-day turnaround on homework keep students up to date regarding their progress in a class. Feedback is far less effective at the end of a project; at that point, when he or she considers the project finished, there is little likelihood the student will learn from feedback. As noted previously, Benchmark teachers evaluate each student's work in comparison to that student's previous score or in comparison to a standard. Students are not evaluated by comparison to other students.

An Example from Benchmark's Summer Program

What a child does depends on what is reinforced and what is neglected. This axiom is vividly illustrated in a story Joyce Ostertag tells about teaching writing to an almost-second-grade struggling reader who was attending Benchmark's summer program for the first time. Helen's early journal writing went something like this: "The cat sat on the mat. Look at the cat. The cat sat." Spelling words correctly had been the main criterion for a good journal entry in her previous school, so she decided on the strategy of using only words she could spell. After a couple days of journal writing, Helen realized that Miss Ostertag had not marked a single misspelling on any student's journal entry, but instead was praising students who wrote honestly and openly about topics about which they cared. Helen's journal quickly turned into a lively account of her adventures that summer.

Examples from the Lower School

When I asked Miss Ostertag how the teachers she supervises at Benchmark handle accountability, she shared these insights:

"Learning is effortful. All students will have some areas in which they excel, and in which they experience the 'flow' that will keep them going in the activity. They will also have other areas in which the going is tough, particularly in the early stages of acquiring competence and automaticity. Teachers at Benchmark set high, but realistic, goals for their students, then set up systems of supervision and feedback, rewards and consequences to ensure that students consistently engage in activities that further these learning goals. For example, most students are expected to read a story a day during their independent reading time and complete some type of response to that reading. In the early grades, close supervision by a support teacher holds the students accountable for staying on task and completing their responses to what was read. As students progress, more of the accountability is turned over to each student. A goal might be set for a student to read one story a day during seatwork time, with a reward such as a sticker or a cumulative reward such as free reading time. If the student chooses to avoid that task during the time allotted, there is the natural consequence of completing the reading and response to reading during recess. This consequence is given very matter-of-factly, saying: 'To become a better reader, you need to do lots and lots of reading; therefore your reading needs to be completed. You may read now or during your free time, it is up to you.' Of course, teachers ensure that the reading can be completed independently or are quick to provide scaffolding and coaching when the student is not able to complete the assignment. There is always the expectation that the student will complete the assignment. Teachers at Benchmark rarely use a 'bad grade' as a consequence for work not completed, because it becomes too easy for the student to say, 'Oh, well, I'll take the poor grade—it's easier than doing the work.' Over time, these high expectations lead students to believe that effort and with the willingness to collaborate with peers and teachers, there is nothing they cannot do."

The next examples illustrate the value of rubrics and anchor papers. Students in a sixth-grade class were working on writing personal narratives. Miss Ostertag had talked about narrowing and focusing the topic, but noticed that many of her students were still producing list-like narratives that moved quickly from one idea to the next, with no elaboration. She realized that modeling how to focus a topic was not making sense to her students. In addition, feedback on a particular narrative improved that narrative but had no carryover to the next piece.

To help her students move forward, Miss Ostertag developed a rubric for evaluating the ideas of a piece, then wrote her own personal experience piece in three ways, each serving as an anchor paper for a level of the rubric. As students read each paper, they compared it to the rubric to decide how to rate it. By the end of the period, Miss Ostertag could sense that many students had had an "aha" experience regarding what she was expecting in their papers. The following day, students evaluated their own papers using the rubric, sharing the score they gave themselves and why. Next, they shared their papers with their writing group. Because the students had already critiqued their own drafts, they focused more on suggestions rather than on the score itself. Students went back to their drafts with renewed enthusiasm and proudly shared the improved draft with the group later in the week.

Lower school teacher Helen Lawrence begins her research report writing unit by giving her students a packet entitled "All You Need to Know about Writing a Research Report." The packet contains a page with the expectations and ordered steps for writing a research report in her class. There is a page explaining how to write a good note card, and examples are shown. The page for writing the bibliography provides examples from each type of source students might use. Mrs. Lawrence guides her class through the process one step at a time, using the packet for class instruction. Students are held accountable for daily tasks (e.g., "Write at least five note cards"; "Write the rough draft of the introduction"; "Write a plan for your first two paragraphs"). Students are given deadlines for each step (e.g., "You must finish reading your first source and taking notes by _____"; "The plan for the rough draft is due _____"; "You must give the teacher the name of the person you will research by tomorrow"). Over the years the staff has learned how critical this explicit process is to the success of our students. Teachers have discovered that the necessity for planning and other self-regulating strategies are not self-evident for most of our struggling readers.

Mrs. Lawrence divides students into groups of four or five and gives them feedback on what they have accomplished each day, as well as works with them to revise as necessary. Students share their writing with group members for feedback as they move through the report-writing process. When students think they have a final draft, they are paired so that each student has an "editor" to read his or her paper for final revisions and to catch any proofreading errors. If a student fails to complete a daily task due to poor use of class time, the natural consequence is to complete the task during what we call "recess-study hall."

An Example from the Middle School

As is true in the Smith/Cummin class, each year Barbara Mistichelli's class completes an Alaska unit, a long-term reading and writing unit. The unit is interactive and involves much research, background building, organization of information, writing, feedback, revision, and reflection. Each assignment and project in the unit is carefully presented so that from the beginning students know what will be expected. Each project is set up in a brainstorming session so that students can activate their background knowledge about the subject. Project materials, such as schedules and rubrics, are given to students. Schedules are often in the form of calendars, on which students are asked to plan their time on the days between the due dates. In planning their use of time, students are instructed to consider other homework, after-school activities, and extracurricular activities (e.g., religious education, family events) as they make their own personalized plan on the calendar.

> T: Here is a calendar showing the key due dates for the Alaska geography research report. You need to keep this calendar in a safe, handy place—like in your binder. Using the calendar blocks between the key due dates that I have written in for you, you need to develop a plan as to how you will accomplish the various parts of the project that occur between the key due dates. For instance, there will be a note check on _____. You need to plan how much time you will spend on taking notes from your sources each day, considering writing period and your time in study halls, after-school guided study, and time at home, so that you will have sufficient notes under the purpose questions (the five themes of geography) by the date of the note check. Be sure to keep in mind your other homework, after-school sports, other activities such as religious education, and family events when you fill in the calendar blocks.

> S: So if I have basketball after school tomorrow and Hebrew school tomorrow evening, I should plan to take more notes tonight when I have less to do?

> T: Exactly! You need to create a realistic plan that will work for you.

Rubrics are designed to show students which parts of the project are more important (i.e., are worth the most points), and what level of effort will result in students achieving a designated number of points. The parts, or stages, of the project are clearly listed on the left-hand column of the rubric, and the levels of effort (usually four or five columns) range along the top of the rubric. The point values go from the highest points possible on the left side to the least amount on the right. When the rubric is presented to the students, they are led to notice the parts of the project on the left, and the levels of points possible for each of the parts in each column across the rubric.

> T: So, what do you notice on the left-hand column of this rubric?

> S: There are categories listed, like notes, plans, content, headings, mechanics and neatness, and bibliography.

> T: How many points are possible for each?

> S: (*Reads the number of points possible for each category.*)

T: The number of points you might receive for each category depends on what?

S: How well you follow the requirements in each block?

T: Yes. This rubric tells you exactly how to earn the most points. However, do we want you to do this project just to get a good grade?

(Laughter from students)

S: No, you want us to do the project well, to learn about the geography of Alaska. You even want us to learn.

T: Do you think you could learn anything else from this project? Think *process*.

S: You want us to practice using the research process and the writing process.

T: Right! Just remember that the points (grades) are really only feedback about how you are doing on a project or a part of the project. You are not working for the points, you are practicing skills and strategies—and you are learning about the geography of Alaska! Right?

Students are held accountable for meeting due dates (reminders are placed on the whiteboard) and are referred back to their schedules and rubrics almost daily. The responsibility for being aware of due dates, along with the various parts of the project, rests with students because they have in their possession the tools they need to be successful and up-to-date with the project. Teachers are always available for clarification, coaching, and feedback at each part of the project.

SUMMARY

The six principles of learning employed by Benchmark teachers as they teach struggling readers can be used as guidelines for all teachers in creating an optimal learning environment for struggling readers. Undoubtedly, these six principles relate equally well to teaching all students how to learn.

1. Learning is an interactive process.
2. Learning is more likely to occur if instruction is explicit.
3. Learning is a social act.
4. Learning occurs at different rates and in different ways.
5. Learning requires motivation.
6. Learning is enhanced by accountability and feedback.

In the next chapter, additional learning principles are presented that the Benchmark staff believes are important for teachers to share with struggling readers.

CHAPTER 9

Learning Principles to Share
with Students

This chapter continues the emphasis on the scientifically based principles that guide learning at Benchmark School, with a focus in this chapter on principles that the staff feels are important to share with students. For example, we want to ensure that students are aware that learning is an interactive process involving person, situation, task, and text variables and that it is their job to be in charge of, or adapt to, these variables. We also discuss with students the value of paying close attention to explicit explanations of procedures for completing tasks and encourage them, as a life skill, to request explanations when they are not provided. We teach students to initiate collaboration because learning is social. Initiating collaboration and seeking explicit explanations are part of our emphasis on teaching students to act as self-advocates who seek out the support they need to succeed.

In addition, students are made aware that all of us learn at different rates and in different ways; therefore, it is the responsibility of each student to pay attention to what works best for him or her in accomplishing tasks both in and out of school. Motivation is another "hot" topic of conversation with students, in which we stress how their beliefs, attitudes, and attributions affect their ability to achieve their goals. The importance of accepting and using feedback is also discussed. These six topics are based on the scientifically based principles discussed in Chapters 7 and 8 and are posted on a chart: "Six Actions for Becoming a Better Learner" (see Figure 9.1). In addition to these six actions, the Benchmark staff explicitly shares with students the active learning principles presented in this chapter (see Figure 9.2). These principles are restated as active learner strategies in Figure 9.3. Teaching students to be active learners is the focus of this chapter.

FIGURE 9.1. Six actions for becoming a better learner.

Six Actions for Becoming a Better Learner
1. Take Charge Take charge of, or adapt to, person, situation, task, and text variables.
2. Request Explanations Pay attention to explicit explanations and seek them when not given.
3. Initiate Collaboration Talk with others about what you are learning.
4. Figure Out What Works Figure out what works best for you in accomplishing tasks.
5. Know What Affects Your Motivation Evaluate the affect of beliefs, attitudes, and attributions on motivation and achievement of your goals.
6. Accept and Use Feedback Ask for feedback before assignments are due.

From *Success with Struggling Readers* by Irene Gaskins. Copyright 2005 by The Guilford Press. See copyright page for photocopying limitations.

FIGURE 9.2. Principles of learning to share with struggling readers.

Principles of Learning to Share with Struggling Readers
1. What people learn is based on what they already know.
2. Metacognitive strategies for monitoring and controlling learning are essential to reaching one's learning goal.
3. New information is easier to understand, remember, and use if it is attached to prior knowledge.
4. Organized knowledge is easier to recall than random information.
5. Information that is thoughtfully and deeply processed is likely to be understood and used.
6. Concepts and strategies that are repeatedly practiced and applied are not easily forgotten.

From *Success with Struggling Readers* by Irene Gaskins. Copyright 2005 by The Guilford Press. See copyright page for photocopying limitations.

FIGURE 9.3. Active learner strategies.

From *Success with Struggling Readers* by Irene Gaskins. Copyright 2005 by The Guilford Press. See copyright page for photocopying limitations.

BECOMING ACTIVE LEARNERS

A person must actively engage his or her mind in thinking about the information that is being presented if learning is to take place (Bransford et al., 2000; Lampert & McCombs, 1998; Marzano, 2003; Matlin, 2003; Silverman & Casazza, 2000; Zimmerman, 2001). Some of the actions that learners exhibit when they are actively involved are listed in Figure 9.3. Benchmark students recognize these actions as flowing directly from the principles of learning taught by their lower school teachers.

Historical Perspective

In the early days of the school, we were struck by the fact that rather than being actively involved in the individualized lessons we had specifically created for them, our struggling readers tended to be off task much of the time. We initiated behavior modification systems in an attempt to entice our students into becoming more actively involved in learning, but with only moderate and temporary results. Then in May 1977, Sally Laird and I heard Barak Rosenshine speak at the International Reading Association conference in Miami. His summary of research about teacher behaviors and student achievement provided us with the keys we needed to increase our students' active involvement in learning. Rosenshine shared drafts of his work in progress as well as recently published works by himself and other researchers. We were thrilled to be in on this cutting-edge research, and the prospect of including these concepts in our teaching was energizing.

For the next several years, the focus of the Benchmark research seminar was on the work of Brophy and Good (1974), Stallings and Kaskowitz (1974), and Rosenshine (1979) and his colleagues (Rosenshine & Furst, 1973; Rosenshine & Berliner, 1978). Some of the conclusions from this research surprised us. For example, we had convinced ourselves that it was in the best interest of our students for teachers to write individualized daily lessons for students to complete on their own, as teachers moved from student to student to provide feedback. However, the research reviewed by Rosenshine suggested that students who spent the most time working alone made the least academic progress because they were less engaged when they were not taught directly by a teacher. The research suggested that whole-class or small-group instruction produced better academic growth. One of the primary lessons learned from this body of research was: What is not taught is not learned (Stallings & Kaskowitz, 1974). Rosenshine suggested that the key factors related to student learning are content covered, student engagement, and direct instruction. Rosenshine (1979) recommended highly structured, teacher-directed classrooms, in which there was a high level of student time on task and where students received immediate feedback. Academic engaged time correlates with progress in learning. One answer to increasing active involvement is *direct teaching*.

Present-Day Perspective on Active Involvement

During the 30 ensuing years, we have fine-tuned and elaborated on the suggestions of Rosenshine, but the main concept remains the same: Engaged academic time correlates with academic progress. Benchmark teachers plan instruction that keeps all students actively and meaningfully engaged, and they orchestrate lessons in which students participate in discussions and activities that emphasize the relationship between active involvement and successful learning. Typically, struggling readers enter Benchmark School either not understanding that learning necessitates active involvement or not knowing how to be actively involved. Some students seem unaware that learning does not occur based on raw intellect alone; rather, the intellect has to be actively *engaged*. This lack of knowledge about how learning works is a barrier to their progress. To overcome this barrier, teachers explicitly address students' lack of knowledge about how learning works, as part of daily strategy lessons about how to learn and how to complete assigned tasks. Each day teachers provide students with a rationale for how the strategies being taught will enhance learning. (Teaching students strategies for learning words and comprehending text is addressed in Chapters 10–13.) The point is always the same: It is what students *do* while learning that shapes what is learned (Gollub et al., 2002).

In addition to teaching students how to be actively involved in applying learning strategies, we also guide them in the development of thinking dispositions. A "thinking disposition" includes the emotional and motivational aspects of thinking that determine how effort is invested—what we call *cognitive style* at Benchmark. Perkins (1995) defines a thinking disposition as "a tendency, habit, or commitment toward thinking in a certain way, for instance the disposition to be open-minded, the disposition to think in an imaginative, adventurous way, or the disposition to seek out evidence" (p. 202).

To this list Shepard (2000) adds the disposition of willingness to persist. These examples of thinking dispositions illustrate, once again, that thinking and learning are active processes.

From the first day students attend class at Benchmark, they begin to learn that being actively involved means actively employing thinking strategies, positive attitudes, and self-management of the mind, including the management of beliefs, dispositions, thoughts, feelings, and actions (Zimmerman & Schunk, 2001). We tell students that they must take charge of their own learning. We refer to the ability to actively manage one's learning as *self-regulation*. A learner who is self-regulated displays personal initiative, perseverance, and adaptive skill in the pursuit of learning (Zimmernan, 2001).

The goal for each Benchmark student is to become increasingly involved in personally initiating strategies to improve learning outcomes and environments. Usually by the time students graduate from eighth grade at Benchmark, and even sooner for some, they are aware that academic learning is something that learners do for themselves rather than something that is done *to* or *for* them. The road to achieving this understanding stretches over many years. It begins with teaching our younger students that reading must make sense and that when it does not, they must take action by using a fix-up strategy. It ends with the third-year middle school program, when students conduct conferences with parents and staff to present their personal plan for learning. Six of the major principles of active involvement that the Benchmark staff shares with students are discussed next and are summarized as active learner strategies in Figure 9.3.

LEARNING PRINCIPLES

What People Learn Is Based on What They Already Know

The foundation for learning is the learner's knowledge and experience (Alexander, 2000; Anderson & Pearson, 1984; Greeno, Collins, & Resnick, 1996; Lambert & McCombs, 1998; Shepard, 2000). In reading the many yellow tech reports that emanated from the Center for the Study of Reading during the early 1980s, we could not miss the emphasis on the importance of the background knowledge that the learner brings to the text. Our understanding of the role background knowledge plays in learning has been enriched by our 20-year collaboration with Richard Anderson and what we have learned from him about the relevance of schema theory to instruction at Benchmark. We have further elaborated our understanding of the role of knowledge through discussions with Patricia Alexander. As a result of these collaborations, we have come to realize that how well students learn and understand depends heavily on what they know about concepts and what they know about cognitive processes. What they know includes knowledge, skills and strategies, beliefs, conceptions, and misconceptions (Gollub et al., 2002). For the Benchmark staff, *knowing* means that students have structures of information and processes that allow them to recognize and construct patterns. We believe that the result of knowing is the ability to understand concepts and to exhibit abilities such as reasoning, problem solving, and using and understanding language (Greeno et al., 1996).

To ultimately achieve high levels of learning, our students begin in their earliest days at Benchmark to develop a foundation of knowledge that will become vast and deep over the years at the school; this knowledge is understood in the context of a conceptual framework and organized in ways that facilitate retrieval and application. A simple example involves the study of American history. We find that students who are well oriented to the location and geographical characteristics of some or all of the 50 states, either as a result of travel experiences or study, tend to achieve higher levels of understanding of American history than students with less background knowledge. Those who can locate the 50 states are able to connect historical happenings to specific locations and geographical conditions. They can grasp the logical connections between geography and how specific areas of the country developed. There is no doubt in the minds of teachers that what students know, or believe they know (whether accurate or inaccurate, real or perceived), provides a conceptual scaffold for learning new information. Of course, if what students know is a misconception, then correction of the misconception must also be addressed.

Knowledge is important because cognitive processes are dependent upon the sheer quantity of knowledge a person possesses (Ceci, 1996). A primary reason that people who are experts in their field perform better than nonexperts is because they know more (Strong, Silver, & Perini, 2001). The goal for Benchmark students, however, is not to passively *acquire* inert information but rather to *construct* knowledge and to *reorganize* it, often transforming significant understandings that they already possess. Several examples follow that illustrate how the Benchmark staff guides students to construct knowledge.

An Example from the Lower School

Realizing that learning is based on the learner's knowledge and experience, lower school teachers select informational books for about 50% of the reading that is completed during daily reading instruction. This practice was initiated to provide students with information about the essential understandings being emphasized (usually in social studies and science). In addition, as part of homework, parents read to their Benchmark student for at least 20 minutes each evening, often using books students select from a classroom library of books that provide background knowledge for the content areas being studied. The staff also shares with students a lifelong learning skill: It is always a good idea to consult a variety of texts about topics they want to study and understand, as well as to watch videos and check multiple online sources. Teachers also suggest relevant movies, plays, and places to visit to parents. We teach students that what they know provides a hook on which to attach what they are learning, and the more they know, the more hooks they have. In other words, the more they know, the more they are able to know.

An Example from a Lower School Math Class

When a student in Cindy Whittle's math class forgot the answer to 4×7, Mrs. Whittle reminded her that she knew a strategy to find 4×7. The student then said, "I know that 2×7 is 14, so I can double it to get 28."

An Example from the Middle School

On a visit to Kristina Reisinger's class in January, I observed the beginning of a geography unit. Mrs. Reisinger asked her students to write a description of a desert. As she walked around the room to survey what each student was writing, she noted who was describing a Saharan desert, who was describing an Arizonan desert, and who was describing an Arctic desert. After a few minutes, she asked students to stop, then called on a few prechosen students to share their descriptions. One student described a Saharan desert, one an Arizonan desert, and one an Arctic desert. After the students shared their descriptions, Mrs. Reisinger led a discussion about deserts. She noted how interesting it was that there were so many different, yet correct, images of deserts, depending on each individual's background knowledge and/or perspective. Mrs. Reisinger made the point that if a students' background knowledge included only one perception of what a desert looks like, it might be difficult to understand all that was discussed about deserts in their text. The class discussed how these differences in background knowledge might come into play as they read, took notes, and discussed. Describing a desert proved to be not only an exercise in understanding the role of background knowledge in the learning process, it also encouraged students to be more respectful of peer contributions to a class discussion that may not, at first, seem to them to be correct or relevant.

Metacognitive Strategies for Monitoring and Taking Control of Learning Are Essential

Successful students monitor and take control of their learning (Bereiter, 2002; Lampert & McCombs, 1998; Silverman & Casazza, 2000; Zimmerman, 2001). An aspect of active involvement that we began hearing a lot about when we attended reading conferences in the early 1980s was metacognition. In fact, *metacognition* was one of the most frequently heard words at the 1982 International Reading Association conference. Those of us who attended from Benchmark came back from the conference determined to share what we understood about metacognition and to enlist the rest of the staff in helping us flesh out how to make metacognition part of our instruction. Speakers at the conference said that metacognition is the knowledge or awareness people have about their own cognitive processes of memory, attention, comprehension, and so on. This notion of metacognition clearly fit with the staff's desire for Benchmark students to understand how learning and thinking work. We also learned that metacognition includes self-monitoring—knowing when we do and do not understand, maintaining awareness of our ongoing comprehension processes. The goal of metacognitive instruction is to teach students to assume the executive or self-control function over their own learning and thinking processes. Some of the strategies that students would need to learn to become metacognitive learners include predicting, self-questioning, visualizing, and self-correcting. We read and shared what we learned about metacognition in our research seminar and tried out our ideas with the reading groups we taught. Becoming metacognitive did not happen quickly for our students; nevertheless, the attempt to teach metacognition provided just enough of a glimmer of understanding among our students to keep us going. As we understood metacognition better, so did our students.

Succinctly put, metacognition is "the capacity to reflect upon one's own thinking and therefore to monitor and manage it" (Greeno et al., 1996, p. 19). Over the years, we have come to the conclusion that to be metacognitive requires knowledge about thinking (e.g., what enhances thinking, and what gets in the way?), knowledge about strategies (e.g., what kinds of strategies are available to use?), and knowledge of task variables (e.g., a recall task vs. a summarizing task). We have observed that our most effective learners become increasingly conscious of how they learn; that is, they expand their strategies and monitor their progress. They develop "executive control" over learning strategies rather than passively reacting to the environment (Joyce & Weil, 2004). These are the ways of thinking that we want to see exhibited by all of our struggling readers. To enhance the chances of this learning taking root, we explicitly teach metacognitive strategies across the curriculum.

One way to think about metacognition is to divide it into three self-regulatory phases: *before*, *during*, and *after* (e.g., Zimmerman, 1998). Some teachers find it convenient to use these three categories when they discuss metacognitive strategies with their students.

1. *Before*: These processes include goal setting (determining what is already known and what else needs to be known), strategic planning, self-efficacy (thinking of the relevant success in the past that suggest this new task is doable), goal orientation, and intrinsic interest (establishing personal reasons to accomplish the task).
2. *During*: The performance-control processes used during the completion of tasks include focusing attention, self-instruction, and self-monitoring.
3. *After*: Self-reflection processes include self-evaluation, attributions (answering the question "What led to my success or difficulty?"), and adaptivity (thinking about how to accomplish the task another way).

A metacognitive approach to learning and thinking helps students understand how to be actively involved in the control of their own learning by teaching them to define learning goals, monitor and control their progress in achieving them, and evaluate how well they did.

Perhaps because metacognition requires reflection, it does not come easily to struggling readers, especially those who have an impulsive style. These students are unlikely to monitor their understanding unless the process is repeatedly taught, modeled, and scaffolded. For example, we provide explicit explanations, modeling, and scaffolding to help students select strategies to use in planning, monitoring, and evaluating thinking processes and for implementing self-initiated metacognitive strategies to control learning experiences. Teachers at Benchmark have found mental modeling (i.e., talking aloud about their thinking processes—think-alouds) to be helpful in making thinking processes visible to students. In fact, teachers model their metacognitive processes in think-alouds and talk about personal examples of metacognition almost daily. Several examples follow.

Examples from the Lower School

I shared this example of metacognition with a group of fourth graders to make the point that even teachers and administrators consciously use strategies to enhance their memory.

T: Yesterday I was showing a researcher around the school when we stopped and talked to Mrs. Laird. She asked the researcher about his recent classroom observation study and what he had learned from it. As Dr. Pressley began to talk, I thought to myself, "This is great stuff—as soon as I get back to my desk, I've got to write it down." Dr. Pressley was ticking off the results of his study so fast that I knew my short-term memory wasn't going to be able to handle all he had to say. So, what do you think I did?

S1: You asked someone for a piece of paper and pencil and wrote down what he said?

S2: You asked him to slow down.

S3: You chunked the things he was saying.

T: All of your ideas are good ones. What I actually did was wait until he took a breath and then made a statement that was something like this: "You have shared a lot of good ideas and I want to hear more. Before you go on, may I summarize what I think you said?" Then, I shared my summary. During this brief discussion, I was pulling out and using a lot of my metacognitive skills. Take 60 seconds and jot down on think pad anything I did that you think was monitoring or taking control of my learning.

Joe, would you please begin the discussion by telling one thing I did that was metacognitive. After Joe tells us one thing, then I'd like someone else to chime in, followed by someone else, and continue in this manner. Try not to repeat what someone has already said.

S1: You showed that you understand about short-term memory.

S2: You had a plan and you monitored how well you were achieving it.

S3: You knew that writing down what you heard would help you remember.

S4: Maybe you thought that if you summarized what he said, you could get that into one chunk in short-term memory.

S5: You took charge of your attention.

T: What good mind readers you are. Can anyone tell me an occasion today when you were metacognitive? (*Several students share instances of being metacognitive.*)

In addition, we guide students in determining the relative effectiveness of different strategies so they can apply those strategies flexibly rather than use the same strategies for all learning tasks. We also guide the development of their awareness about when and how to use skills and strategies. To acquire this awareness, students are taught to apply self-reflective practices, including self-assessment. Benchmark students reflect and self-assess to reveal problems, misunderstandings, and confusions, as well as to determine new directions (Strong et al., 2001).

Beginning about fifth grade, when assessments are implemented at Benchmark, teachers design their assessment systems so that they are transparent, enabling students to know the criteria by which their work will be assessed and to learn to evaluate their own work in the same way that their teacher would (Shepard, 2000). The teacher's assessment system (employing rubrics and exemplars) provides the basis for developing metacognitive awareness of the important characteristics of such school tasks as good problem solving, good writing, and good literary analysis. Students are also guided to become aware of mental habits that support learning.

Students take control of the learning process by applying strategies appropriate to the learning task and to the way they learn best. For example, we teach students to summarize in their own words what they have read or heard, to take notes in a form that works best for them, to read easier texts to gain background knowledge, and to spread learning time over several study sessions. Strategies for learning and understanding that are taught at Benchmark are discussed in Chapters 12 and 13. The next principle to be discussed gained prominence in the late 1970s as the result of schema theory.

New Information Is Easier to Understand, Remember, and Use If It Is Attached to Prior Knowledge

Fitting new information into knowledge that one has already learned makes the new information easier to understand, remember, and use (Bransford et al., 2000; Gollub et al., 2002; Greeno et al., 1996; Joyce & Weil, 2004; Pressley & Block, 2002). The rationale for this principle comes from schema theory (Anderson & Pearson, 1984). A schema, I learned from Richard Anderson early in the 1980s, is an abstract knowledge structure that summarizes what is known about a variety of cases that differ in many particulars. For example, a schema for the word *lawyer* summarizes all the information an individual knows about what it is to be a lawyer, including information from TV programs (e.g., "The Practice"), books with lawyers as characters (e.g., *To Kill a Mocking Bird*), and life experiences with lawyers (e.g., the lawyer your dad hired to help write his will). In simpler language, a *schema* contains knowledge about a topic that is already stored in memory; *comprehension* involves the interaction of new information with old knowledge. This interaction requires activity on the part of the learner.

Consequently, in addition to being metacognitive, we want students to be actively involved in learning by relating what they are reading or learning to what they already know. Prior knowledge (schema) provides the hook to which the learner attaches new information. Constructing meaning involves more than appending new concepts and processes to existing knowledge; it also involves conceptual change and the creation of rich, integrated knowledge structures. Possessing prior knowledge is especially important when attempting to learn information that is conceptually dense. Without related prior knowledge and experience, there may be too much new information that requires attention simultaneously. When the cognitive load becomes too great, pieces of information drop out of short-term memory, and learning may be incomplete or confused.

Examples from the Lower School

Benchmark teachers gauge what learners already know about a subject and seek ways to build on that knowledge. They explicitly teach students to survey pictures and headings prior to reading as a way of assessing related prior knowledge to which they can attach the information they are going to read or discuss. Based on surveying the text, students share their prior knowledge and set purposes for reading. As already mentioned, to help students cope with conceptually dense topics, teachers guide students to find books on the topic being studied that are written several reading levels below the classroom text they want to understand. These lower-level books usually provide the major ideas that students need to have as background knowledge to be able to understand conceptually dense texts.

Examples from the Middle School

An example of how Benchmark teachers guide students to become aware of, and use, background information comes from a discussion with Barbara Mistichelli, a teacher of first-year middle school students. Mrs. Mistichelli commented that whenever she begins a new topic with her class, she asks students to brainstorm what they already know about it. As students share, she records their ideas on the chalkboard. After the brainstorming is concluded, the students organize the information on the board to form a framework, with the teacher pointing out main ideas and concepts related to the topic they will soon be studying. One day when I was visiting in the classroom, I witnessed Mrs. Mistichelli conducting a version of such a lesson. Her class was about to begin a unit on Alaska. She asked students to brainstorm what they knew about Alaska by putting each piece of information on a small sticky note. (Mrs. M handed out stacks of stickies to each student.) Once the students had completed writing what they knew about Alaska on stickies, she placed students in small groups to organize their stickies by category and then use them to make a concept map. The students were amazed at how much they already knew about Alaska, as well as how many misconceptions they had about the state (e.g., Alaska has little daylight; penguins live in Alaska; it is cold 12 months of the year).

A second example of attaching new information to old information occurred in Mrs. Reisinger's middle school language arts class. Mrs. Reisinger conducted an experiment with her second-year class, based on an experiment Richard Anderson reported when he conducted inservice training at Benchmark in the 1980s. This is the scenario of that class session that she shared with me.

> "During class one day, I assigned groups of students to three different roles in a memory activity. Students were unaware of the assignments given to other groups of students. One group was instructed to pretend they were lawyers, one group pretended they were parents, and another pretended they were musicians in a rock band. Next, I asked my students to listen carefully as I read aloud an article about the recording industry suing thousands of parents for allowing their children to illegally download songs from the Internet. When I was finished reading, I asked my students to work with the other students assigned to their group (i.e., lawyers, parents, musicians). I gave the groups a few minutes to write down everything they remembered from the article before I asked them to share; then the groups shared their information while I noted patterns about the information each group remembered. When the groups were finished reporting, I pointed out to my class the following patterns. The lawyers remembered impersonal information such as the number of lawsuits filed and the amount of money demanded for an out-of-court settlement. The parents' group was much more emotional; they remembered the outrage of some parents who were being held financially responsible for their

Accessing and organizing background knowledge help prepare students to be actively involved in their reading.

children's illegal actions. The musicians' group was passionate about its right to sue for damages done to the recording industry through illegal downloading."

Mrs. Reisinger next led a discussion on the first lesson to be learned from this activity. They concluded that our perspective, goals, and wants influence what we remember and learn. By virtue of their discussion, they also discovered the second lesson to be learned from this activity: Information is more easily remembered when it is attached to prior knowledge.

Students learn a similar lesson about prior knowledge in Dr. MacDonald's third-year class. Prior to reading the novel *Animal Farm*, each student is assigned a topic to research related to the Russian Revolution. Students write research reports on their topics and develop presentations to teach what they have learned to others in the class. As the class reads the novel, students make connections between the research the class has completed and what is happening in the novel. Students become excited about their ability to understand the deeper meaning of *Animal Farm*, as a result of the research they did.

Later in the year, during an author study of work by Neil Simon, Dr. MacDonald's students again realized the value of connecting new information to old. During the Simon unit the class reads seven of his plays. The main goal of the unit was for students to examine the plays to identify the characteristics of Simon's style. While reading the seventh play, *Lost in Yonkers*, students were able to connect what they were reading to the previous plays they had read by Simon and realize that it is through the unique characterizations that the author develops that the plot unfolds. Prior knowledge made the difference.

The second-year social studies program taught by Dr. MacDonald is designed so that students will continually make connections from what has been studied previously to the new information they are encountering. The class spends the first weeks of the school year learning basic principles of good government, such as the ideas of

Locke, Montesquieu, and others. Each unit builds on these principles. The class studies the development of monarchies in France and England and the presence or absence of the principles; they research the American colonies and Revolution, analyzing how these principles played out in this country. The class then examines the Constitutional Convention to see the ways these principles were woven into our Constitution and the compromises that were made for expedience. Prior knowledge of other governments enabled students to understand our Constitution in a much deeper way.

Organized Knowledge Is Easier to Recall Than Random Information

Grouping bits of information based on some commonality makes it easier to remember (Bereiter, 2002; Bransford et al., 2000; Gee, 2003). When Michael Pressley visited one of the Psych 101 classes (Gaskins & Elliot, 1991) I taught in the late 1980s, I told the class that Dr. Pressley had discovered a way to beat Miller's rule that people can only hold seven, plus or minus two, numbers in mind at a time. Then I said a string of 16 numbers (e.g., 1-8-4-9-1-7-7-6-0-7-0-3-1-9-4-1), which Dr. Pressley promptly repeated back for the class. They were impressed and asked him how he had managed such a feat. His response went something like this:

> "I organized the numbers into chunks so they wouldn't take up so much space in short-term memory. As I listened to the numbers, I looked for patterns—groups of numbers that had meaning for me. For 1-8-4-9, I thought about the gold rush and, for 1-7-7-6, I thought of the Declaration of Independence; 0–7 made me think of 1607, the settling of Jamestown, and 0–3 made me think of 1803, the U.S. purchase of the Louisiana Territory from France. The last four numbers were 1-9-4-1, which was the year the United States entered World War II."

As illustrated by Michael Pressley, another way of staying actively involved in the learning process is via a deliberate and effortful organization of what is being learned. Students for whom learning seems to come easily in a particular discipline are almost always pattern seekers. They look for the way information is organized. They also impose organization on what they are learning by grouping bits of information around key principles and concepts (Alexander & Jetton, 2000; Strong et al., 2001). It is by this principled and coherent way of thinking that expertise develops in a field of study. It has been our experience that struggling readers, however, tend to *not* take action to organize information and instead accumulate a random assortment of information. In discussing this phenomenon with my lower school Learning and Thinking (LAT) classes and my middle school Psych 101 classes, I have often had a discussion similar to the one below.

T: After a snowstorm, which do you think would be easier for me to find in your snowy backyard, a specific snowflake or a snowball?

S: A snowball.

T: Your brain is like your backyard. The bits and pieces of information coming at you all day are snowflakes. If you don't organize the snowflakes in your brain into a snowball, you are going to have a hard time finding the little snowflakes of information. I'm wondering how many of you put effort into making snowballs out of the snowflakes of information you hear and read throughout the day. Take 60 seconds and jot on your think pad an instance when you turned snowflakes of information into snowballs. (*Students write for 60 seconds.*) Who would like to share? (*Several students share instances in which they noted how a text was organized and then framed their recall of the main points in the same hierarchy.*) Just as experts organize new information around major concepts and principles of a content area or discipline, so should you. (*The discussion continues about ways to organize information for easier recall.*)

The Benchmark staff has learned that it is difficult for students to organize information around core concepts and principles if the curriculum emphasizes breadth of coverage and recall of facts. Therefore, we stress depth of learning in the content areas because depth lends itself to students learning the concepts and essential understandings that form the organizing structures of each domain. We have designed instruction in the content areas around key concepts and essential understandings. We teach students how to use these as the "snowballs" to which they attach the "snowflakes" of information they are learning. Benchmark's conceptually based programs are discussed in Chapter 14.

An Example from the Middle School

Mrs. Mistichelli teaches students how to develop an organized note-taking sheet to use while reading. For example, one of the goals of her animal unit is for students to record information in a way that they will be able to understand and use later. Students brainstorm important categories about animals. These categories become pages of a learning log, in which students record information throughout the reading of the entire book. The information they record in their learning logs is used in a culminating activity of their choice (i.e., essay, poem, or creative project). Not only does information need to be organized to aid recall, but it also needs to be thoughtfully and deeply processed. This topic is explored in the next section.

Information That Is Thoughtfully and Deeply Processed Is Likely to Be Understood and Used

Taking time to critically analyze, reorganize, or elaborate on information that is being learned usually results in better understanding and the ability to use the information (Gee, 2003; Marzano, 2003; Pressley, 1995). Benchmark's receipt of a James S. McDonnell cognitive science grant in 1988 provided Betsy Cunicelli and me with the opportunity to work with and learn from other McDonnell researchers, including Ann Brown, Joe Campione, John Bransford, Carl Bereiter, Marlene Scardamalia, Robert Sternberg, and Howard Gardner. One important point we learned was that they all believed that the goal of instruction was thoughtful and deep processing of information, as opposed to breath of coverage. Coverage was a common goal in most schools in the final decades of the 20th century, and these McDonnell researchers wanted to change the trend. Active involvement for McDonnell researchers meant developing learners who were not satisfied with a superficial understanding, but rather actively probed for connections to other concepts and generated and analyzed personal theories about topics under study. The researchers believed that without thoughtful and deep processing, information becomes inert; it is stored in memory but serves no function in students' lives (Bereiter & Scardamalia, 1993). By contrast, thoughtfully and deeply processed information is information that can be accessed and applied.

The researchers of the 1990s saw the role of teachers as developing students who want to know the "why" behind the facts; students who ask questions of others (and of themselves) that require deeper processing than sheer memorization (Pressley, 1995); students who think analytically, creatively, and practically (Sternberg, 2003). The pathway to this goal begins during the elementary years with the gradual, systematic, and explicit introduction of strategies to help students think more thoughtfully and deeply about a text or topic. These strategies include summarizing, stating the main idea of nonfiction, deciding on the theme of a piece of fiction, drawing conclusions, evaluating, and synthesizing (Duffy, 2003). Compare/contrast, imagery, critical analysis, and application are other high-level processes that require thoughtful reflection and deep processing and should be introduced at the intermediate grades and above. Because it is deep understanding of subject matter that transforms factual information into usable knowledge (Bransford et al., 2000), Benchmark teachers explicitly explain the difference between surface understanding and the deep understanding necessary to be able to use information effectively. In fact, they explain to students that if they are having difficulty applying what they learned, they probably only have a superficial understanding.

An Example from the Lower School

One way we guide students to process information deeply in social studies classes is by asking them to view historical information through several lenses. The concept of lenses facilitates the generation of different perspectives. For example, in studying the gold rush of 1849, students were asked to think of the events they studied from perspectives posted on their lenses chart: social, political/governmental, economic, technological, religious, cultural, and geographical. During a discussion in one of Benchmark's classrooms, I saw students scan the lenses chart and then make comments about changes brought about by the California gold rush.

> T: Looking through one of our seven lenses, I'd like each of you to discuss changes in California that resulted from the gold rush. On your think pad, jot down the lens through which you choose to look, as well as a few notes about what you want to say. (*Gives students 2 minutes to write their notes. As the students write, the teacher circulates to scaffold the thinking and note writing for students who seem to be experiencing difficulty coming up with ideas. After all students have written something, the teacher continues.*) Harry, please begin the discussion of changes that resulted from the California gold rush. After Harry has made a contribution, others should chime in.

> S1: Economically the Chinese proved to be clever. The white men searching for gold did their best to not allow the Chinese to pan for gold, so the Chinese made money by providing services that were needed by the men in the min-

ing towns. One change was that the Chinese began running restaurants and laundries for the miners.

S2: What you just said could also be viewed through a social and a cultural lens. Socially the Chinese were not viewed as equals and culturally the Chinese had different values. They came to America to earn money to send back to their families. They did not come to America to settle like most of the white men. A change was that lots of people hurried West hoping to get rich, and all these people turned San Francisco into a big city.

S3: I'm looking through the geographical lens. Some mining towns in other states in the West became ghost towns in a few years, but people who came to California in search of gold settled there even if they didn't find gold. Some stayed in California because of the pleasant climate and the good seaport.

S4: Because of the gold rush, better technology was created. Men invented crude machines to separate the gold from the sand. These machines took the place of panning for gold.

S5: Looking through the government lens, the miners realized that there were too many fights and problems. The men with the most power appointed others to enforce laws about people's rights. (*The discussion continues in this manner, with the teacher reminding students of key events that might be viewed from one of the lenses.*)

Encouraging students to view what they were learning from different perspectives created the need to delve more deeply into information than mere recitation of facts from the text would have required. The result was not only deeper understanding but also a better recall of what was learned.

An Example from Support Services

Kim Munday of our support services staff encourages students to ask questions aimed at developing a deeper understanding of a concept being discussed during class meetings. In a discussion with Kim, she had this to share with me:

"We were discussing how to keep thoughts about peer relationships from interfering with completing homework. I suggested leaving difficulties at school and not bringing them home. Someone said, 'How do you do that?' One of the girls shared that she leaves the problems she has with another student behind the bookcase in my office. She turned an abstract concept into a concrete example."

An Example from Middle School Math

Amy Cuthbertson talked about students needing to process deeply in math. She told of students who, after they had solved for the variables in a system of equations, were asked what the numbers represented. The students could not explain; they seemed to feel that getting the "answer" was sufficient. Mrs. Cuthbertson told the class that clearly they did not have a deep understanding of what they were learning and that the goal was not simply to find the "answer" but to understand what the answer represented.

An Example from the Middle School

In the example from Dr. MacDonald's author study, students needed to use analytical reasoning to develop a sense of the author's style across seven plays. They applied such strategies as compare/contrast, critical analysis, drawing conclusions, evaluating, and synthesizing. For example, after reading *The Odd Couple*, the students were expected to read another version that Simon wrote (i.e., the female version of the screenplay, *The Odd Couple II*), then compare the variation to the original. Needless to say, a lot of teaching and learning about critical analysis went on during the 2 months of author study. Clearly thoughtful and deep processing have to be practiced if students are to develop a comfort level in thinking this way.

Concepts and Strategies That Are Repeatedly Practiced and Applied Are Not Easily Forgotten

Repeated practice and application are essential to learning (Gee, 2003; Marzano, 2003; Pressley, 1995). By 1973 Benchmark had become an independent day school with a grades 1–8 curriculum. Teaching a full-day curriculum to struggling readers was the beginning of our understanding that there is more to teaching poor readers than teaching them how to read! Our students knew that they were supposed to practice what they were learning, but they did not understand exactly what practice was. They passed their eyes over text and turned pages and thought they were practicing reading, even though they often could not accurately reread or discuss what they had just "read." They studied for content-area tests by "looking over" the text and their notes and then were amazed when they did poorly on tests—after all, they had "studied." Over 30 years later, this phenomenon still continues to be true for most of our new-to-Benchmark students and even for some of our veteran students. Over the years we have studied educational psychology journals and texts for insights into this problem. As we gained insights about meaningful practice, we shared them with our students.

First, we taught our struggling readers that practice entails active involvement. We explained that when learners practice, they routinely and conscientiously organize and react to what is being learned and that mindlessly passing their eyes over the text does not qualify as practice. We also had to differentiate practice in performance-based fields, such as music, athletics, and chess, from practice in academic domains. Twenty minutes a day of practicing piano scales in various keys may seem mindless, yet it still has a great payoff when performing a piano concerto. By contrast, expertise in cognitive endeavors requires mindful, thoughtful practice. For example, to become an expert physicist, composer, or teacher requires both a depth of understanding of the domain and "a blend of creative (generate ideas), analytical (evaluate the ideas), and practical thinking (make the ideas work and convince others of their worth) that goes substantially beyond deliberate practice" (Sternberg, 2003, p. 6).

Second, we explained to our students that the more time engaged in processing and applying information, the greater the achievement. For example, one result of mindful practice is pattern recognition. Good thinking in a domain takes years to attain because of the need to build up a vast library of patterns (e.g., common orthographic patterns in words, common patterns among themes in literature). People more rapidly recognize patterns in areas in which they have great experience. At the core of expertise are years of practice recognizing patterns and applying what one has learned (Perkins, 1995). In fact, the amount of practice and application acquired over time are two factors that separate experts from novices. Students who spend the most time engaged in multiple exposures and complex interactions with knowledge are the ones who learn the most (Marzano, 2003) and eventually develop expertise in the domain being practiced (Hatano & Oura, 2003).

Third, we discussed with students the impact practice has on memory. Multiple exposures are required to integrate and retain knowledge in permanent memory. Students are taught that they must regularly practice using their conceptual understandings and applying strategy knowledge or they will forget what they have learned. For strategies and other procedural knowledge to be used effectively, they must be learned to a level of either automaticity or controlled processing. This requires practice. Ideally, practice thinking about topics being learned and using newly acquired strategies should occur, at most, only a few days apart, and the types of experiences should be varied from exposure to exposure. Our goal is to lead students to conclude that what matters is not the amount of time spent doing something, but, rather, what one does with the time. Without mindful practice, real competence is not possible (Marzano, 2003). Several examples follow that illustrate this point.

An Example from Support Services

In class meetings Mrs. Munday talks about how a person cannot change other people, but he or she *can* change how he or she responds to someone. The more opportunities (i.e., in lunch group, class meeting, individual sessions) Mrs. Munday gives students to practice this concept, the more they can take charge of it and make it their own.

Examples from the Middle School

Students who are exposed to explicit strategy instruction when they enter Benchmark sometimes think that they do not have to apply the strategies they have been taught until they leave Benchmark and attend high school. Without sufficient regular practice, of course, they are unlikely to be able to apply these strategies when they are needed. Year after year, the staff scaffolds student use of learning and thinking strategies and leads them through applying them. The middle school staff deals with this problem by providing opportunities in the second- and third-year programs in which students must use the strategies they have learned or they will not be able to succeed. Our teachers have found that it is when students actually *need* to use strategies to succeed that they begin to develop a sense of how to apply the strategies independently. This actualization only comes through high expectations that hold students accountable for using the strategies, opportunities to "fail" by not using the strategies, and reflection on what they are doing that works and what they are doing that is not working for them. An example of this process occurred in Dr. MacDonald's English class.

George took a quiz about the previous night's reading. When Dr. MacDonald glanced at the quiz, there was absolutely nothing correct. Dr. MacDonald asked George if he had read the assignment. George replied that he had, but he "didn't really understand it." Dr. MacDonald asked him what he had done about it. Had he taken notes? No, he had not taken notes, nor had he done anything to rectify his difficulty with comprehension. Dr. MacDonald suggested that George reread and take notes, which he did. He retook the quiz and did better. A few days later Dr. MacDonald and George had a debriefing conference to reflect on what had happened and what he had learned from the experience.

Despite advice to the contrary, our struggling readers want to believe that they can put off until the last minute practicing and applying what was taught in previous lessons and still successfully put together projects and cram for tests. The end result, more often than not, is superficial understanding and a poor product. Managing self-regulation over a period of time is a common roadblock among our students. A century of psychological experiments has revealed that paced learning (i.e., distributed practice) brings about greater learning than the same amount of time massed into one session (Pressley, 1995). To help our students in fifth grade and above understand the *spaced-practice principle*, we ask them to write self-reflections upon the completion of a project and when the project or test is graded and returned to them. The first self-reflection explains what students did to complete the project or prepare for the test, what they think that they should have done differently, and the grade they think they earned. The second self-reflection is completed after students receive feedback from the teacher. In this reflection students explain how they think they should complete the next project or prepare for the next test. We want students to assess which practice schedule and type of active involvement work best for them and which do not, and then to make a plan for the next project or test. The goal is for students to learn how to manage a long-term project.

SUMMARY

A common misconception among students, particularly struggling readers, is that if they show up at school and teachers do their jobs, learning will happen. Neither research, theory, nor experience support such wishful thinking. As much as some of us might like it to be different, learning requires intent and intelligent effort. Students must enter classrooms intending to learn. Furthermore, because learning does not occur by osmosis, nor is it automatic, intent alone is not enough. The learner must also be actively involved in achieving the goal of the learning process—the goal to create meaningful, coherent representations of knowledge. It is the learner's job to be actively involved in constructing meaning from two sources: from information and experiences presented in the classroom, and from what is already in his or her head, including thoughts and beliefs. Learning is accomplished by linking new information and experiences with existing knowledge in meaningful ways.

Learning, then, is a complex, interactive process that requires the intent, or goal, to create meaning, plus the mental activity to achieve the learning goal. To reach the learning goal, the learner needs to employ a repertoire of thinking and reasoning strategies, as well as self-regulation strategies for selecting and monitoring mental operations. These are all actions of a student who accepts personal responsibility for his or her learning. Six learning principles that teachers should share with students are:

1. *Develop and access background knowledge.* Learning is based on the learner's knowledge and experience.
2. *Monitor and take control.* Metacognitive strategies for monitoring and controlling learning are essential to reaching one's learning goals.
3. *Attach new information to what is already known.* New information is easier to understand, remember, and use if it can be attached to prior knowledge.
4. *Organize bits and pieces of information.* Organized knowledge is easier to recall than random information.
5. *Process information thoughtfully and deeply.* Information that is thoughtfully and deeply processed is more likely to be understood and used.
6. *Practice and apply what is being learned.* Concepts and strategies that are repeatedly practiced and applied are not easily forgotten.

PART III

CLASSROOM IMPLEMENTATION

Autonomy is fostered by teaching students strategies for decoding and comprehending.

CHAPTER 10

Strategies for Reading Words

Teaching Phonemic Awareness, Decoding, and Fluency

Children who struggle in learning to read often exhibit difficulties in phonemic awareness, decoding, and fluency (Torgesen & Burgess, 1998). Some experts even suggest that these difficulties comprise the struggling readers' "core deficit" (Stanovich, 1988). At Benchmark it is typical for students who are new to the school, regardless of their reading level, to exhibit difficulty in segmenting spoken words into their component sounds and to lack a systematic approach for unlocking the pronunciation of unknown words. As a result, they often are unable to read with fluency, and, without fluency, their ability to comprehend is compromised.

This chapter summarizes insights the Benchmark staff has gained about phonemic awareness, decoding, and fluency during 35 years of teaching struggling readers. The staff's early attempts to teach word-learning skills and strategies are described, as well as our theories about what worked and did not work and why. Dissatisfaction with these early attempts led to Benchmark's research and development project with Patricia Cunningham and Richard Anderson and later to a word-learning project with Linnea Ehri. These projects and what we learned from them about phonemic awareness, decoding, and fluency are also discussed. During the first project in the mid-1980s, we developed the Benchmark Word Identification (BWI) program, an analogy approach to decoding. In the second project a decade later, we added several previously missing elements to BWI to improve students' learning of sight words. These changes in our instruction resulted in significant improvement for our struggling readers with regard to decoding and spelling. The evolution and elements of what became the Word Detectives approach are outlined in this chapter and the next.

EARLY ATTEMPTS TO TEACH PHONEMIC AWARENESS AND DECODING

Throughout the history of Benchmark School we have employed many approaches to help children develop an awareness that words are composed of individual sounds that can be matched to letters or letter patterns. The approaches we have used range from analyzing letter–sound matches in whole words as a way to discover generalizations about how our language works, to learning sound–letter matches in isolation and blending those sounds to decode words. Strickland (1998) describes the first of these approaches as whole to part and the second as part to whole. Each of these general approaches proved helpful for some of our students some of the time. Once again, a reminder that there is no one approach that is a good fit for all students.

This section describes a few of the specific approaches we have used with our struggling readers and suggests several reasons why approaches that work for most beginning readers may not work for children who are struggling with learning to read. Specific approaches reviewed include writing with invented spelling, completing workbooks/worksheets, analyzing sight words, synthesizing sounds, and guessing unknown words based on context and initial consonants.

Writing with Invented Spelling

Daily writing experiences provide our students with the opportunity to experiment with sounds and letters. Even our students who are beginning readers write daily in their journals. Their journal entries may be responses to books their parents read to them or expositions on topics about which they know a lot. As students write, teachers and other adult helpers circulate to assist students in their attempts to segment the words they want to write into sounds and then to match letters to those sounds. Initially, this support requires that the adults in the room move quickly from student to student. However, in only a matter of weeks, students become more independent and begin to take seriously such teacher coaching as "Just write down the letters for the sounds you hear and draw a line for the sound–letter matches you don't know; we can fill in the missing letters later" or "We are not worried about spelling right now; let's just get all your good ideas written down."

In the first month or 2 of the school year, it is not uncommon to find that most of the writing of our beginning readers is composed of "words" written with initial consonants and lines. However, as students realize that invented spellings are acceptable—in fact, applauded—their voices can be heard attempting to segment the sounds in the words they want to write. This process of writing initial consonants and lines, as well as invented spellings, has played (and continues to play) an important role in helping our struggling readers develop phonemic awareness at a pace that is appropriate for each student. However, although these initial attempts to express themselves in writing may prove sufficient to launch some young children into the world of reading and writing, they surely have not proved sufficient for students who struggle with learning to read. Although writing with invented spellings is an important step toward understanding how our language works, something more is necessary for struggling readers.

Completing Workbooks/Worksheets

In the early days of the school, we tried building a program of phonemic awareness and decoding around published phonics workbooks and ditto masters. This approach was unsuccessful for several reasons. One was that workbooks and dittoed worksheets resembled the materials with which our students had already failed, so students resisted completing them. A second and more important reason was that students did not see any reason for completing them. In fact, many students regard workbooks and worksheets as having no connection to "real" reading, but rather as something teachers use to keep them busy. Most of the workbook/worksheet activities involved only *writing* letters for sounds, or *circling* pictures, letters, or words, rather than necessitating that students *produce* sounds that matched letters, as occurs in reading words. In addition, the organization of these activities was not systematic (i.e., concepts were not introduced in a logical order, nor did they build on each other with embedded review). Furthermore, the sound–letter matches in the workbook/worksheet activities were usually not accompanied by reading in real texts, which would have provided practice applying the concepts introduced in the pencil-and-paper tasks. Without a rationale that made sense to them, our struggling readers found ways to complete the pages without gaining useable knowledge of sound–letter matches. We quickly realized that independent completion of these tasks was not the best way to teach struggling readers about sound–letter relationships. We concluded that students needed more explicit teacher guidance to learn what they had not figured out on their own about sound–letter relationships.

Analyzing Known Words

Another early approach we used was analytic phonics. From the words students knew as sight words, teachers selected words that shared a commonality in letter–sound matches, then challenged students to develop generalizations about these matches. For example, for one day's lesson early in the school year each student was given an envelope with a set of index cards containing one of each of the following words: *be, bet, go, got, no, not, we, wet*. Students were asked to sort the words into two lists, with each list containing words that were alike in some way. After students had sorted their words into two lists, the teacher asked for volunteers to share their lists with the class. Students usually shared that *be, go, no,* and *we* were alike. The teacher circulated among the students, commenting that most of them had generated the same list of words. Next, the teacher asked if someone would explain how the words were alike. Some responses led to helpful discoveries about the relationships between sounds and letters, whereas others did not. For example, sharing that all the words in the list have two letters is correct but does not lead to an insight about how our language works. Insightful responses included "All the words end in a vowel" and "I hear the name of the vowel at the end of each word." The teacher then asked, "Would anyone like to make a statement that connects what you see [a vowel at the end of each word] with what you hear [the vowel's name]?" With scaffolding, the teacher led students to notice that when there is only one vowel in a word and it is at the end of the word, the vowel *may* say its name. The next step was for students to apply this generalization to words or word parts they had not previously decoded or learned as sight words (e.g., *hi, lo, ye, quo, pi, fro*). In addition, *to* and *do* were discussed as examples that generalizations work most of the time, but not all of the time. More advanced students were led to understand that the generalization that they had just made also applied to syllables containing one vowel at the end of the syllable (e.g., *halo, silo, hotel, alto, limbo*). A similar procedure for developing a generalization was used with the list containing *bet, got, not*, and *wet*.

Our students enjoy sorting words and making generalizations. However, although opportunities occurred when students could apply these generalizations, they often did not do so when reading in group or on their own—despite the fact that a generalization was posted on the wall in the classroom after it was discovered. It appeared that these isolated lessons to create generalizations about letter–sound matches were not sufficient for our students to recognize opportunities to apply them, even with daily reminders. We wondered why this process was not as successful with our students as we had hoped it would be and hypothesized that those who did not actively participate in developing a generalization might not understand it and thus could not apply it. We needed an approach that involved every student, not just a few, in making discoveries about how our language works. Furthermore, it appeared that our students needed immediate and repeated practice in connected text to use what they had just learned. Incidental instruction and one or two occasional applications were not going to be enough. Clearly we needed a more systematic approach (Strickland & Snow, 2002).

Synthesizing Sounds

To address the weaknesses found in these isolated lessons, we adopted a program in which we explicitly and systematically taught students the sounds that matched each letter or letter pattern (i.e., two or more letters that represent one sound) in our language, including the many sound–letter(s) matches for vowels. Posted in each classroom at the beginning of the school year were 42 large cards with their blank sides facing toward the class. As the teacher introduced each sound–letter match, a card was turned toward the class to reveal a picture associated with one of the approximately 42 sounds in our language. Also on each card was the letter or letter patterns that represented each sound (e.g., both *ue* and *oo* can represent the vowel sound we hear in *glue* and *zoo*, so *ue* and *oo* were written on the card with a picture depicting howling wind). This program, accompanied by workbooks and readers that provided immediate application of the sound–letter relationships taught each day, seemed to combine just the ingredients we wanted. But as time passed, we noticed that some of our students were not matching sounds to all the letters. Rather they were attempting to read words based on the shape of the word or a distinctive feature, whereas others matched sounds to only a few of the letters and guessed based on these partial clues. Other students matched all the sounds to letters but could not synthesize the sounds on their own to recognize a word that was in their speaking vocabulary. For example, students could match sounds to letters in *met* (e.g., sound out /m/ /e/ /t/) but could not recognize as a word the elongated sounds they produced. Expecting all of our students to respond in the same way (i.e., sounding and blending isolated sounds into recognizable words) on the same time schedule was not proving to be realistic.

Contextual Guessing

During Benchmark School's first decade, it seemed that our most successful approach to teaching decoding to beginning readers involved coaching them to use the initial consonant of an unknown word and the sense of the sentence to guess the pronunciation of an unknown word. This approach worked quite well for students who were reading at first- or second-grade level. However, learning words by using the initial consonant and context did not prove satisfactory when students were reading to gain information that was not already part of their background knowledge or when the vocabulary load became dense. Although contextual guessing worked some of the time, we knew that we had to come up with a better method for teaching students how to read words. That method needed to include having students learn about sound–letter matches in all positions in a word (i.e., not just initial consonants) and learn at a pace that was appropriate for each student.

WHAT WE LEARNED

Students appreciate being allowed to write using initial consonants and lines and/or invented spellings. This method seems to help them codify their understanding of sound–letter relationships, and learning takes place according to each child's personal timetable. On the other hand, workbooks/worksheets can, at best, play only a peripheral role in helping children learn to decode, because they do not address the principal task of teaching children to blend sounds together well enough to aid word recognition (Bereiter, 2002). Discovering generalizations about how our language works has potential for helping struggling readers, but only if the approach is systematic rather than incidental. What we were beginning to realize during Benchmark's first decade was that programs for special populations, such as struggling readers, need to be intense, with large blocks of time devoted to teaching and learning and conducted by teachers who know a lot about teaching reading (Pearson, 1999).

Because struggling readers intuitively know that the method used in their previous schools was a poor match to their phase of development, preferred way of learning, or pace, they generally like any approach to phonemic awareness and decoding that is different from the way they were previously taught. This also may be the case because students who had already experienced difficulty in understanding the relationship between letters and sounds were not willing to risk putting forth effort to use an approach that had proved unsuccessful previously. Whatever the reason, it is clear that our struggling readers like being given the chance to start over, using an approach that is new to them.

During the 1970s, the approach used most frequently in kindergarten and first grade in the schools that our students had attended prior to Benchmark was that of learning and blending isolated sound–letter matches. This approach proved difficult for most of our struggling readers. We observed that most of our students could segment the one-syllable words they heard into two parts: the initial consonant and the vowel–consonant pattern that followed (e.g., /f/ /un/). However, more often than not, they experienced difficulty when asked to segment these same words into their smallest sound units (e.g., /f/ /u/ /n/). We also discovered that students usually could supply rhyming words for a word they heard (e.g., *let, met, bet* for *set*) and blend onset and rime (/l/ /et/), but most had serious difficulty when asked to blend more than two phonemes, even when the phonemes were supplied by the teacher (e.g., blend /l/ /e/ /t/ to decode *let*).

As a result of a decade of employing a variety of approaches to phonemic awareness and word learning, we concluded that we needed to develop an approach that was unlike the programs in which our students had already failed, one that featured explicit explanations of what students were expected to learn, why it was important, when it could be used, and how to do it. Also important would be modeling the thinking process that we wanted students to use in analyzing and decoding words. Furthermore, most or all of the daily activities needed to be teacher directed and provide ways to keep every student actively involved in thinking about sound–letter matches, in producing the sounds associated with letters or letter patterns, and in applying what they were learning to decode words. Our goal was to create a systematic, year-long program that emphasized phonemic awareness, provided a consistent process for students to use in decoding unknown words, and gave students opportunities to practice what they were learning in connected text. In addition, our approach needed to provide many opportunities and reminders for students to apply what was taught to decoding and writing of words throughout the day.

Research and Development

In the early 1980s, we conducted a review of research looking for insights that might guide us in developing an approach to phonemic awareness, decoding, and fluency for our struggling readers. Our review of the literature revealed that good readers use an automatic analogy process when they encounter unfamiliar words (Cunningham, 1975–1976; Glushko, 1979; Perfetti, 1985). Children who are good readers use their knowledge of vowel–consonant patterns in the words they know how to read to decode unknown words in which these patterns are encountered (Fowler, Napps, & Feldman, 1985; Gibson & Levin, 1975; McClelland & Johnston, 1977; Torgesen, 1985; Vellutino & Scanlon, 1984). Our review of the literature also confirmed an observation that we had made: Struggling readers often do not discover on their own what teachers leave unsaid about sound–letter relationships. Students depend on explicit instruction to learn these relationships (Barr & Dreeben, 1983; Calfee & Drum, 1986; Johnson & Baumann, 1984). Using insights from our review of the literature and what we had learned from our experience with other approaches, we set out to develop an analogy approach to decoding.

An Analogy Approach

In 1984 we invited Patricia Cunningham to work with us as a consultant to develop an analogy approach to decoding. After our initial year, Richard Anderson, from the Center for the Study of Reading, joined us in developing what became the Benchmark Word Identification research and development project (Gaskins et al., 1988; Gaskins, Gaskins, Anderson, & Schommer, 1995). During daily 20-minute lessons that were an adjunct to traditional guided reading lessons and process writing instruction, emphasis was placed on two areas: developing phonemic awareness and acquiring a basic sight vocabulary of 120 key words that could be used to decode unknown words by analogy. Our key words are high-frequency words that contain the major spelling patterns (phonograms) found in our language. Three to five new key words were introduced each week and, after a week as our featured words, were placed on the word wall. These words were used to decode unknown words, as well as to explore sound–letter matches and to identify and produce rhyming words.

Unknown words used for practice in applying the analogy approach were usually presented in context. For example, students might be asked to decode the underlined word in the sentence: We visited a splendid castle. As students followed along, the teacher would read the sentence to the class, saying *blank* for the underlined word. Next, she would ask: "What spelling patterns do you see?" "What key words do you know with the same spelling patterns?" Students would identify the *e-n* and *i-d* spelling patterns and supply the key words *ten* and *did*. In choral response, students would say, "If I know *ten*, then I know *splen*. If I know *did*, then I know *did*. The word is *splendid*." At that point the teacher would usually beam with pride and tell these beginning readers that they had just decoded a "college" word. Daily teacher-directed and every-pupil-response (EPR) phonemic awareness and decoding activities were followed by students writing key words beneath each underlined word on a page with 6 to 12 sentences. As students called to mind and wrote key words, the teacher circulated to listen to individual students pronounce target words and to assess their accuracy in using key words to read the underlined words.

Lessons were fast-paced and game-like, using an explicit-explanation model (Gaskins, Downer, & Gaskins, 1986). Teachers told students what they were going to teach them, why it was important, when they could use it, and how to do it. They modeled their thinking about how to decode by analogy, then provided guided practice, followed by a gradual releasing of responsibility to the students. Student engagement and active involvement were fostered by the use of EPR activities, visual–auditory–kinesthetic processing, and individual student checks.

Our research revealed that Benchmark students who were taught to decode by analogy significantly outperformed our struggling readers who had not been taught this strategy (Gaskins, et al., 1995). We were delighted! In addition, Marilyn Adam's (1990) extensive review of how children learn to read confirmed that word recognition depends upon pattern recognition as encouraged by an analogy approach. Nevertheless, during the school year 1993–1994, we began to wonder if something might be missing in our analogy approach to phonemic awareness and decoding. About 15% of our middle school students who had been taught to decode by analogy were slow readers and tended to spell phonetically but not necessarily accurately. We wondered if their reading and spelling problems were due to difficulty in calling to mind the analogous words they needed to decode and spell unknown words. These students had been successful decoders when they were in our lower school. Throughout those years, students received daily word-identification instruction in classrooms with word walls of key words, and they were encouraged to use the analogy approach across the curriculum. In analyzing our data from the middle school, we hypothesized that the problems some of our middle school students experienced in decoding and spelling might be due to their having depended on the word wall as a source of analogous words, rather than having stored the key words in memory. They could not call to mind known words that contained the same spelling patterns they found in words they wanted to decode or spell. It turned out to be a little more complicated than that, but we were on the right track.

A Second Literature Review

We again studied the research related to how children learn words to find clues about how we might improve our approach to teaching phonemic awareness, decoding, and fluency. Two principles stood out as we conducted this review of the literature. One was that readers use at least four different ways to read words, and all of these ways require that students, at some point in their development as readers, fully analyze words for sound–letter matches. Although our program included some of these elements, we knew we could do more. A second principle was that children move through phases with regard to the letters or parts of a word to which they pay attention. The next sections summarize what we learned from our literature review about the various ways in which words are read and the phases of word learning.

Ways to Read Words

From studying the research of Ehri and her colleagues (summarized in Ehri, 1991), we learned that children learn to read words in four ways: contextual guessing, letter–sound decoding, analogy, and sight. Our experience and the work of Cunningham (2000) suggested that successful readers use all four ways. Furthermore, we had observed that the way our struggling readers choose to read a word seemed to depend on their background knowledge and developmental level, as well as on features of the word and the context in which it appeared. The four ways to read words are summarized below.

One way to read a word is by *contextual guessing*, a method that has great appeal to our struggling readers. Contextual guessing occurs when students read most of the words in a text as sight words and use meaning and grammar cues to guess unknown words. For instance, in a story about a visit to grandmother's house, located in the mountains, there is the unknown word *woods* in the sentence: "Jack hid in the woods." To guess the unknown word, a student needs (1) appropriate background knowledge that will cue retrieval of the word, and (2) knowledge of letter–sound relationships. Without knowledge of letter–sound relationships, contextual guessing, even with a picture, is not reliable. For example, the word *woods* may be read as *forest* or *trees* or even *water*. In another case, after examining a picture of a farm, accompanied by the sentence "I see the . . . ," a student read the unknown word as *duck* instead of the correct word *pig*. The child ignored the letter–sound matches in *pig* and relied on what made sense based on the picture and the context.

Another way to read words is by *letter–sound decoding*. This method involves identifying an unknown word by using a few select sound–letter matches, as well as matching *all* the letters or letter patterns in the word to sounds. Using only one or a few letter–sound matches in a word may lead to a miscalled word. For example, reading the word *country* for *county*. On the other hand, a correct match between just one letter and sound is sufficient for some students to combine background knowledge, context, and letter–sound knowledge to read correctly the final word in the sentence: "She ran fast in the race." Using a few select letter–sound matches is another approach that seems to have natural appeal for our students. However, using only partial cues often leads to miscalled words.

A more mature level of letter–sound decoding occurs when a reader looks all the way through a word and matches sounds to each letter or letter pattern and successfully blends those sounds to pronounce the word, as in decoding /ch/ /a/ /t/. Some children, however, may match all the letters or letter patterns to sounds, yet not make sufficient closure in the blending process to recognize the word (e.g., blend /sh/ /ou/ /t/, but not be able to blend the sounds together quickly and smoothly enough to recognize the word *shout*). This closure difficulty is found among some of our struggling readers.

A third way to read unknown words is by *analogy* to a known sight word, the process we attempted to teach our students explicitly. For example, when students encounter an unknown word with a familiar spelling pattern, they think of a word they know with the same spelling pattern (i.e., the vowel and letters that follow). If the unknown word were *slot*, students might think of *not* and say to themselves, "If I know *not*, then I know *slot*." Similarly, students might use the known words *in* and *blow* to decode *window*. To be successful in using the analogy approach independently, a child must have stored in memory known words in a fully analyzed way (Ehri, 1991). In cases in which a child has not fully analyzed a known word, the child may attempt to decode an unknown word using a known word that has a different but similar spelling pattern from the unknown word. For example, he or she may attempt to use *tent* to decode *plant* or *in* to decode *Stan*.

A fourth way that children read words is by *sight*; they just recognize the word as soon as they see it. Knowing a word as a sight word is the goal of the word-learning process. The process of sight-word reading is different from that of using letters and sounds to decode unknown words. In sight word reading, the words are read from memory, not from conscious and deliberate decoding and blending operations. Fluency in sight word reading is increased in proportion to the number of words read, especially in books in which almost all of the words are sight words. Fluency is also enhanced by repeated reading, echo reading, choral reading, partner reading, and readers theater.

Phases of Word Reading

As children develop as readers, they go through phases of word learning (Bear, Invernizzi, Templeton, & Johnston, 1996; Ehri, 1995) (see Figure 10.1). In the first phase, the *prealphabetic or visual-cue phase*, children remember a word based on distinctive and purely visual cues. Children in this phase may, for example, identify *baby* based on the "tail" of the letter located at the end of the word. As a result, other words with a tail may also be called *baby*; thus, *donkey* and even *king* may be read as *baby*. Relying on purely visual cues is commonplace among our young struggling readers.

Children in the second phase, the *partial alphabetic phase*, are not yet using all the letter–sound information in a word. This is another phase that is common to struggling readers. Students remember and apply a few letter–sound matches that capture their attention, such as remembering only the letter–sound matches for *r* and *y* in the word *ready*. In a story about getting ready for a party, students who may have noticed only the letter–sound matches for *r* and *y* may be successful in correctly reading *ready*. How-

FIGURE 10.1. Phases of sight-word learning.

Prealphabetic Phase (Remembering a distinctive, purely *visual* cue) Example: tall posts	ye**ll**ow
Partial Alphabetic Phase (Remembering limited matches between salient letter–sounds) Example: matches between *K* and *N* only	**K** itte **N** | | k it n
Full Alphabetic Phase (Remembering matches between *all* letters and sounds) Example: 4 letter units matched to 4 sound units	C L O CK | | | | k l o k
Consolidated Alphabetic Phase (Remembering matches between multiletter units and syllabic units) Example: matching onset and rime units	CR ATE | | kr at

From Gaskins et al. (1996). Copyright 1996 by Benchmark Press. Reprinted by permission in *Success with Struggling Readers* by Irene Gaskins (2005). See copyright page for photocopying limitations.

ever, when they later read a story with the sentence "Sue really likes ice cream," some of them may misread the sentence as "Sue ready likes ice cream."

The third phase is the *full alphabetic phase*. Students in this phase of sight-word learning notice and remember all the letter–sound matches in a word. They can decode words such as *coax* because, in reading other words, they have matched the letters and sounds for *c* (when followed by any letter except *e*, *i*, or *y*), *oa* (two vowels together), and *x* (as in *box*). Also, they can decode words such as *coax* because, in decoding the word, they have looked all the way through the word and matched a sound to each letter or letter pattern. The vast majority of Benchmark's struggling readers has not attained this phase at the point of entering our school. In revising BWI, we knew we had to devise a way to scaffold word learning to pull students into and through the full alphabetic phase.

The final phase, the *consolidated alphabetic phase,* is the most efficient; it is the phase in which we commonly find mature readers. In this phase readers have consolidated their letter–sound knowledge and remember matches between multiletter units and syllabic units. For example, they match onset and rime units, as in decoding the unknown word *shade* by recognizing the letter–sound matches from the onset of a known word (e.g., *ship*) and the rime of a known word (e.g., *made*).

Based on what we had learned about ways to read words and the phases of word learning, we decided that some changes were necessary in our approach to teaching phonemic awareness, decoding, and fluency. We needed to allow each struggling reader to begin where he or she was in the development of word knowledge. That meant that students should be encouraged to read words in any of the four ways appropriate for their phase of development and the characteristics of the word, with the ultimate goal being movement into the consolidated alphabetic phase.

Revising Our Approach

Goals

We decided to add the word-analysis procedures and activities to the BWI that we believed would provide the foundation students needed to reach the consolidated alphabetic phase. Our ultimate goal was for students to be able to automatically use consolidated word parts such as spelling patterns to decode words, as well as use letter–sound decoding and contextual guessing to supplement the decoding process when an analogy approach did not work. As noted, the addition of word analysis processes was needed because calling key words to mind without the word wall seemed to be difficult for our students. We now suspected that our middle school students who were slow readers and phonetic spellers had not looked carefully at the letters that composed each word, but rather remembered the characteristics of each word that were most salient, suggesting that they were stuck in the early phases of word learning. We believed that in order for our struggling readers to call to mind a word with the same spelling pattern as a word they wished to decode, they would need to learn that word by listening to every sound in the word and matching the sounds to the letters or letter patterns in the word.

Collaboration

Keeping in mind our newly acquired understandings about word learning, we decided that the best approach to improving our program would be to focus our initial efforts on word-identification instruction in Benchmark's class of first- and second-grade beginning readers. As our task we set the challenge of changing or adding to the BWI program in a way that would ensure that students got the key words into memory in a fully analyzed way. We also wanted to make any changes that were necessary to meet the needs of students who were at different phases of development in word learning. Thus, in the fall of 1994 we embarked on a journey to revise and expand our analogy program. A team of collaborators was assembled, including Sherry Cress, the classroom teacher of our youngest students, supervisor Colleen O'Hara, research assistant Katharine Donnelly, and myself. Each day for over a year the four of us were in the classroom for (or watched a video tape of) the approximately 60-minute word identification lesson. We also planned lessons together and took turns teaching. We were fortunate to engage Linnea Ehri as our consultant and relished the days when she observed with us and shared her perceptions. Her input led to a significant improvement in our program.

Dr. Ehri convinced us that for these students to use the analogy strategy and eventually work independent of the word wall, we needed to help them advance to the full alphabetic phase in sight-word learning. To foster students moving out of the visual-cue phase and through the other phases, Dr. Ehri suggested that we should discontinue writing key words on cards that were cut in shapes that cued the identity of the word (e.g., *cat* written on a card cut in the shape of a cat's head or *boat* on a card cut in the shape of a boat). With key words displayed on cards that cued the identity of the word, students had little need to carefully analyze the letter–sound matches. We felt certain that once our struggling readers developed the habit of processing all the letters and their related sounds in printed words, they would be able to store the key words in memory as fully analyzed sight words and access them to read unfamiliar words sharing the same letters. Our goal was for students to function independent of the word wall by the end of the school year. We were beginning to understand that both automaticity of calling words to mind and fluency were determined by the quality of each word's representation in memory. Our challenge was to figure out which processes we could add to the program to help students get key words into memory in a fully analyzed way. We finally had a pretty good idea about what needed changing and what was missing in our program.

Overview of the Word-Learning Process

We set about designing processes to add to the BWI that would teach students how to analyze and talk about the key words they were learning (Gaskins, Ehri, Cress, O'Hara, & Donnelly, 1996–1997, 1997). These processes needed to provide students with teacher-mediated opportunities to stretch out and hear individual sounds in words and to talk about the sound–letter matches they observed. Ninety-three of the BWI key words were selected to be analyzed over the course of the school year. The order of introducing these words was determined by the frequency of the key word's spelling pattern in the English language. In general, our word-learning processes required that students accomplish the following:

1. Stretch out the pronunciation of the word to analyze its constituent sounds.
2. Talk about the matches between sounds and letters or letter patterns.
3. Discover similarities between sound–letter matches in words.
4. Practice reading and spelling words with the high-frequency spelling patterns represented in key words (see Figure 10.2).

FIGURE 10.2. Talk-to-Yourself Chart.

1. The word is _____.

2. Stretch the word.
   I hear _____ sounds.

3. I see _____ letters because _____.
   (Students reconcile the number of letters they see
   with the number of sounds they hear.)

4. The spelling pattern is _____.

5. This is what I know about the vowel
   _____.

6. Another word on the word wall with the same
   vowel sound is _____.

From Gaskins et al. (1996). Copyright 1996 by Benchmark Press. Reprinted by permission in *Success with Struggling Readers* by Irene Gaskins (2005). See copyright page for photocopying limitations.

Fully Analyzing Words

Stretching and Counting Sounds

Working out how to teach the four processes took some trial and error to discover what made the most sense to our students. For example, when we introduced the "fully analyzing procedure," we initially placed the card containing the new key word on the chalkboard, then asked students to stretch the word, saying and counting with their fingers the sounds that they heard. The first week, when we introduced *in*, *and*, and *up*, this procedure seemed to work. However, in the second week, when *king* (/k/ /i/ /ng) and *long* (/l/ /o/ /ng/) were introduced students tried to convince themselves that they heard four sounds in *king* and *long*. They wanted to believe that there were as many sounds as there were letters. We suspected that seeing the word as they analyzed the sounds had influenced the number of sounds students thought they heard.

The third week, when *day* and *will* were two of the words introduced, we tried a different procedure. We had students stretch the sounds *before* the word card was placed on the chalkboard. The teacher and students stretched /d/ and /a/, putting up a finger for each sound they heard. This was followed by the teacher asking: "Students, I want each of you to rest your elbow on the desk with your hand up and in a fist. When I say 'show' at the end of 'Ready, set, show,' I want you to hold up your fingers to show me the number of sounds you heard in *day*." The teacher said, "Ready, set, show." Immediately every child put up two fingers.

We had made an important discovery. Seeing a word prior to stretching and counting sounds influenced what children thought they heard. The following week our hunch was confirmed when *truck* was stretched and its sounds counted before students saw the word. All agreed they heard four sounds.

Led by a teacher, students fully analyze words "to get them stuck in their heads," with the sounds matched to letters or letter patterns.

Sound–Letter Matches

The next step of fully analyzing words is for students to match the sounds they hear to the letters they see in the key word. For example, after students counted the sounds in *day*, the teacher drew two sound boxes on the chalkboard and placed the word card with *day* next to the sound boxes. She said, "Mmmmm, we have three letters and only two sound boxes. How are we going to solve this puzzle?" Someone suggested, "Well, in *king*, it took two letters to stand for one sound. Maybe that is what is going on here." The teacher asked the class to say the first sound in *day*, then she asked what letter or letters they thought represented that sound and belonged in the first sound box. All eventually agreed that it was *d*. The class said the next sound in unison, /a/. The teacher asked, "What letter or letters do you think represents that sound?" After some discussion about there being only one box left, students agreed that it took both *a* and *y* to represent the /a/ sound in *day*.

Next, students were asked to identify the spelling pattern of the key word. The spelling pattern is the vowel or vowel pattern and the consonants that follow (e.g., *a-y* in *day*, *u-c-k* in *truck*, *e-a-t* in *treat*). Students also generated rhyming words for each key word. As children suggested words that had the same spelling pattern as a key word, the words were written under the key word. If a child suggested a rhyming word that is spelled differently from the key word, the word was written on the chalkboard away from the rhyming lists, so that the class could see that although the words rhyme, the letters that comprise the spelling patterns are different. For example, in supplying rhyming words for *slide*, one student suggested *lied*. The teacher praised her for contributing a rhyming word and placed *lied* on the chalkboard as an example of another way the sounds in *slide* could be represented. Once students generated rhyming words for all the key words, they read them as the teacher pointed to the words, moving across spelling patterns, because reading words with different spelling patterns (e.g., *ride*, *hit*, *got*) requires deeper processing than reading down a rhyming list of words (e.g., *side*, *ride*, *hide*). Students use the form, "If I know _____ [saying the key word], then I know _____ [saying the rhyming word]."

Finally, students were asked to tell what they noticed about the vowel, using as a guide the poster in the classroom that lists the letters that always represent vowel sounds, plus the two additional letters that sometime represent vowel sounds or are part of a vowel pattern (i.e., *y* and *w*). With regard to *in*, *and*, and *up*, students concluded that there was one vowel in each word, and that vowel is followed by a consonant. The following week they commented that the same is true of *king*, *long*, and *jump*. When *day* was introduced, students commented that it took two letters to represent the vowel sound.

Discover Similarities

Another component of fully analyzing words is discovering similarities. For example, during the second week of instruction, when *king* was introduced, the teacher asked "Is there another word on the word wall with the same vowel sound?" The students had only three words on the word wall to search (i.e., *in*, *and*, *up*). Nevertheless, with teacher guidance, students were successful in discovering that *king* has the same vowel sound as *in*. They also discovered that *jump* has the same vowel sound as *up*.

By midyear, students had been introduced to approximately 45 key words and were making amazing discoveries about sounds and letters. For example, they noticed that *a* is the only vowel in the word *car* and that it is followed by a consonant; and they noticed that *a* does not represent the same sound in *car* that it does in *cat, map,* and *can.* Several lessons later they made a similar discovery about the *e* in *her* and the *o* in *for.* Guided skillfully by teacher scaffolding, students discovered that when a vowel is followed by *r,* it usually does not represent the expected sound. The purpose of making these letter–sound discoveries is not to teach students the correct pronunciation of words, but rather to help them match letters and letter patterns to *the way they pronounce each word* (Johnston, 2001). Teachers therefore need to be mindful of regional differences in letter–sound matches (e.g., the word pairs *not / caught* and *scout / route* rhyme in some dialects, sounding to some children like *not/cot* and *scout/rout,* just as *pin* and *pen* may be pronounced the same). Because making discoveries about how our language works is at the heart of our program, we named the approach we use *Word Detectives.*

OVERVIEW OF WORD DETECTIVES

Practice Reading and Spelling

Sustained practice of the exact concepts being taught was missing in the programs that we had implemented previously. Struggling readers need multiple and varied opportunities to apply and practice what they are learning. Daily application of phonemic awareness and decoding concepts is a key to helping students develop mature habits of word reading and become fluent readers. In the Beginning Word Detectives Program (Gaskins et al., 1996) students (1) participate in teacher modeling of words on sentence strips; (2) repeatedly read predictable-rhyme and echo-reading books containing words with the spelling patterns they have learned; (3) write words with the high-frequency spelling patterns that have been introduced; and (4) as they read, keep a log of discoveries they make about how our language works. Each of these opportunities to practice what they are learning is discussed next.

Sentence Strips

On the first day of the lesson cycle the teacher models the process of decoding by analogy, using a sentence containing an unknown word that students can decode using what they know about the key words they have learned. The sentence is written on a sentence strip and attached to the chalkboard with magnets. The teacher thinks aloud so that students hear the thinking process she uses when she encounters an unknown word in text. For example, one teacher modeled the decoding of *slapdash* in the sentence "John sometimes completes his work in a *slapdash* manner." The teacher's instruction went something like this:

> "Boys and girls, please take out a piece of scrap paper and on it copy the underlined word you see on the sentence strip. I am going to need your help in decoding this college word. I'm thinking to myself: When I come to a word that I don't know, I look at all the letters in the word, then I ask myself: 'What is the first vowel in the

word?' What letter should I be thinking to myself? Can you all say it together? [Students respond.] Yes, it is *a*. Next I ask myself: 'What is the letter that comes after the vowel?' Can you help me with this and answer all together? [Students respond.] Yes, *p* comes after the vowel. Next, I think: 'What is the spelling pattern—the part of the word that contains the vowel and what comes after it in one chunk of a word?' Can you say it with me? [Students chant *a-p*.] Then I say to myself: 'What word do I know that has the same spelling pattern as this word?' Who can pull from your head, or help me find the word on the word wall, the word that has the *a-p* spelling pattern? [Students search the word wall and as they find the word, they write it on their scrap paper below the first chunk of *slapdash*.] Let's say it together. The word with the same spelling pattern is . . . [students chant *map*, and the teacher writes *map* beneath *slap*]. I next think: 'Are there any other vowels in the word?' Yes, there is another vowel. Put your hand up if you see it. [The teacher asks students to say the vowel together.] Now I'm thinking: 'What are the letters that come after the vowel?' I bet you noticed that the letters are *s-h*. What question should I be thinking next? [Students respond.] Yes, I would ask myself, 'What is the spelling pattern?' Who can tell me? [Student responds.] Yes, it is *a-s-h*. Now I am thinking: 'What word on the wall has the same spelling pattern?' Who can help me find that word? [Students search the word wall and as they find the word, they write it on their scrap paper beneath the second chunk of *slapdash*; meanwhile, the teacher writes *smash* on the chalkboard under *dash*.] Now I am thinking 'If I know *map*, then I know *slap*. If I know *smash*, then I know *dash*.' What is the college word? [Students respond in unison.] Yes, the word is *slapdash*. I'm going to read the sentence to see if *slapdash* makes sense in the sentence. 'John sometimes completes his work in a slapdash manner.' *Slapdash* means fast and not too carefully. Does *slapdash* make sense in the sentence?"

Students love the big words and usually cannot resist chiming in when the teacher is modeling. It would be rare for a teacher to get through the entire modeling process without a lot of help from her students. From a distance it may sound like chanting, but it is music to the teacher's ears.

Predictable Rhymes

Believing that students must immediately put into practice the word knowledge they gain each day, as well as do a great deal of reading to become fluent, we have written a predictable rhyme "little book" for each week. Each book features words with the same spelling patterns as the key words for the week. In addition, there are words with spelling patterns that were introduced in previous weeks and high-frequency words that students are reading in their beginning readers. Initially, the vocabulary of the stories is limited because the students have been introduced to only a few spelling patterns. However, as the year progresses and more spelling patterns are introduced, the stories contain many "college" words that struggling readers find more interesting and challenging than those usually found in beginning readers. For example, during the 4th month of the first year of the Word Detectives program, students read a story about a boy's room that concludes: "Just ask William—he'll tell you, his room is magnificent. It's a place where he doesn't need consent to make a mess of great proportionment" (see Figure 10.3). Students who were once deemed poor readers feel good about themselves when they can dazzle their parents and grandparents by reading words such as *magnificent* and *proportionment*—and our struggling readers can do just that! Developing fluency becomes less of a problem when students look for opportunities to show off their new-found ability to read hard words. And parents are impressed by, and proud of, this long-awaited ability to read!

The teacher introduces these predictable rhyme little books to the class just as he or she would introduce any good story. The title is read and predictions are made about the story. The pictures are examined and further predictions are made. Students set purposes for listening to the story, then the teacher reads it aloud, pausing occasionally to ask students if they can predict what the next word will be, based on the rhyme and rhythm of the previous words. For example, after reading "There's even a tent in William's room! The tent is round—but, it can't always be . . . ," the teacher might ask students what they expect the next word to be, based on what they have learned about William's messy room. Next, the teacher reads the story again as students complete a

FIGURE 10.3. An example of a predictable rhyme "little book"
that contains two "college" words.

"William's Room"
by Irene West Gaskins

William's room is full of toys.
They're everywhere—
In his bed, on the floor,
Even piled high in a chair.

There's even a tent in William's room!
The tent is round—
but, it can't always be found.
Yesterday his tent disappeared.
Susan found it—it was under:
father's black skate,
ten stuffed animals,
an old broken plate,
his sister's Monopoly game,
a heater grate,
and lots and lots of trucks and cars.

Just ask William—he'll tell you,
His room is magnificent.
It's a place where he doesn't need consent
To make a mess of great proportionment.

Key words: tent   round   skate   ten

From Gaskins et al. (1996). Copyright 1996 by Benchmark Press. Reprinted by permission in *Success with Struggling Readers* by Irene Gaskins (2005). See copyright page for photocopying limitations.

response sheet on which they write missing components for 10–15 select words in the story. For example, *skate*, *grate*, and *plate* are words in the story "William's Room." The spelling pattern -*ate* is written on the response sheet three times, and students fill in *sk*, *gr*, and *pl* as each of these words is read in the story.

Finally, students are given copies of the little book. As the teacher reads the predictable rhyme one more time, students point to each word and chime in with the teacher on words they recognize or remember. The little book is added to each student's "books-in-bag" (a plastic carryall) of Word Detective stories that are read at home each evening. A one-page typed copy of the text in the book is also placed in each student's word-identification folder at school and is read at school throughout the week.

Echo Reading

To provide students with additional practice reading words with the same spelling patterns as the key words for the week, a second set of books is provided. These books have less story and more of the lilt of a nursery rhyme and work very well for developing fluency by echo reading. The books often contain some dialogue, and students love taking parts and reading their roles with expression. We divide the class into two or three heterogeneous reading groups for echo reading, each led by an adult. Echo reading is an activity that students and adults enjoy, so it is not difficult to convince a library aide, parent, or supervisor to join us for 15 minutes of echo reading once or twice a week. The adult leaders introduce the book to a group in much the same way the predictable-rhyme books are introduced: by surveying the title and pictures, asking for predictions, and setting a purpose for listening to the story. The adult reads the book once to the students, modeling his or her thought processes as he or she reacts to the storyline and words. His or her self-talk, interspersed as the story *Ferdinand's Commands* is read, might sound something like this:

> "Dublin, hmmmm. I wonder if that is the city in Ireland or a city in the United States."
> "This boy is pretty demanding—I wonder why he is asking for such a lot of different things."
> "Stirrups—I'm having a hard time picturing exactly what they look like. Maybe I can ask someone to explain exactly what they look like."

After the adult leader finishes reading the book, students comment on the storyline and discuss words whose pronunciation or meaning are unfamiliar. Then the adult leader asks if the students noticed any familiar patterns in the story. Next, students are given copies of the book. They point to the words as the adult leader reads the first sentence, then the students echo the first line, pointing to each word as they read. The adult leader reads the second line, and students again echo that line as they point to each word. This procedure is continued for the entire book, with occasional pauses to talk about rhymes and patterns in words. Students like to point out words with familiar spelling patterns after having read a page.

The echo-reading book *Ferdinand's Commands* features the spelling patterns *in*, *and*, and *up*. The teacher reads, "A boy who's almost nine is who this tale's about." Students echo the line. The teacher then reads, "He lives in Dublin and he loves to shout." The students echo the line, followed by the teacher reading and students echoing: "Get me teacups, pickups, I want lots of cups. Get me stirrups, too—I think I'll saddle up." After echo reading the book, the students choral read the book, and then parts are often assigned for the third reading of the book. The echo-reading book is added to the plastic bag containing Word Detectives books.

We believe that students' partial word-recognition units are continually refined by interaction with print and that frequency of exposure to words reflecting certain featured patterns aids the recall of words. The reading aloud of stories in the little books, as students point to each word and join in, according to their individual abilities, accomplishes several purposes. First, this reading provides exposure to what it feels like to read fluently; it allows children to feel successful and to see that words and reading can be fun. Second, it demonstrates to students that reading is meaning driven and requires saying the words that are written on the page. Pointing to each word as they read helps students develop the concept of word and focuses their attention on the phonemic structure of words by virtue of rhyme, alliteration, and word play. Finally, the little books contain interesting words that offer opportunities to students to make discoveries about how our language works. It is our experience that students who read the little books aloud repeatedly, especially to parents or other adults who sit with the child to assure accuracy, make the most progress in phonemic awareness, decoding, and fluency. Stated differently: The number of words read correlates with progress in reading.

Spelling Chant and Check

Another practice activity is "spelling chant and check." With the words on the word wall in view, the teacher gives a "spelling test." Students write the words on a sheet that has the exact number of sound boxes that are needed for each word that will be spelled. The teacher encourages students "to get the word from your head," but, if they feel the need, they may look at the word wall for assistance. The teacher pronounces each word, then stretches it. Next, she stretches just the first sound, which is the students' cue to write in the first sound box the letter or letters to match that sound. She then stretches the first two sounds of the word, and students write in the second sound box the letter or letters that represent the second sound. She proceeds through the entire word in a similar manner. After the three or four words for the week are written, she asks students to read each one to make sure that they wrote the word they intended. Finally, the students and teacher chant the words that were just written: "in—i-n; next word, *and*—a-n-d; next word, *up*—u-p." The use of sound boxes really seems to help our students understand the concept of sound–letter matches.

Filling in sound boxes becomes a little more complicated when words contain sounds represented by two or more letters. For example, for *skate*, the student would write S, K, A, T in the four boxes; there would be no box for E because it does not represent a sound. We teach students to write a small E in the same box with the T to indicate that the E is part of the pattern A–consonant–e that tells the reader that A will say its own name, but that e cannot have a sound box because it does not represent a sound. When written in boxes, the word appears: S K A Te. The word *right* would have three boxes and be written: R Igh T. We have found that placing letters in boxes that represent the number of sounds in words helps our students remember how letters are matched to the sounds in words. Once students are taught to fully analyze words, they write their spelling words in sound boxes for the first two spelling "tests" of the week. Later in the week, they spell the words without the structure provided by sound boxes, but following the chant-and-check procedure described earlier.

Word Detectives

The job of word detectives is to look for clues that provide information about patterns in our language and to practice applying these patterns. Students are encouraged to look for consistencies in the way sounds and letters are matched and to analyze the surrounding letters in which these sound–letter matches are found for clues that might alert them to expect a specific sound. As a result of noticing the match between combinations of letters and sounds, students begin to share their theories about how our language works. For example, one theory that students advance early in the year is: "Consonant sounds are usually represented only one way, but vowel sounds often are represented by several letter combinations" (e.g., -ain, -ate, -ay). It is usually not too long after that theory is advanced that a student discovers that the words *she* and *he* both have two sounds, but *she* has three letters. The student word detective then proclaims, "Sometimes it takes two consonants to represent one sound." The next discovery may be that *cat* and *king* sound the same at the beginning, but the sound is represented by different letters. By the time students have encountered *city*, *can*, *cent*, *cut*, and even *cyclone* in the many little books that they read, they suggest such theories as: "Some consonants can have more than one sound," "*c* doesn't have a sound of its own—it takes the sound of *k* or *s*," or "I think the letter that comes after *c* has something to do with its sound."

Each day the word-identification block ends with the teacher asking students: "What did you discover today about how your language works?" Sometimes students share a discovery they made during the lesson or when reading their Word Detective book at home. At other times a teacher may cue specific students to share a discovery made during reading group or writing. During this sharing time, students describe their discoveries as theories or hypotheses and are encouraged to continue looking for words that support or oppose those theories/hypotheses. Teachers accept the language each student uses to describe his or her observations, rather than trying to formalize students' observations by making them into abstract rules. We have learned that students express their discoveries in ways that make sense to them and that someone else's way of stating a generalization often does not make sense to them. For example, our beginning readers have never heard of an "*r*-controlled vowel," yet they talk about observing that when there is a vowel followed by an *r*, the vowel does not have the sound they would expect. In fact, knowing that, by definition, every word must have a vowel sound, yet not hearing the vowel sound when *r* follows the vowel, we find students saying things like: "When there is an *r* after a vowel, the *r* talks so loud you can't hear the vowel"; or "*R* is such a loudmouth that the vowel can't be heard, even though it is trying to say something" or "When there is an *r* after a vowel, the vowel just makes a peep."

Some of our struggling readers who enter Benchmark in the visual-cue phase make very rudimentary discoveries. For example, we were surprised and pleased when one day Nathan had an "aha" experience. After several students shared discoveries about two letters representing one sound, he exclaimed, "My name has *t-h* and it makes one sound." The next day he could hardly wait to share and said: "In *Nathan, t-h* makes one sound, and in *smash, s-h* makes one sound." Nathan's discoveries for weeks to come were all about two consonants that represent one sound—and he never ceased being excited about each one.

By midyear, students are making amazing discoveries, and it is not uncommon for a student to make an observation about a word in a predictable rhyme that has gone completely unnoticed by the teacher. For example, when reading *Frog Ball*, one of the little books written to accompany the Word Detectives program, a student noticed the words *old* and *stroll*. He commented that he was surprised that the *o* in *old* did not have the sound that *o* usually has when the pattern is one vowel followed by a consonant (e.g., *not*). He said that when he noticed the vowel saying its name in *old*, he just assumed it was a word that did not fit a pattern. However, when he read *stroll*, he noticed that the *o* in that word also said its name, and that the *o* in both words is followed by an *l*. The theory he suggested was that maybe when there is the *o-l* pattern, the *o* will say its name. Over several days he continued this line of thought and suggested that *l* might hold power over other vowels, too, because the *a* in *ball* did not sound like the *a* in *cat* and *can*. At this point, another child entered the discussion to remind the class that a few weeks ago he had shared his discovery that the *i* in *child* is the only vowel in the word and is followed by a consonant, but it did not have the expected sound. Now he realized that *child* fit the same pattern as *stroll, old,* and *ball.*

Awarding certificates for attaining significant personal goals is one way to communicate progress to students and parents.

There is no doubt that these students were very alert Word Detectives, and each one made discoveries at his or her own phase of development. Students who discover, learn, and use patterns are able to "self-teach" for word identification (Strickland & Snow, 2002).

SUMMARY

Because difficulties in phonemic awareness, decoding, and fluency are common among struggling readers, the Benchmark staff has employed many methods in an attempt to teach its students an effective and systematic way of decoding. The methods that work best are those that combine elements of several approaches and allow students to use what they are learning about how their language works and what works for them. In any Benchmark classroom you might see a student decode a word using context and several salient letters in the word, whereas another student uses the spelling pattern in a known word to decode an unknown word. Still another student may slowly work his or her way through an unknown word, matching sounds to letters, then blending those sounds to decode the word. Another student may be able to pronounce an unknown word beginning with *c* because he or she remembers the generalization that *c* usually represents the /s/ sound when followed by *i*, *y*, or *e*.

All students should have this arsenal of strategies. Students who learn to read using the Word Detectives approach have systematically acquired a knowledge of how their language works and have many strategies at their disposal. Systematically guiding students through the stages of word learning is one of the secrets to achieving successful word learning for all students. Chapter 10 was devoted to explaining the development and approach of the Word Detectives program. Chapter 11 describes the many reinforcement activities.

Activities That Reinforce
Word Detective Practices

As we developed the Word Detectives program we came to realize that struggling readers need to have word-learning concepts reinforced over and over again, in many different forms and settings, before these concepts become their own. Activities that have become part of our systematic week-by-week emphasis on word learning include those described below. Some were part of BWI, many are new to Word Detectives. We do not use these activities in isolation but as reinforcement for the sound–letter concepts being taught via the key words. A systematic, coordinated program is crucial to word learning for struggling readers, who tend to need one concept presented many times in a variety of brief activities. A brisk pace, frequent use of an every-pupil response (EPR) approach, and frequent change of activity to reinforce a concept tend to keep students actively involved and interested.

BEGINNING WORD DETECTIVES ACTIVITIES

Structured Language-Experience Story

During the early weeks of the school year, students compose structured language-experience stories as a class, using the key words that are introduced each week and words with the same spelling patterns. The teacher uses the writing of the language-experience story to acquaint students with the structure of stories and to teach them how to plan their writing. We call these language-experience stories "structured" because teachers guide students by providing a framework and helping them plan and rehearse ideas to include in the class story. Teachers use basic story elements as their framework for writing. The terms students see posted on the chalkboard are *characters*, *setting*, *story problem*, and *resolution of the story problem*. Students, with teacher guidance, flesh out the details of these story elements before they begin composing their story. After the story is planned, quite often using the students in the class as characters, and after generation of words that rhyme with the key words that might be used in the

story, the students suggest sentences for the story and critique one another's suggestions. Once written, the story is typed and students are given copies to read throughout
the week.

Ready–Set–Show (Rhyming and Initial Consonants)

Playing word games is one way to emphasize awareness of sounds in rhyming words
and in words that begin with the same sound or sounds. One of the students' favorites
is Ready–Set–Show. During this game, the teacher discusses the concept of rhyme and
models how to play Ready–Set–Show. Students have a card on their desk with a smiling face on one side and a frowning face on the other side. The teacher says a pair of
words; if the words rhyme, students hold up the smiling face after the teacher says,
"Ready, set, show." The game is played similarly for recognizing words that sound the
same or different at the beginning. The value of this game is enhanced by giving students ample time to reflect before saying, "Ready, set, show," and by modeling what
should be going on in the students' heads as they compare the sounds of the two words
they have heard.

Tongue Twisters

To help students develop an awareness of the relationship between initial consonant
sounds and the letters that represent them and to help them develop the concept of
word, we have students echo read while pointing to the words in a sentence in which
most words begin with the same letter. For example, early in the school year students
echo read, "Susie's sister sipped seven sodas sewing seams." In this application of echo
reading, the teacher first reads the sentence as students point to each word, then the
students read the sentence with the teacher, pointing to each word as they read. Reading three or four tongue twisters is usually followed by playing Ready–Set–Show, fea-
turing the same consonant sounds as in the tongue twisters.

Talk-to-Yourself Charts

Each day, using several different charts, students assess their word knowledge by talking to themselves or a partner about the sound–letter matches in words. On some days,
they assess their knowledge of the words learned that week; on other days, they assess
to see how much they remember about a word on the wall. Students are instructed to
select a word that they have a hard time calling to mind when they need it for decoding
or spelling. Just as they did in the original full analysis of the word, they stretch the
word, count the sounds they hear, match the sounds they hear to the letters they see,
talk to themselves about the vowel and spelling pattern, and find a word on the wall
that is like the word they are analyzing with regard to sound–letter matches. Finally,
without looking at the word, they stretch the sounds in the word and write the letters
that represent each sound that they hear. Thus a child might say:

> "My word is *vine*. Stretch the word—/v/ /i/ /n/. I hear three sounds. I see four let-
> ters because the *e* does not make a sound. The spelling pattern is *i-n-e*. This is what
> I know about the vowel. The vowels are *i* and *e*. The *e* does not make a sound. It is

there to signal that the vowel will say its name. Another word on the word wall like *vine* is *name*. They are alike because they both have the pattern vowel–consonant–final *e*, and the first vowel in both words says its name."

Following this talk-to-yourself routine, the student stretches out the sounds and writes the word.

Three times a week, after students have fully analyzed a word, they are given the opportunity to share what they know about that word with a partner. On each occasion they write the word they will share on a card. They show the card to their partner as they tell their partner about the word. On one day they share the information listed on the Talk-to-Yourself Chart. Another day they follow the partner-sharing chart in Figure 11.1. After one partner shares, the other has a turn sharing his or her word. A partner-sharing exchange might sound like this:

"My word is *pig*. My word wall word is *it*. The words are alike because they both have one vowel, *i*, followed by a consonant, and both *i*'s say /i/. Do you agree?"

The partner would agree with that information, then share about the word on his or her card.

The students' favorite partner-sharing activity is making a word. The chart for this activity is shown in Figure 11.2. A partner-sharing exchange might sound like this:

"My word is *treat*. My new word is *trot*. I made this word because I know that in *treat*, it takes two letters *e* and *a*, to make the vowel sound, so I took out the two letters and put in an *o*. I know that when an *o* is followed by a consonant, it will probably have the same sound as in *not*. The new word also has the same spelling pattern as the key word *not*. Do you agree?"

FIGURE 11.1. Partner-sharing chart.

Comparing Words

Person #1:

1. My word is _____.

2. My word wall word is _____.

3. The words are alike because _____.

4. Do you agree?

Person #2:

Give one of these answers:

Yes/No, because _____.

Switch roles.

From Gaskins et al. (1996). Copyright 1996 by Benchmark Press. Reprinted by permission in *Success with Struggling Readers* by Irene Gaskins (2005). See copyright page for photocopying limitations.

FIGURE 11.2. Partner-sharing chart.

Making Words

Person #1:

1. My word is _____.

2. My new word is _____.

3. I made this word because I know

_____.

4. Do you agree?

Person #2:

Give one of these answers:

Yes/No, because _____.

Switch roles.

*If you finish early, pick other word-wall words and
make them into new words.*

From Gaskins et al. (1996). Copyright 1996 by Benchmark Press. Reprinted by permission in *Success with Struggling Readers* by Irene Gaskins (2005). See copyright page for photocopying limitations.

Homework: Books-in-Bags and Language Logs

Language logs play a crucial role in fostering the discovery of generalizations about how letters and sounds are matched. During nightly reading, students are instructed to pay attention to interesting patterns in words and dictate discoveries about these patterns to their parents, who write them in the language log. The next day in school a few students share their favorite discoveries. By discussing the letter–sound relationships students notice in words, they begin to solidify their understanding of letter–sound consistencies in our language. Parents are an important key to this process, as children are usually anxious to share their discoveries with their parents after they complete reading a few of their books-in-bags. For example, after reading in the little book *William's Room* that William's toys were "In his bed, on the floor, even piled high in a chair," one child dictated: "The *i* in *high* works the same way the *i* does in *right*, and in both words the *i* is followed by *g-h*." Another child shared with her mother, "In the word *his*, the *s* sounds like a *z*." These beginning readers like being word detectives and sharing their discoveries with the class the next day. The language log is a tool to help these discussions take place. As parents record their child's important discoveries about words in the language log, the child builds his or her word knowledge. This process also facilitates parent–child discussions about discoveries. In addition, the language log allows parents and child to review earlier discoveries and to note the child's development in word knowledge over time.

Language logs are used to make several types of word discoveries. Using the predictable-rhyme and echo-reading books, as well as print in the child's environment, each school night parents jot down the information their children discover about how our language works. It seems to be most meaningful and useful for the child to provide specific words with each discovery. For example, rather than stating that *c* has two sounds, /k/ and /s/, an entry in the language log would give an example for each of these instances. "In the word *cat*, *c* sounds like /k/. In the word *city*, *c* sounds like /s/." Another way that children and parents use language logs is to describe how a child has decoded a particular word: "If I know *and*, then I know *stand*." Some children list rhyming pairs of words they have discovered. An additional benefit of analyzing the words in the predictable-rhyme and echo-reading books is that, for those students who take their role as word detectives seriously, these stories are not just rotely memorized. Students have really looked at each word and are able to recognize most of the words in or out of the little books—this is especially true of the words the students consider "college words."

During the Word Detectives lessons, students are encouraged to gather data about the letters necessary to represent the sounds they hear in words. Rather than repeat rules or generalizations they may have memorized but not understood, we ask students to put their discoveries and theories in their own words and give specific examples of what they noticed about particular sound–letter matches. An example of noting a sound–letter match, rather than a generalization, would be: "In the word *black*, I noticed that I don't hear the *c*. It takes the *ck* to represent the /k/ sound." This information is written in the log.

The log is handed in to the teacher on the first day of each 5-day cycle. This is a time to check to see that language discussions are taking place at home and that no misconceptions are embedded in these discussions. The teacher reads through the logs quickly, noting how much parents and children are discussing words and the kinds of discoveries children are making. Inaccuracies in several logs might prompt the teacher

Encouraging students to record and share the consistent sound–letter relationships they discover fosters growth in phonemic awareness and knowledge of how our language works.

to initiate a discussion with the whole class. If only one child seems confused, the teacher clears up the misconception during a private discussion. It seems to take the teacher about 1 or 2 minutes per log to read the information from the previous week and write an encouraging note, such as "I was amazed you discovered that. . . . " Some teachers read half the logs one week and the other half the following week.

Five to eight weeks after language logs have been introduced, children usually move from noticing just sound–letter matches to noticing patterns of language. These are recorded in the logs. This transition to patterns happens naturally as the children's knowledge of sound–letter relationships increases. Even so, they should continue to give examples of these patterns. An example might be: "When I see the pattern vowel–consonant–*e* in a word, the first vowel usually says its name and the *e* is quiet. This is true for words like *make, name,* and *vine.*" Although making discoveries to record in language logs may develop slowly, language logs often become a vehicle for wonderful conversations between teachers and students and between parents and children.

Each day the teacher reminds students to spend about 10 minutes in the evening being Word Detectives with a parent:

> "As you read the predictable-rhyme and echo-reading books with your parents, be good detectives and notice how our language works in the words you are reading. Share your discoveries with a parent. Your parent will write your discoveries in your language log."

Partner Read

As a special treat, on the 5th day of the Word Detectives cycle, students spend about 15 minutes reading with a partner from their notebooks of 1-page copies of their predictable-rhyme and echo-reading books and their language-experience stories. The text from the books is arranged in four-line verses. One student reads and points to a verse while the partner follows and points in his or her copy of the text. Then, for the next verse, roles are reversed. Students are asked not to supply a word for a partner; rather, if a word is miscalled or unknown, the partner is to give clues just as a teacher would. For example, if in *Ferdinand's Commands* a student were stuck on *martins* (the bird species), the partner might ask how many chunks he or she thought the word had. Once the word is divided into two parts, the student coaches his or her partner to identify the first spelling pattern and think of a key word; then they move on to the second spelling pattern.

What's in My Head?

Almost daily the teacher conducts a game of What's in My Head? The purpose of this game is to provide students with additional practice analyzing words. The teacher thinks of one of the words on the word wall and gives students five clues about the word. Students number 1–5 on a piece of paper and write a word for each clue the teacher gives. For example, the first clue might be, "My word has five letters." Students scan the word wall and write any word that has five letters; thus any word with five letter would be correct (i.e., *truck, black, round, skate, right, slide, smash, brave*). "Number two: My word has four sounds." (Students must write a word that fits both the first and second clues.) Again, there is more than one correct response (i.e., all of the previous responses except *right* have four sounds). "Number three: My word contains two letters to represent one consonant sound." There is still more than one correct answer (i.e., *truck, black, smash*). "Number four: My word has only one vowel, and the vowel has the same sound that I hear in *cat*." This time there are two correct responses possible (i.e., *black, smash*). "Number five: If we 'blank' the cardboard box, it will fit in the trash can." A student may be lucky and guess the correct word on the first clue. More than likely, more clues will be needed. No one can be absolutely sure what the word is until the final clue. The teacher calls on students to read the five words they wrote, and as students read their words, the teacher makes a mental note of anyone who has written words that do not fit the clues. Later the teacher will find a time to review the clues with these students. Students love this activity because it provides them with an opportunity to review concepts about how their language works.

Word Sort

To complete a word sort, students are given a worksheet with a word bank of words that have the same spelling patterns as the three or four key words for the week. These words appear in random order, and students are asked to write each word from the word bank on the lines below the key word with the same spelling pattern. For example, during the week that *it*, *not*, and *slide* are introduced, the word bank contain these words: *dot, bit, hide, fit, got, ride*. If a student were writing *dot* from the word bank, he or she looks for the key word with the same vowel–consonant pattern as *dot* and writes *dot* beneath that key word—in this case, *not*. Once all the word-bank words are written under the key words, students read the word bank words to the teacher, or to one another, in random order, saying "If I know _____ [reading the key word], then I know _____ [reading the word-bank word]."

Individual Student Checkout

Students complete a decoding worksheet that contains 10 sentences, each with an underlined word that has the same spelling pattern as one of the key words for the week. Students circle the spelling pattern in the underlined word, then, on the line below the underlined word, they write the key word that has the same spelling pattern. Once students have written a key word for each underlined word, they practice using the analogy approach to decode the underlined word. After they practice decoding each word, the teacher "checks out" each student. The student says, "If I know _____ [saying the key word], then I know _____ [saying the underlined word]." Then the teacher reads the sentence, hesitating at the underlined word. When the teacher hesitates, the student identifies the word. Once a student has been checked out, the teacher will often let that student check out other students.

Looking through Words

Another one of our students' favorite activities is Looking through Words. To impress upon students the necessity of looking at every single letter in a word, rather than looking at the initial consonant and guessing, as so many of our students prefer to do and is

FIGURE 11.3. Looking through words.

and	not	her
an	noc	her mom
at	noc go	her mom he
ath	noc o	her mom e
bath	noc o skate	her mom e her
bath tent	noc o kate	her mom e ter
bath ten	noc o late	ther mom e ter
bath tub	choc o late	thermometer
bathtub		

From Gaskins et al. (1996). Copyright 1996 by Benchmark Press. Reprinted by permission in *Success with Struggling Readers* by Irene Gaskins (2005). See copyright page for photocopying limitations.

typical of students in the partial alphabetic phase, we designed Looking through Words (see Figure 11.3). This is an activity in which students read down a list of words and pseudowords in which each word in the list is different from the one before it by just one letter. The word at the head of the list is a key word. This activity is introduced when students learn the first set of key words *in*, *and*, and *up*. The first list on the Looking through Words page is composed of *in*, *ip*, and *dip*. Students place an index card under the first word in the first list. The teacher calls on a student to read the first word. Cards are moved down and placed under the second word or pseudoword. A student is asked to first tell how the second word is different from the first, then to pronounce the new word or pseudoword. The reply would be, "The *n* was taken off and a *p* was put in its place. The new word is *ip*." Cards are moved down again, and another child is asked to tell what is different this time. The child would say, "*D* has been added to the front of the word. The new word is *dip*." After several simple lists such as *in-ip-dip*, students read: *and*, *an*, *am*, *amp*, *ramp*, *tramp*. In several weeks students are reading word lists that end with words such as *thermometer*. By that time they are beginning to believe that, given enough time, they can figure out any "college word."

Word Hunt

The day after the predictable rhyme is introduced, students go on a word hunt in the predictable rhyme looking for words they can decode because they either know a key word with the same spelling pattern or they have discovered something about how their language works that will help them figure out the word. Students are given a one-page copy of the text of the predictable-rhyme book that features the key words for the week. They circle the spelling patterns in the words they can decode because the words have the same spelling pattern as key words. After about 5 minutes, the teacher calls a stop to the word hunt and, moving through the story verse by verse, gives students the opportunity to share the words they can read. Students respond in this form: "I can read _____ because I know _____." Thus, after looking through *William's Room*, a student said, "I can read *grate* because I know *skate*." Another student said, "I can read *heater* because I know *treat* and *her*."

MAINTENANCE

Follow-up studies of students who received intensive remedial interventions suggest that they often do not maintain the gains they made while in the program (Center, Wheldall, Freeman, Outhred, & McNaught, 1995; Hiebert, 1994; Shanahan & Barr, 1995). This finding suggests that struggling readers may need longer periods of intensive instruction and practice than is currently the norm, if they are to develop the skills and strategies they are learning to the level of automaticity (Strickland, Ganske, & Monroe, 2002). For this reason, Benchmark provides Word Detectives maintenance programs for our struggling readers through grade 6. During the first period of each day, students in grades 2–6 are regrouped for 30 minutes of word study based on their decoding and spelling strengths and needs.

The first maintenance level is the Word Detectives Transition Program (O'Hara & Gaskins, 1999). Students make discoveries about not-yet-introduced aspects of our language (e.g., patterns for chunking words; vowel sounds in unstressed chunks; common chunks in special-feature words such as *picture, special,* and *mission*; and flexibility in applying sound–letter knowledge). For each 5-day cycle of lessons in the transition program, a nonfiction text is written to provide practice in applying the word-learning concepts emphasized that week. This text is read repeatedly because developing fluency is still a focus at the transition level. The text also provides background information for science and social studies concepts usually taught in third or fourth grade. The transition program has two forms and may be taught for two consecutive years, depending on the needs of each student.

The next maintenance level is Intermediate Word Detectives (Gaskins, 2000, 2002), also consisting of two forms that can be taught for 2 years. The goal of the intermediate program is for students to develop automaticity and flexibility in the application of the four ways of reading words, as well as to apply their knowledge of how our language works to spelling words that are appropriate for each student's phase of development. The intermediate program provides for review and extension of the concepts taught at the beginning and transition levels. By the time students reach the intermediate levels, they generally are more proficient in applying their language knowledge to decoding than to spelling. Therefore, in contrast to the earlier levels, in which the primary emphasis is decoding and students spell only five words a day that contain the featured spelling patterns, more emphasis is placed on spelling than on decoding. Spelling words are drawn from the 3,000 most frequent words in our language (Fry, Fountoukidis, & Polk, 1985). The text for both forms of the intermediate level is nonfiction, as it is for the transition program, although the amount of text read each week during intermediate decoding and spelling lessons is considerably greater. For each cycle of lessons, students complete a pretest consisting of 15–25 high-frequency words featured in the nonfiction text; then each student fully analyzes and makes discoveries about five of the words he or she misspelled on the pretest. Students also participate in daily activities and teacher modeling that draw attention to characteristics of our language represented in the spelling words. A posttest is given at the end of the cycle. Moving back and forth between reading and spelling helps our students see how their alphabetic and word-structure knowledge is connected.

SUMMARY

The Word Detectives program for learning to read and spell that is currently taught at Benchmark School is implemented as one block of a grades 1–6 literacy program that also includes blocks for daily process writing, guided reading and strategy lessons, independent reading with written response, and teacher read-aloud. Over the years, our approach to teaching word-learning processes to struggling readers has changed considerably, as we observed what seemed to work and what seemed to be missing. This same process of reflection and change continues today. Word Detectives is a dynamic program, continually evolving and improving.

Although we are convinced that many beginning readers learn to read *despite* a teacher's approach to word learning, we are equally convinced that at-risk and struggling readers need a program that provides flexibility in teaching students how our language works and how to apply that knowledge in a way that is appropriate for their phase of development. Struggling readers need to be taught by teachers who know a lot about how our language works; teachers who can fill in the knowledge gaps that students do not figure out on their own (Strickland & Snow, 2002). The conclusion from the First Grade Reading Studies that the teacher makes the difference, not the materials, is as true today as it was when the studies were published (Bond & Dykstra, 1967).

In the early years of Benchmark School we purchased materials and programs and hoped that by following them, we would be able to teach struggling readers to segment words into sounds, unlock the pronunciation of words, and read fluently. At that time we did not have sufficient knowledge about how children learn words to be able to fill in the gaps in the programs we were using. Fortunately, in the more recent past, researchers have provided information about how children read words. Now teachers who are aware of that information can develop systematic programs based on knowledge about how our language works, how children learn words, and how children move through phases of word learning.

Teachers need ample opportunities to study the form and structure of language. Without this foundation they are handicapped as they try to teach children phonemic awareness, decoding, and fluency (Stickland & Snow, 2002). To help Benchmark teachers gain in-depth knowledge about word learning and how our language works, we have written manuals that address these professional development topics (Gaskins, 1996). These manuals outline a sequence of word learning based on the frequency of phonograms in children's reading material. Also outlined is a systematic approach to strengthening phonemic awareness, decoding, and fluency that meets the criteria suggested by the National Reading Panel (2000) and matches how children develop the ability to read words. Sample lessons taught by Benchmark teachers are provided. In preparation for tailoring their own daily lesson plans to the struggling readers they teach, teachers are encouraged to study the manual for background information about the language concepts in each lesson. The focus of instruction is on understanding the alphabetic principle and how it works rather than on mastering a specific set of letter–sound correspondences within a particular methodological frame (Pearson, 1999).

As a result of the knowledge gained from reviews of literature and our research and development projects, as well as Benchmark's 35 years of teaching struggling readers, we have developed 11 principles of instruction (see Figure 11.4). Following each principle is a brief summary of how the principle applies to teaching phonemic awareness, decoding, and fluency.

Materials do not teach, *teachers* teach. It is time to discontinue the search for commercial programs that produce successful readers. Instead we need to search for a deep understanding of how our language works and for research-based principles to guide our teaching of what we know. The key to improved phonemic awareness, decoding, and fluency among our struggling readers is *professional development*, not materials.

FIGURE 11.4. Principles of learning applied to teaching decoding.

Principle	Action
1. Struggling readers learn what you teach and often do not figure out what is not taught.	Teach students explicitly how to examine and learn words by segmenting words into their component sounds and matching letters to sounds. Encourage students to notice patterns among words so they can learn this self-teaching process.
2. Children learn at different rates and exhibit different strengths and needs.	Begin where students are functioning developmentally and provide opportunities and scaffolding that will lead them from one phase of development in word learning to the next. Schedule the school day so that more than the usual amount of time is dedicated to an intense word-learning program. This intensity is necessary because struggling readers are playing catch-up, and word learning is often their greatest deficit.
3. There is more than one way to learn.	Teach students to be flexible in their approach to word learning by showing them how to recognize that different words and contexts lend themselves to different ways of reading a word. Encourage students to learn words as sight words as well as by contextual guessing, matching sounds to letters, and analogizing.
4. Organized knowledge is easier to recall and use than random information, such as lists of words, rules or facts.	Teachers should guide students to see the systematic nature of our language and to share their discoveries about how our language works. Our English spelling system is much more systematic than is usually acknowledged. This system is especially evident when spelling patterns that are larger than the correspondences between sounds and letters are considered. Teach children to look for patterns among words, including phonograms (i.e., spelling patterns), affixes, syllables, and roots. Also teach students to be flexible in the application of known word parts, so that they are willing to try several possibilities and to accept approximations that come close enough to reveal the word (e.g., using *rain* to decode the last chunk of *captain*).
5. It is easier to understand and remember information if you attach what you are learning to what you know.	Guide students to fully analyze words that they need to learn and to compare an analyzed word to other words they already know to notice and remember similarities in letters and sounds. Teach decoding of unknown words by thinking of known words that have the same parts.
6. Knowledge is socially constructed.	Provide instruction that is interactive (i.e., features teacher–student and student–student discourse), rather than instruction characterized by "teacher talk" or students working independently. Encourage students to share what they discover about how our language works. Foster a collaborative community in which students are encouraged to value and capitalize on one another's strengths and knowledge and provide mutual support. In such a community, students read with partners and are taught how to cue one another regarding strategies to use or concepts to apply when words are unknown.
7. Active involvement facilitates learning.	Design EPR activities that keep all students involved in the learning experience, rather than expect them to be passive recipients of knowledge. EPR activities include Ready–Set–Show, What's in My Head?, self-assessments, partner-sharing charts, and choral and echo reading.

From *Success with Struggling Readers* by Irene Gaskins. Copyright 2005 by The Guilford Press. See copyright page for photocopying limitations.

FIGURE 11.4 *(continued)*

Principle	Action
8. Information that is deeply and thoughtfully processed is more likely to be understood and applied than information that is dutifully accepted at face value and/or memorized.	Teach students to (a) talk to themselves, develop theories, and collect supporting data about the relationship between sounds and letters; (b) notice familiar spelling patterns in words, then use words they know with the same spelling patterns to decode unknown words; and (c) self-check for sense. Word detectives tend to have a useable knowledge of how our language works because they discuss discoveries in their own language and are discouraged from quoting phonics "rules" they have learned from someone else.
9. Strategies, skills, and concepts that are not immediately and repeatedly applied are easily forgotten.	Provide teacher coaching and immediate opportunities to help students apply the strategies, skills, and concepts they are learning to the everyday reading they encounter across the curriculum. In addition, ensure that students repeatedly read many stories each week that contain both the spelling patterns and concepts currently being discussed as well as the patterns and concepts learned earlier. Teacher coaching while students are reading and writing throughout the day enhances the chances of powerful results.
10. Accountability and immediate one-to-one feedback support the learning process.	Devise a system of accountability that assures that students are checked individually each day and each is given feedback about his or her ability to apply what is taught. For example, have students check out with a teacher or student after completing the rhyming word sort and sentence-decoding worksheets and encourage them to "show off" during story reading and the looking through words exercise.
11. Collaboration, choice, and competence are keys to motivation.	Design activities that are motivating because they allow students to (a) learn at different rates, (b) employ different approaches, (c) chose the level of collaborative support they need, and (d) meet with success. Teach in such a way that students feel successful because the responses they give at their phase of development are accepted and supported. For example, competence is scaffolded as teachers and students repeatedly echo read and choral read the stories for the week. Students point to each word and chime in when they can. Some students learn to decode or read on sight most of the words in the stories, whereas others learn to decode a few words and rely on their memory of the story for the rest. As a result, all feel like good readers by the end of each week.

CHAPTER 12

Comprehension Strategies

Is the job of a teacher of struggling readers finished when students can read words? Definitely not. Forty-five years of teaching struggling readers have convinced me that there is more to a reading problem than poor reading. I believed this in the early years of Benchmark School (Gaskins, 1984), and 14 years later I was still singing a variation of the same tune when I wrote "There's More to Teaching At-Risk and Delayed Readers Than Good Reading Instruction" (Gaskins, 1998). Today I am even more convinced that to treat only the delay in learning words is to under threat, perhaps mistreat, the problem. Who would know better than I? I was once one of those reading teachers under treating students with reading problems. As was true of most reading teachers in the 1960s, I taught struggling readers how to read words and fill in blanks on workbook pages and worksheets. These were the skill areas in which my students scored poorly, so that was what got remediated. Although, over time, most of my students earned higher scores on reading tests that measured what I taught them, these same students often did not do well in regular classrooms. I had not given them the tools they needed to construct meaning from all kinds of texts, particularly content-area texts. And, even when they could read and understand the textbooks, they still had great difficulty expressing in writing what they understood from their reading.

The prognosis was no different when I started Benchmark School. Just teaching students to read words did not prepare them to be successful in regular classrooms. Because the majority of our students seemed to comprehend well the literature that was read aloud, we assumed that the key to classroom success was improved written expression. In the mid-1970s, in an attempt to remedy our students' problems with written expression, we began to search professional journals for new ideas about how to teach writing. We came across the work of Donald Graves and enlisted him as our consultant. Our writing program improved immensely under Graves's guidance (Gaskins, 1982). Implementing a process approach to instruction in writing resulted in students who actually enjoyed writing and who wrote wonderful stories about their personal experiences and interests. But there was still something missing. Written work in response to what students read in basal readers, novels, and content-area texts did not improve nearly as much as personal-experience writing.

EVOLUTION OF COMPREHENSION STRATEGIES INSTRUCTION

About the same time that I was pondering why written responses to text were not improving, I read a study by Dolores Durkin (1978–1979) and I realized what was missing. Durkin reported on a large classroom observation study in which she found that it was rare for teachers to explain to students how to accomplish the comprehension tasks they assigned. As each Benchmark teacher read the Durkin study and discussed it during our research seminar, there was an "aha." That was what was missing in our instruction—explicit explanations of exactly how to do the tasks we assigned. One of the tasks we assigned throughout the day was constructing meaning from text and writing responses about this sense making. Durkin's message was clear: We needed to explicitly teach students how to comprehend texts and how to write responses about what they had read.

Explicit Explanations

It appears that many students in classrooms throughout the country figure out on their own tasks such as how to break the code, find the main idea, make inferences, write a report using three sources, and learn from content-area textbooks. However, it was becoming increasingly clear to us that most of the students who attended Benchmark School were not among those students. Explicit explanations of how to complete school tasks became our main emphasis. Fortunately for us, the Center for the Study of Reading at the University of Illinois was conducting research about this very topic, particularly as it related to reading comprehension. We read everything we could obtain about teaching students how to learn and think based on what they read in texts. In addition, a guest expert was invited to Benchmark once a month to provide inservice training to the staff on the topic of constructing meaning from text. Dolores Durkin kicked off our thrust toward explicit explanations when she visited in October of 1980 to present an inservice program and to answer questions. She also met with some of us at the annual conference of the International Reading Association during the spring of 1981. We had spent the 6 months since Durkin's initial visit piloting our approach to providing explicit explanations and were anxious to share our successes and hear her ideas about how we could do an even better job. The follow-up session with Durkin was immensely helpful!

In October of 1981 Robert Tierney of the Center for the Study of Reading visited Benchmark to share some of the latest findings from the center's research on the provision of explanations to students about how to be actively involved in, and take charge of, their own reading and learning. Tierney's input allowed us to fine-tune what we were trying to accomplish. And so we continued to invite the best and the brightest who were thinking about explicit explanations, and with each bit of input we continued to refine our approach to explaining how to comprehend and learn from text. Marjorie Lipson visited during the 1982–1983 school year to share what she had learned from her dissertation research about informed instruction; David Pearson visited just a month later to talk about scaffolded instruction and gradual release of responsibility. Our heads were swimming with their helpful ideas.

Gerald Duffy was the first to visit who actually taught demonstration lessons so that we could see what an expert thought explicit explanation of strategies actually looked like. That was in February of 1984. Donna Ogle, Annemarie Palincsar, and Beth Davey all visited during the fall of 1984 to talk about strategies for constructing meaning from text. With each bit of input and critique of our lessons by these experts, our strategies-across-the-curriculum program was improving. By the time Richard Anderson visited for the first time in March 1985, we were able to show him the nucleus of what was growing into an exciting approach to helping our struggling readers succeed in all areas of the curriculum. We were doing a lot more than teaching students to read well; we were teaching them to be metacognitive. We were learning how to put students in charge of their own learning, thinking, and problem solving by discussing with them strategies for taking control of person, situation, task, and text variables and explaining how strategies helped their brains do a better job for them.

Other experts continued to present inservice programs at Benchmark during the next few years, and a strategies-across-the-curriculum program began to take hold throughout the school. No longer were just a few of us piloting explicit explanations of comprehension strategies and discussing how the brain works. Now the entire staff was excited about the impact strategy instruction was having on our student body. Others who advised us on our strategies program prior to 1988 included Taffy Raphael (who also taught demonstration lessons), Jane Hansen, Peter Johnston, Isabel Beck, Karen Wixson, Lee Indrisano, Chuck Perfetti, Scott Paris, and Donna Alvermann.

A Grant Proposal

Standing on the shoulders of these giants who had helped us understand how to teach struggling readers to construct meaning from text, Jan Frisch (Benchmark's development director in 1987) and I spent a hectic several weeks in October of 1987 writing a proposal to the James S. McDonnell Foundation for a grant in their Cognitive Studies for Educational Practice program. Richard Anderson agreed to be the research design consultant for our proposed research and development project. Approximately ten grants were to be awarded, and we had heard that most of the prominent cognitive psychologists in the United States and Canada were applying. (It turned out there were over 100 proposals submitted.) Most people would agree, including us, that our application was a long shot.

However, just a few weeks after mailing the grant proposal, Jan was notified that we had made the "short list" and that I was invited to come to Carnegie Mellon University in mid-November to present our proposal to a panel of cognitive scientists. The other finalists included some of the country's best known and widely published cognitive scientists (e.g., John Bransford, Ann Brown, and Robert Sternberg). Of the 18 finalists I was the last to present. I arrived only minutes before the appointed time, so I did not even have time to become nervous. After being coached for 8 years about explicit explanation of comprehension strategies by the top people in the field of reading, and having spent those years with my staff developing a program of explicit explanation of metacognitive and cognitive strategies, I could have talked for hours about our program—but the panel gave me less than an hour and most of that was spent answering their questions about classroom applications of cognitive and metacognitive strategies. By the time I boarded a plane and flew back to Philadelphia, Jill Larkin, director of the James S. McDonnell Foundation Cognitive Studies for Educational Practice, had already called Benchmark to give my secretary the news that Benchmark had been awarded a 3-year grant of $342,730. What a thrill! The press release from the James S. McDonnell Foundation read:

> Dr. Irene Gaskins, head of the school, and her faculty will develop a curriculum to be used in all subject areas to teach metacognitive skills, i.e., what children have to know and do to be able to learn. Benchmark will be assisted in this project by R. Anderson (University of Illinois). Several other grantees in the JSMF program will serve as consultants. Benchmark may serve as a research and evaluation site for a number of projects in the program "Cognitive Studies for Educational Practice."

Help from Experts

Our first reaction was excitement, then reality set in. I needed someone as a consultant to Benchmark who knew strategy research inside out and backward—someone who would visit often and help us formalize and codify the strategies program we had been developing since we had first read the Durkin (1978–1979) study. Michael Pressley came to mind. I had read everything I could find that he had written and felt that he had a broad knowledge of psychology and the workings of the mind, but I had never met him. I approached Pressley at the annual meeting of the National Reading Conference in December 1987. He did not say yes or no to my plea for help. He merely handed me two manuscripts he had just completed and informed me that everything he knew about strategy instruction was in those two papers. I raced to my room and read both from cover to cover. After reading the manuscripts I was certain that Pressley was the one to help us codify our instructional program. Pressley and I chatted the next day at NRC, and he agreed to visit Benchmark in October of 1988. In the meantime he recommended that Benchmark rely on two people whose work he greatly admired, Gerald Duffy and Laura Roehler, to help us kick off the McDonnell project.

Duffy and Roehler visited for several days in February 1988, working with me late into the night to coach me on explicit explanations and modeling of the tasks I wanted students in my middle school social studies class to be able to do. The next day we co-taught the strategy lessons we had planned as part of a social studies lesson. It was on that day that I finally felt sure I knew how explicit explanations could be successfully integrated into more than just reading lessons. And I was convinced that that was what had to be done if struggling readers were to return to regular classrooms and be successful. Students had to be explicitly taught how to use strategies to solve reading and learning problems as they arose in specific texts in specific content domains.

This chapter and the next summarize insights the Benchmark staff has gained about teaching students how to take charge of the tasks, especially comprehension tasks, that are expected of learners, thinkers, and problem solvers in the world of school as well as in real life. I begin by discussing the staff's preparation and rationale for teaching specific strategies across the curriculum, personal examples that illustrate strategy use, and guidelines for explaining strategies. In Chapter 13 I describe our current strategy instruction in Benchmark's lower school and middle schools.

DEVELOPMENT OF STRATEGIES ACROSS THE CURRICULUM

Our McDonnell grant was to develop an across-the-curriculum program that taught students in grades 1–8 how to be metacognitive. Our first task was to collaborate as a staff to understand exactly what it meant to teach students to be metacognitive. We did not want to make the mistake Judith Orasanu related in her series preface to Ruth Garner's (1987) book about metacognition. In it she stated that too many educational efforts are based on an incomplete understanding of what is to be taught because there has been a concern for method in the absence of a concern for understanding. Our understanding of metacognition had to precede learning methods for teaching it. One of the books that we found helpful in understanding metacognition and developing our McDonnell strategies program was *Metacognition and Reading Comprehension* by Ruth Garner (1987). Garner divided metacognition into three parts: (1) knowledge (about ourselves, our tasks, and the strategies we know), (2) awareness (of our cognitive successes and failures), and (3) fix-up resources (what to do in case of failures). Stated in the simplest terms, metacognition is thinking about our own thinking. More recently metacognition has been defined in IRA's *Literacy Dictionary* (Harris & Hodges, 1995) as "awareness and knowledge of one's mental processes such that one can monitor, regulate, and direct them to a desired end; self-mediation" (p. 153). Metacognitive awareness in reading is "knowing when what one is reading makes sense by monitoring and controlling one's own comprehension" (Harris & Hodges, 1995, p. 153). In their definition of metacognitive awareness these authors go on to say: "Good readers appear from an early age to possess metacognitive awareness that allows them to adjust their reading strategies; poor readers do not" (p. 153). In working with our struggling readers, we had certainly experienced that phenomenon. Now we had to figure out what to do about it.

Teacher Planning and Retreats

We decided that we first needed to develop an understanding of two aspects of metacognition. As stated in the book describing our first 3-year McDonnell grant (Gaskins & Elliot, 1991), we needed to understand:

1. How task, person, strategy, and environmental variables affect learning
2. How executive processing or *control* carries out the work of the mind, the planning, implementing, monitoring, and assessing. (p. 21)

Once we had a basic understanding of those two aspects of metacognition, the goal was to provide students with an awareness of the variables that affect learning and procedures that would put them in control of their learning. We also wanted both teachers and students to have a basic understanding of how their minds work. We wanted them to know, for instance, that between input and output of information, cognitive processes are involved in taking in information, performing mental operations on it, and storing it. Furthermore, we wanted them to know that we could teach students control strategies that would permit more efficient use of their limited-capacity processing systems, especially when accompanied by teacher-guided practice and feedback. Our goal was for students to become goal driven, planful, self-assessing, and strategic. It was our suspicion, at least in relation to our struggling readers who had adequate decoding skills, that their poor oral and written responses to text were related to failure to participate actively and strategically in the reading process.

Armed with what we had consolidated from 8 years of study and inservice training, plus my epiphany under the tutelage of Duffy and Roehler, I scheduled weekend retreats at my house to create prototype lessons of what metacognitive and cognitive instruction might look like as part of reading, social studies, science, mathematics, and health classes. Attendance by the Benchmark staff was voluntary. The first retreat was held on a Saturday, from 8:30 in the morning until 10:00 at night. Nine teachers attended. They brought their lunches; I cooked dinner. We spent the morning deciding on a lesson format to use initially in writing lesson plans. Based on our review of the literature, we concluded that effective explanations of reading strategies should explain:

1. Why the strategy should be learned and how it would help the brain be an efficient learner, thinker, and problem solver
2. What the strategy was
3. How to implement the strategy
4. When and where the strategy could be used

Each lesson was to begin with an objective (goal) and include an explanation for implementing a strategy that the teacher thought would enhance the likelihood that students would meet the objective of the lesson *and* learn how to accomplish school tasks. The nine teachers set up study areas throughout the house. Secluded from interruptions, they reflected on what they had learned about metacognition and explicit explanations from 8 years of inservice work and study of the research and applied that knowledge to writing lessons they would pilot the following week. As teachers ran into problems in constructing their lessons, they would seek a collaborator. I encouraged teachers to collaborate with me, because I wanted to understand any concerns or problems teachers had in designing lessons that taught students how to be metacognitive. We also shared our problems and victories as we ate lunch and dinner. An invigorated group left my house at 10:00 that evening, promising to return at 9:30 the next morning to tie up lots of loose ends. On Sunday we worked until 6:00 P.M. Some of the teachers agreed to share their lessons, including comments about how the lessons went when they taught them. We had made a good start. More retreats and lesson planning followed. Subsequent retreats stayed within more reasonable hours than the first and, with the sharing of lessons that seemed to be working, our strategies instruction improved.

Rationale for Students' Learning Specific Strategies

Our study of the literature as well as discussions with experts suggested that the success of our program might rest on our ability to provide students with a convincing rationale for implementing each of the strategies we would teach. Implementing strategies is effortful, so students needed to be convinced of their value so that they would be willing to put forth the effort to learn and practice them. We soon discovered that the more complete a teacher's knowledge of how the brain works in the process of learning and remembering, the easier it was for the teacher to lead a fruitful discussion with students about how strategy use would benefit them. We learned that when the rationale for a strategy was too general or involved results that were too far in the future, students were not motivated to learn or use the strategy. Students wanted the payoff for strategy use to be immediate. Telling them that use of a strategy would make them smarter or help them in their next school simply did not work.

Jim Benedict and I had learned that lesson during the 1987–1988 school year when we teamed up to teach social studies. Jim was "Content Man," teaching social studies, and I was "Strategy Lady," who taught students strategies for completing the tasks that Jim assigned. Our class was just one mini-experiment after another that proved to students that when they used the strategies we taught, they understood and could apply the information they were learning in social studies. Students began calling my part of the social studies lesson Psych 101. We liked the Psych 101 idea so much that, beginning in the fall of 1988 and for many years thereafter, we called the course I taught to middle school students Psych 101. Teachers remained in the classroom as my co-teachers while I taught Psych 101. Before long they were using Psych 101 concepts as a rationale for the strategies they taught in reading, social studies, science, and other content areas. I was thrilled. See Gaskins and Elliot (1991) for a chapter about Jim's and my co-teaching and for a chapter about Psych 101.

When students were convinced of the rationale for using a strategy, there was a much greater likelihood they would apply it. Therefore, in teaching strategies we were careful to explain "why" the strategy would make them a more successful learner, thinker, and problem solver and how the strategy helped their brains function more efficiently. Figure 12.1 includes strategies that a teacher might explain and the possible reasons for using the strategy. What follows is the way I introduced the rationale for strategy instruction to a class of middle school students at the beginning of one school year.

"All day, every day of our lives, our senses are being bombarded with information. That information goes to processing centers in our brain. You are not conscious that it is even happening. Based on your past experiences, some of that information may be passed on to your working memory. If you choose not to pay attention to the information once it enters your working memory, it is lost. Some information you will probably pay attention to just enough to know it is there, and you may even say to yourself, 'That's important, I'd better remember it.' However, if that is all you do about remembering it, the information will probably be pushed out of working memory by new information as it comes in. This happens because, for young people your age, working memory has room for only about five bits of information. And even adults only have room for approximately seven bits of information. If you don't consciously process the information that is in your working memory to get it into long-term memory, you lose it. Because we don't want to lose important information that is in working memory, we use strategies to help us:

1. Pay attention to the information.
2. Think about the information that is in working memory to make a decision about whether it should be moved to long-term memory.
3. Process and learn the information that we want to move to long-term memory.

FIGURE 12.1. Explaining why a strategy should be used.

STRATEGY	WHY WE TEACH THE STRATEGY	HOW THE STRATEGY HELPS THE BRAIN
Survey	We survey to get a sense of what the text (story/selection) is about and to hook our interest. Surveying provides a framework we can fill in as we read.	Surveying tells our brains what background knowledge to get ready to help us understand the new information.
Access Background Knowledge	We access background knowledge to help us become actively involved by relating what we are reading to what we know.	We use background information to make sense of the selection, because our brains don't remember things that don't make sense. We also want to hook new information to what we already know, because it is easier to get information back out of our brain if it is hooked to what we already know.
Predict	We predict to stay actively involved and to check our understanding of what we are reading. If we are going to remember what we read, it has to make sense.	The brain doesn't put information in long-term memory if it doesn't make sense.
Set a Purpose	Having a goal or purpose makes us pay attention to what we are trying to find out. Without a purpose, we might daydream.	If we aren't paying attention, the words will go in one side of our brain and out the other. We have to do something with the information we are reading or it won't get stored in memory.
Ask Questions	We ask ourselves questions to check our understanding. We ask our teachers and our classmates questions to clarify what we don't understand. Asking questions shows that we intend to understand.	If we don't understand, our brain will allow the information we are reading or learning to escape.
Identify Story Elements	We look for story elements (setting, character, problem, and solution) to help us recall the most important information in fiction.	The brain likes structure, and story elements are the structure of a story. Structures that form patterns, as story elements do, are easier for the brain to remember than individual facts.
Create Mental Images	We create mental images or pictures in the brain to check our understanding. If we can't see a clear picture of what is being read, we know we need to use a fix-up strategy.	The more senses that we involve as we read, the better the brain can remember and retrieve what was read.
Monitor Understanding	We monitor (pay attention to) what we are reading to make sure it is making sense. Unless we consciously think about and monitor what we are reading, nothing we read will stick in our brain.	If what we are reading isn't making sense, our brain will not accept the information, because our brain only accepts what makes sense.
Summarize	We summarize to check our understanding—if we can't summarize what we've read, we probably didn't understand it.	Summarizing is a way to rehearse what we want to save from working memory and put into long-term memory.

(continued)

From *Success with Struggling Readers* by Irene Gaskins. Copyright 2005 by The Guilford Press. See copyright page for photocopying limitations.

FIGURE 12.1 (*continued*)

STRATEGY	WHY WE TEACH THE STRATEGY	HOW THE STRATEGY HELPS THE BRAIN
Make Inferences	We make inferences to fill in gaps in the text. Authors often do not tell us everything that is needed to completely understand a text. They expect us to be actively involved in using our background knowledge to fill in gaps. If we aren't aware that text doesn't always tell everything and that we need to make an inference, we may not be able to make sense of a text.	When what we are reading doesn't make sense, our brain will not save the information. The more knowledge we have stored in our brain, the better the inferences we can make.
Identify Character Traits	We think about how a character in a story or novel usually acts in order to better understand the character, and to connect the character traits to the story problem, key events, or story resolution.	By being actively involved in thinking about the characteristics of the character, we are helping the brain remember and figure out what is happening in the story.
Take Notes	We take notes to help our working memory. If we didn't take notes, we would forget a lot of what we read or hear.	We take notes because our working memory is only able to hold and think about approximately five ideas at a time.
Put Notes in Own Words	We paraphrase, or put notes in our own words, to assist understanding and recall by deeply processing what we want to remember, rather than unthinkingly writing exactly what the text said. Putting something in our own words takes more thinking than copying ideas.	The more we think about something, the more likely the information will be moved from working memory to long-term memory and can be called upon when we want to use it.

A few of the strategies we learn as beginning readers, and which are helpful for the rest of our lives, are listed on the chalkboard." (Listed on the chalkboard were a few of the strategies noted in Figure 12.1.)

Personal Examples of Strategy Use

In addition to explaining how a strategy will help the brain work better to learn and remember, we often tell students a story about someone who did or did not use a particular strategy. Often the story is personal. For example, one of my favorite stories about note taking actually took place in a middle school social studies classes I taught. The bell had rung for the start of class and students were searching through their binders to find their social studies notes, when one student initiated a complaint about note taking. It went something like this:

S1: Can we not take notes today? We've learned how to take notes and we'll be able to do it if our next school makes kids take notes.

S2: He's right. We all know how to take notes. Besides, it's a lot of work and it gets boring taking notes on what we read and what we talk about in class. Anyway, it doesn't really work for me.

T: Have you found a better way to remember what you have heard and read?

S2: Yeah, when my mom reads the social studies assignment to me, that's when I remember it best.

S3: I don't need my mom to read it to me. I remember what I read without taking notes.

T: Does anyone else have a different point of view? (*No one responds, but mumbling is heard about not wanting to take notes.*) Okay, I'll make a deal with you. For two-thirds of the class period today, we will do it your way, and for one-third of the period I would like you to do it my way and take notes on just the major ideas in one section.

The text to be discussed that day was divided into three sections. The first section I read to the class. I told them they could either sit back and just listen or they were welcome to implement any of the strategies they knew for learning and remembering. Everyone appeared to just listen. For the next section, I asked the class to turn the section heading into a purpose question, then read to themselves to answer the purpose question. Again, I encouraged them to use any of the strategies they thought would help them learn and remember. When everyone had finished reading, we moved on to the next section. This time I told the class that they had to take notes because that was the deal we had made. They were to read the next section and write in their own words a sentence or phrase stating the major idea of each paragraph. All students dutifully complied, a task that took them until the end of the period.

The next day when the class entered, I gave them a three-question self-assessment to determine which method of learning and remembering information from text had worked for each of them. Most students could not satisfactorily recall the information from the first two sections of the previous day's text, but they all had quite accurate recall of the important information in the third section of the text. We had a discussion about what they had learned from the mini-experiment.

T: What did yesterday's mini-experiment tell you about learning and remembering?

S1: That we remember more about what we read when we put what we have read in our own words.

Decoding and comprehension strategies provide the foundation for students to write well about what they are learning.

S2: That taking notes takes longer than just listening or reading.

S3: That if you really want to learn something, you'd better do more with the information than just listen or pass your eyes over it.

T: You have surely heard me say that before. So could someone sum up what we have learned?

S4: You want us to say we learn more when we take notes and are actively involved. I know it helps my brain remember stuff, but it's a lot of work. [It was pretty clear that the class knew that they would learn more if they were actively involved. My job was to keep them interested. One way was by relating what we were learning to happenings in their world.]

Personal experiences that illustrate the value of applying cognitive and metacognitive strategies are well received by our students, and often these stories are referred to when students are self-assessing. Next, I review some additional guidelines for teaching procedural knowledge.

GUIDELINES

This chapter tells the story of the incredible heritage of the Benchmark strategies-across-the-curriculum program and the decades that the staff has spent developing it. I conclude the chapter with Benchmark's interpretation of Garner's (1987) admonitions to teachers about effective strategy instruction. These guidelines shaped our strategy instruction during 1988 and continue to be useful today. Guidelines for teaching strategies for comprehension and completing other school tasks are summarized in Figure 12.2.

Applying these guidelines, we developed a continuum of strategy instruction that enhanced the completion of school tasks from first through eighth grades. Strategies for word learning were discussed in Chapters 10 and 11. Strategies for comprehension and completing other school tasks in grades 1–8 are discussed in Chapter 13.

FIGURE 12.2. Teaching strategies for task completion: Guidelines for the teacher.

1. **Lesson Preparation**
   Analyze into its component parts the procedure (strategy) you suggest that students use to complete the assigned task.

2. **Explain How**
   Explain explicitly how to complete the assigned task.

3. **Think Aloud and Model**
   Think aloud while modeling how to complete the task.

4. **Explain Why**
   Explain why the strategy or strategies being suggested are useful (i.e., how they will help the brain work more efficiently).

5. **Explain When**
   Present each strategy as applicable to texts and tasks in more than one domain.

6. **Continue to Teach and Cue**
   Teach and cue strategy use over the entire school year, not just in a single lesson or unit in which a strategy or strategies are introduced. Ideally, students should be expected to use the strategies in all future school years.

7. **Provide Practice Opportunities**
   Provide students with many opportunities to practice the strategies they have been taught and to receive teacher guidance and feedback.

8. **Wholly Intertwine Instruction**
   Wholly intertwine strategy instruction with subject-area instruction.

9. **Encourage Strategy Instruction**
   Encourage students to teach each other about strategies for understanding and learning that work for them.

From *Success with Struggling Readers* by Irene Gaskins. Copyright 2005 by The Guilford Press. See copyright page for photocopying limitations.

CHAPTER 13

Explicit Explanations of Comprehension Strategies for Grades 1–8

Strategy instruction at Benchmark looks quite different today compared to the 1988–1989 school year, when McDonnell researchers tape-recorded strategy lessons taught in our classrooms, transcribed the tapes, shared the lessons, and revised lessons to combine what worked best. During the early 1990s we again studied transcripts of Benchmark teachers' lessons—this time to discover the "moves" that teachers made during strategy lessons. We discovered that eight "moves" were typical of good strategy instruction (Gaskins et al., 1993). The first four were discussions of *what*, *why*, *when*, and *how*. These discussions were followed by teacher modeling of how to use the strategy, the sharing of personal experiences about strategy use, guided and scaffolded practice of the strategy, and cued use of the strategy (Figure 13.1). What Benchmark teachers were doing during strategy instruction lined up well with Garner's (1987) advice for teaching strategies presented in Chapter 12, with the added Benchmark touch of teachers sharing personal experiences about the value of using each strategy. And so the program-development process proceeded, as the staff collaborated to create an across-the-curriculum strategies program for struggling readers in grades 1–8.

By the mid-1990s teachers of students who had been at Benchmark for 4 or more years began to comment that they arrived in their classes able to orchestrate strategies in much more sophisticated ways than had been the case with earlier students. Strategy use seemed to be almost second nature to many of these students. This was exciting news. This is how we think that happened.

All teachers at Benchmark had become so familiar with the strategies introduced by the teachers who taught the levels that preceded theirs that they knew what to build on—and build they did. It was the consistency of strategy instruction year in and year out, and the expectation by every teacher that strategies be used, that seemed to make the difference. We also learned that 1 or 2 years of strategy instruction was not enough for students to make strategy use part of their way of operating in classrooms. More scaffolded practice would be necessary for that to happen.

FIGURE 13.1. Eight moves of good strategy instruction.

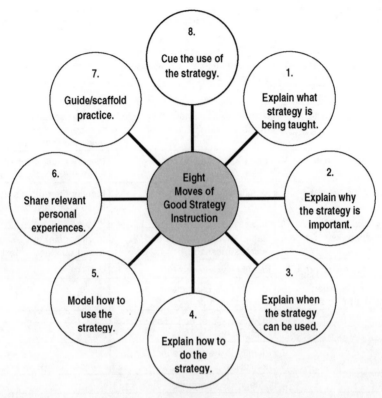

From *Success with Struggling Readers* by Irene Gaskins. Copyright 2005 by The Guilford Press. See copyright page for photocopying limitations.

CURRENT STRATEGY INSTRUCTION IN BENCHMARK'S LOWER SCHOOL

Teachers begin strategy instruction at a very basic level, teaching one strategy at a time and teaching it thoroughly. Once a strategy is fairly well learned, it is combined with the ones taught previously to compile, over time, a substantial portfolio of strategies. The comprehension strategies taught at Benchmark fall into three categories: monitoring for sense, looking for patterns, and making inferences. A sampling of strategies found in each category is shown in Figure 13.2. In the next section I describe how Benchmark's primary-level teachers begin to accomplish the task of helping students build a portfolio of strategies.

Primary-Level Strategies Instruction

Strategies in the primary grades, for the most part, focus on two aspects of reading (see Figure 13.3). The first involves processing the words in text efficiently (as discussed in Chapters 10 and 11). Processing text includes acquiring a sight vocabulary, reading text fluently, decoding words efficiently, recognizing unfamiliar words, and taking action to

FIGURE 13.2. Framework for learning and understanding. Based on Pearson (1993).

Monitor for Sense	Look for Patterns	Make Inferences
Check to be sure that what I hear or read makes sense and use fix-up strategies, as needed.	Look for spelling and number patterns; story elements, genre characteristics, or text structure; and major concepts/theme.	Connect clues (from author or speaker) with background knowledge.
Sample Strategies	*Sample Strategies*	*Sample Strategies*
Use context to check sense of word decoded.	Use words you know to decode words you don't know.	Support statements, inferences, and conclusions by finding evidence in the text.
Summarize story elements.	Identify story elements.	Identify character traits based on what character does and says.
Make and describe mental pictures.	Identify elements of genre.	Identify the author's message, lesson, or universal truth based on genre or clues in text.
Self-question about key elements.	Gather clues to theme and author's message.	Identify point of view or bias based on clues in text.
Discuss your understanding.	Identify key events.	
Use fix-up strategies when reading does not make sense.	Identify how character traits influence events.	
	Identify topic of nonfiction paragraph.	
	Identify text structure in nonfiction.	
	Categorize information.	

From *Success with Struggling Readers* by Irene Gaskins. Copyright 2005 by The Guilford Press. See copyright page for photocopying limitations.

figure out what those words mean. The second aspect of reading emphasized in the primary grades is comprehension. We want our students to be able to construct meaning from text, beginning with the gist and including inferences. At the primary level we expect students to be able to identify important points in text and read "between the lines," using the text and background knowledge to construct inferences.

Now let's take a look at the strategies taught by the three teachers of the youngest students at Benchmark as an example of primary-level strategy instruction. Sherry

FIGURE 13.3. Benchmark's major reading goals for the primary grades.

Word Knowledge	Comprehension
• Acquire a sight vocabulary. • Read text fluently. • Decode words efficiently. • Recognize unfamiliar words and take action to figure out the words.	• Construct meaning, beginning with the gist. • Identify important points in text. • Construct inferences using information in the text and background knowledge.

From *Success with Struggling Readers* by Irene Gaskins. Copyright 2005 by The Guilford Press. See copyright page for photocopying limitations.

Cress teaches the incoming first and second graders; the following year her class moves, intact, to become Theresa Scott's class. Karen Berry teaches the incoming third and fourth graders, most of whom are reading at first-grade reading levels, with a few at second-grade reading levels.

Mrs. Cress begins the year discussing the objective that "reading must make sense." Day in and day out she walks her students through the process of surveying, accessing background knowledge, predicting, and setting a purpose for reading. While doing this, she also explicitly teaches self-questioning for sense, using the story elements (setting, characters, problem, and solution). The emphasis is on the dictum "reading must make sense." A copy of one of Benchmark's story elements charts appears in Figure 13.4. Theresa Scott follows up a year later with the same students by teaching and/or reviewing the strategies noted in Figure 13.5. Karen Berry teaches a combination of the strategies taught by Cress and Scott.

FIGURE 13.4. Identifying story elements.

Characters

Who are the important people or animals in the story?

Setting

Where and when does the story take place?

Problem

What does the main character want, need, think, or feel? What is getting in the way?

Solution

How is the problem solved?

Copyright 2001 by Benchmark Press. Reprinted by permission in *Success with Struggling Readers* by Irene Gaskins (2005). See copyright page for photocopying limitations.

FIGURE 13.5. Theresa Scott's format for explaining comprehension strategies taught initially in grade 1–3.

Survey

What strategy are we learning?	To survey the story (fiction) or selection (nonfiction) before we read.
Why is the strategy important?	Surveying:

- Gives you a sense of the story or selection.
- Provides a framework that you fill in as you read.
- Triggers background knowledge that helps you get involved in reading.

When can you use this strategy?	Whenever you read.
How do you do this strategy?	Read the title.

Read the author's name.

Look at the pictures (headings and captions for nonfiction) to get a sense of what the story or selection will be about.

Access Background Knowledge

What strategy are you learning?	To access our background knowledge as we survey a text.
Why is the strategy important?	Accessing background knowledge:

- Helps you get involved.
- Provides you with additional information that you use to understand the story or selection.
- Lets you hook what you are learning to what you already know so it is easier to remember.

When can you use this strategy?	Whenever you read.
How do you do this strategy?	Read the title.

Read the author's name.

Look at the pictures (headings and captions for nonfiction) to get a sense of what the story (or selection) will be about.

Ask yourself what you already know about the genre, characters, setting, author, situation (topic for nonfiction).

Predict

What strategy are you learning?	To make predictions as we read.
Why is the strategy important?	Making predictions:

- Keeps you actively involved while you read.
- Helps you check out your understanding.

When can you use this strategy?	Whenever you read.
How do you do this strategy?	Read the title.

Read the author's name.

Look at the pictures (headings and captions) to get a sense of what the piece will be about.

Ask yourself what you already know about the genre, characters, setting, author, situation (topic for nonfiction).

Use the information you gathered from surveying and activating background knowledge to make educated guesses.

As you read, use text clues to confirm or reject your predictions. If you reject a prediction, revise it or make a new one.

We can make predictions about:

- The problem
- The solution
- Key events
- What may be discussed next

(continued)

From *Success with Struggling Readers* by Irene Gaskins. Copyright 2005 by The Guilford Press. See copyright page for photocopying limitations.

FIGURE 13.5 *(continued)*

Set a Purpose

What strategy are you learning?	To set a purpose for reading.
Why is the strategy important?	Reading with a useful purpose:

- Keeps you involved.
- Gives you a reason to read, so reading is not aimless.

When can you use this strategy?	Whenever you read.
How do you do this strategy?	Read the title.

Read the author's name.

Look at the pictures (headings and captions) to get a sense of what the text will be about.

Ask yourself what you already know about the genre, characters, setting, author, situation (topic for nonfiction).

Use the information you gathered from surveying and activating background knowledge to make educated guesses.

Think about what you want to find out about the story or selection.

As you read, use text clues to confirm, reject, or revise your predictions and to answer your purpose questions.

Summarize Nonfiction

What strategy are you learning?   To summarize nonfiction. (A summary is a short retelling of a portion of text that includes the important information.)

Why is the strategy important?   Summarizing nonfiction helps you:

- Check your understanding—if you can't summarize what you heard or read, you probably don't understand it.
- Rehearse what you want to remember.
- Focus on important information.
- Concisely share what you learned with others.

When can you use this strategy?   Whenever you read nonfiction.

How do you do this strategy?   After you have read a portion of the text:

- Read and retell (in your own words).
- Collect notes on important ideas.
- Reflect and organize the notes into a few sentences that tell about what you have read.

Summarize Fiction

What strategy are you learning?   To summarize fiction. (A summary is a short retelling of a story that includes the important information.)

Why is the strategy important?   Summarizing fiction helps you:

- Check your understanding—if you can't summarize what you heard or read, you probably don't understand it.
- Rehearse what you want to remember.
- Focus on important information.
- Concisely share what you read with others.

When can you use this strategy?   Whenever you read fiction.

How do you do this strategy?   As you read, collect clues about characters, setting, story problem, story resolution, and key events. How do I know if something is a key event?

- It provides a clue to the problem or resolution.
- It tells something important about the main character(s).
- It moves the action along and connects the problem with the resolution of the problem.

After you read, reflect on the clues and weave them into several sentences that tell about the story.

(continued)

FIGURE 13.5 *(continued)*

Identify Character Traits

What strategy are you learning?	To identify character traits. (A character trait is a way of acting, such as brave or clever or generous. It describes the way a character usually acts.)
Why is the strategy important?	If you know how a character usually acts: • It helps you understand the character. • It helps you connect the character traits to the story problem, key events, or the story resolution. • It helps you understand the story.
When can you use this strategy?	Whenever you read fiction.
How do you do this strategy?	Read the text and ask yourself, "What did the character do, say, think?" Connect the text clues to your background knowledge. Infer the character trait (i.e., what word(s) describe the way the character is acting?). Connect the character trait to the story problem, key events, or story resolution.

Make Inferences

What strategy are you learning?	To make inferences when you read. (An inference is something you conclude based on text clues and background knowledge.)
Why is the strategy important?	Many times authors do not tell us everything we need to know to completely understand a text. Authors believe readers have background knowledge that they will use to fill in those gaps. When you make an inference (or fill in the gaps), you have a richer understanding of a text.
When can you use this strategy?	You can make inferences whenever you read fiction or nonfiction and you want to have a rich understanding of a text. You can make inferences before you read, as you read, or after you read.
How do you do this strategy?	Read sections of the text. If you are confused, and you are sure you read accurately, ask yourself: • What did I read? • What has the author left out that he or she expects me to know? • What do I know that I can use to help me fill in the gaps? • What can I conclude or infer? • Does my inference fit all the available information?

Introducing Monitoring for Sense

Cress, Scott, and Berry all teach the strategy "monitor for sense." With the help of their supervisor, Colleen O'Hara, they have worked out a framework for teaching students that reading must make sense and what to do when it does not make sense. On the day the monitor-for-sense strategy is introduced, the teacher's conversation with the class might sound something like this:

T: Today we are going to learn a new strategy. It is called "monitor for sense." Does anyone have an idea of what *monitor for sense* means?

S1: It means that what you read has got to make sense.

T: Yes, reading does have to make sense. Any ideas about what *monitor* means? We are going to *monitor* for sense.

S2:   Pay attention to make sure that it makes sense?

T: That sounds pretty good to me. Let's see how close Joe's definition is to the dictionary definition. Joe thinks that "pay attention to" is a meaning for monitor. I brought my dictionary with me to reading group and have a bookmark where I found the word *monitor*. It says "To check, watch, or keep track of." Joe said "pay attention to"—that sounds like he was thinking of the same thing as the author of the dictionary. I'll write the definition on the chalkboard to help you remember what *monitor* means. (*Writes "to check, watch, keep track of, or pay attention to.*") When I hear the word *monitor,* I think of someone who stands on a hill as a lookout to alert people if an enemy is coming. A lookout is sometimes called a monitor. Can anyone tell me what you think we are going to do when we monitor for sense?

S3:   We are going to be lookouts for what doesn't make sense.

S4:   We are going to check to make sure that what we read is making sense?

T: How do you think you are going to do that?

S2:   If I am reading along in a story about going to the zoo and I read something that doesn't fit with being at the zoo, I'm going to say to myself, "This doesn't make sense."

S1:   Yeah, you can just look at the pictures, and if what you just read doesn't fit with the pictures and the title, you gotta think "I must have read something wrong."

T: Why do you think it is important to monitor for sense?

S3:   Reading is supposed to make sense. If it is not making sense, you are not really reading.

S4:   When reading is not making sense, you've got to do something to get it to make sense so you will understand it.

T: Wow, you are way ahead of me. I haven't even told you the whole strategy and you knew that you had to do something to get what you are reading to make sense. The whole strategy is called: monitor our reading for sense and take action when reading does not make sense. What kind of action do you think you might take?

S3:   We could reread the part that doesn't make sense.

S1:   We could ask someone else what they thought it meant.

S2:   When I am reading, I keep on reading a little bit more to see if I can figure it out.

T: You are doing a great job telling me about our new strategy. Let me sum up what you have been saying. I have put the what, why, when, and how of the strategy on separate pieces of posterboard to help you remember the strategy. It looks as if I have an awful lot of information on these cards, but don't panic.

We will work on the "how" part, piece by piece. (*Reads the questions and answers from the what, why, when, and how cards.*)

What strategy are we learning?

- To monitor our reading for sense and then take action when reading does not make sense.

Why is the strategy important?

- Monitoring for sense and taking action when reading does not make sense helps us understand what we are reading. If we don't understand it, we can't get it stuck in our brain.

When can we use the strategy?

- Any time we read fiction or nonfiction. We monitor as we go along and at the end.
- We monitor each sentence and paragraph as we read it and take action if a sentence or paragraph doesn't make sense. When we finish a selection or part of a selection, we monitor again to make sure that the whole thing fits together and makes sense.

How do we do the strategy?

- We read, then we talk to ourselves to retell what happened in the part we read. (In fiction, we can also name the characters and tell what they did.)
- We say to ourselves:
  1. What I read fits with what is happening in the story because
  2. What I read fits with the pictures because I see
  3. What I read fits with my background knowledge because I know
- When reading does not make sense, we take action:
  1. We reread the part that does not make sense.
  2. We read on to get more information.
  3. We ask questions to see what others know.

After explaining the what, why, when, and how of the strategy, the teacher models the "how" part. For example, using a think-aloud strategy she might read a paragraph from the class read-aloud book, beginning where she stopped reading to the class the previous day. While reading, she might misread a word that changes the meaning of the text and read on to the end of the sentence. She then might say aloud: "Something isn't making sense. What I just read doesn't fit with the rest of the story. I think I had better reread that sentence." The teacher rereads, corrects her error, and continues reading. On another day, she might model reading a section of text perfectly, retelling what happened in the text, and concluding that what she read makes sense. On some days the teacher may tell a personal story to make the point about why monitoring for sense is so important. Students tend to like authentic, personal examples that show students that well-educated adults use the same strategies that we are teaching them to use.

There is not one "right" set of words or phrases to use in explaining a strategy. In fact, we find that we sometimes have to experiment with several ways of explaining a strategy, especially with respect to the "how." Teaching struggling readers in primary grades a strategy for monitoring has proved particularly difficult, and there are subtle differences in the approaches Benchmark teachers use.

Practicing Monitoring for Sense

In one class where, almost daily, students quickly finished the assigned reading and claimed they understood what they had read, the teacher began handing students a pencil and note card as each finished reading silently. On the card students were to write brief notes that answered the four questions on a poster on the chalkboard, which read:

1. Who is the story mostly about?
2. When and where does the story take place?
3. What is the main character trying to do?
   - What does the main character want or need?
   - What gets in his or her way?
   - Why can't the main character get what he or she wants?
4. How does the main character get what he or she wants?

Often a student in this reading group will sit poised with pencil in hand for a minute or so, then hand the pencil and card back to the teacher saying, "I think I'd better reread." The teacher tells students each day that talking to themselves about what they read is the way they should be monitoring all the reading they do. If they can't talk about it, they probably haven't understood it.

Students who have attended Benchmark for at least a year may be ready to add more strategies to their repertoire. However, that does not mean they should stop applying the strategies taught previously. Students are cued to implement the strategies they learned during previous years, with special emphasis on combining them into bundles of strategies to accomplish sophisticated tasks.

Intermediate-Level Strategies Instruction

As students move into the intermediate levels, expectations are raised. Efficient text processing and construction of meaning continue to be important goals, and new goals are added as well, including searching for information and noticing patterns in text (see Figure 13.6). These latter goals necessitate analyzing texts for deeper meaning and structure than was expected at earlier levels. At the intermediate levels students discuss character analysis, theme/author's message, human universals, perspective, and principles. Another new set of goals relates to *appreciation*: We would like students to engage emotionally and critically with text by participating in voluntary reading, making personal/emotional connections to texts, sharing reflections about selections with

FIGURE 13.6. Benchmark's major reading goals for the intermediate grades.

Comprehension	Appreciation
• Search for information. • Notice patterns in text. • In fiction discuss character analysis, imagery, theme/author's message and point of view, human universals, perspective, and principles. • Take notes about important ideas and classify them using charts, concept maps, and mini-reports. • Evaluate ideas presented in text and hypertext.	• Engage emotionally and critically with text by participating in voluntary reading. • Make personal/emotional connections to text. • Share reflections about selections with others. • Critically evaluate author's effectiveness and authenticity.

From *Success with Struggling Readers* by Irene Gaskins. Copyright 2005 by The Guilford Press. See copyright page for photocopying limitations.

others, and critically evaluating an author's effectiveness and authenticity. Some of these intermediate goals are discussed next.

Teaching Strategies for Gathering Information

Strategies for gathering information are introduced during the primary grades when students are walked through the steps of summarizing nonfiction for 6–8 weeks in reading group; then they are given charts or planning sheets on which to collect notes during seatwork as they read simple nonfiction books. The charts or planning sheets usually follow the same steps, which the teacher verbally scaffolds each day in reading group. One method Ms. Scott and Mrs. Berry use to introduce note taking from nonfiction books is to have students read the same section of text several times for different purposes. The first time they read the text to determine what the section is mostly about. The second time they read the same section, paragraph by paragraph, and compose a sentence for each paragraph telling what the paragraph is about. Finally, students collect notes on only the important information they wrote in the sentences about each paragraph. These steps are repeated for each section of text. When all the notes for the book are collected, students use their notes to write a summary of the book.

With a background of note taking similar to the one described above, the intermediate-level students learn to set purposes as a way to focus their note taking. For example, Mrs. Sheridan's version of basic-level note taking for her fifth graders included this explanation of how to take notes on a nonfiction library book that was written at (approximately) the third level.

"We survey the text by looking at the table of contents, pictures, captions, bold print, and section headings to get a sense of what the book is about. Let's all do that step together with the new nonfiction book I have set in front of you. (*She and students survey the new book, occasionally commenting to each other about the interesting information they will be reading.*) Who can tell me what this book is mostly about? (*Several students give responses.*)

"The next step after surveying the book is to write purpose questions on your response sheet. (*She hands out response sheets.*) The purpose questions you write should be about the important ideas you think you will learn from reading this book. Before you write, let's share some ideas you have for purpose questions based on your survey of the book. You can see that I have left space on the response sheet for three purpose questions. The decision to have three purpose questions was based on my survey of the book and my prediction that the author will make three important points. When we finish reading the book, we will have to check to see how accurate my prediction was. Who knows, we may need more lines for purpose questions. (*Students suggest purpose questions and critique one another's questions.*)

"Take a minute now and write two or three purpose questions that you think will lead you to the important points in this book. (*Students write for about a minute.*) The next step is to read to find answers to your purpose questions, and to take notes on any other important information in the text. You will notice that below the space where you wrote your first purpose question, there are several lines on which you can write your answer to the purpose question. Below that there are three lines for important related ideas. I am going to let you go back to your seats now to read and take notes. After I have worked with my other group, I will call you back to the reading table and we will discuss together what you believe to be the most important ideas in your notes. Then we will weave those important ideas into a summary of the important information in the book."

The next step is to motivate students to take notes using charts, concept maps, and other visual devices for displaying important ideas. These graphic organizers are introduced as soon as students seem to have a grasp of what is meant by "important information." Helping students understand "importance" takes place in daily discussions like the one conducted by Mrs. Sheridan. The secret of Benchmark strategy instruction is not in the charts and response sheets that teachers devise to explain strategies and to record data, but rather in the teacher's interactive dialogue with students about strategies as they scaffold instruction in a manner that gives students the support they need to apply strategies and learn concepts such as "important information."

Approximately 50% of the in-class reading that is completed during Benchmark's lower school language arts block is in nonfiction. This nonfiction reading often relates to the concepts that students are learning in social studies or science. The notes taken during the language arts block are then used during discussions in content-area classes. For example, when a class was studying planets in science, planets was the topic of the books students were reading and taking notes on during the language arts block. The question students wanted to answer was: What are the environmental conditions on each planet that could affect life? The teacher used this opportunity to teach students how to construct a four-column note-taking chart. At the head of the columns students wrote: *page number, planet, condition, how it affects life.*

Many hours of scaffolded instruction precede asking students to take notes independently. Taking notes that will be beneficial to students after the text is finished is a high-level skill that we have found is best developed by hours of scaffolded instruction and collaborative dialogue, in which the teacher and students explain why one note about a paragraph or section of text is more helpful for a specific purpose than another.

Teachers also explicitly explain to students how to evaluate ideas presented in text and hypertext to (1) select only ideas that are important to a specific purpose, (2) identify the author's point of view and bias, and (3) evaluate the nature and reliability of the evidence and the validity of sources. Making pictures (imagery) and identifying themes in literature are also strategies taught at the intermediate levels. These are discussed next, followed by strategies for self-regulation.

Teaching Imagery

Making pictures in the mind, or imagery, is a valuable strategy that we often teach immediately after the primary-level strategies. This is how an introductory lesson in imagery might sound:

> T: The strategy that we are going to learn today is imagery making, or making pictures in your mind, about what is happening in the selection you are reading. Why do you think picturing things is important?
>
> S1: If you can see pictures, it is like watching TV, so reading is more interesting.
>
> S2: If I can picture something, I can remember it better.
>
> T: Let me tell you a little about how picturing helps your brain be more efficient. Making pictures in your mind helps your brain store and remember the information you are reading. When you use all your senses, the information is stored in more than one place in your brain; therefore, it is easier to remember. Picturing also helps you monitor your understanding. If you can't picture what you are reading, you probably don't understand it. As you read, descriptions in the text may bring to mind some other pictures stored in your brain that are related to what you are reading. You can connect what you are reading to those pictures to help your brain organize the new information. When do you think you would use the picturing strategy?
>
> S3: When authors used juicy words that are easy to picture.
>
> S4: When you are having trouble understanding something, it might make it easier to understand if you tried to picture it.
>
> T: Sounds like you can use picturing any time you read, but especially when you want to make it easier to understand or remember something. Now let's talk about how to do the picturing strategy. Today we will talk about picturing as it applies to reading fiction. Let me model how I use imagery while I read a few paragraphs from our read-aloud book. (*Reads aloud, stopping periodically to describe to students what she is picturing and the words in the text that led to those pictures. She also occasionally invites students to share what they are picturing.*)
>   So this is how we make pictures in our minds:
>
> 1. We think about what the characters are doing or saying and in our minds we see and hear them.
> 2. We think about the setting and in our minds we not only see, we also hear, feel, taste, and smell things that are in the setting.
> 3. We look for words in the text that will help us make our pictures clearer, such as words that describe colors, shapes, sizes, how things feel, or actions.

In summary, we picture the characters, setting, and events in our mind as we read. This will enrich the reading experience, so that we will experience what we read at a deeper level. Next, the teacher reads a portion of a read-aloud book to students and asks them to share the pictures they are making in their minds. This is followed by students reading a short story, page by page, and at the conclusion of each page, sharing with the group the pictures they are making. The lesson usually ends with the teacher asking: "What strategy are we learning? Why is the strategy important? When can we use it? How do we do this strategy?"

Once students are comfortable reading chapter books and are reading at a strong fourth-reader level, Benchmark teachers introduce the strategy of identifying themes in fiction. This strategy is one in a series of strategies that is used to teach students how to gather clues in texts to interpret and draw conclusions. One approach to teaching this strategy is discussed in the next section.

Teaching Theme

In teaching theme at the intermediate level, we share with students that thinking about the major ideas, or themes, in literature allows them to go beneath the surface-level meaning of what happened in the text to get at the author's message. Children who have been read to from a young age or who watched "Sesame Street" are probably unaware that they have been hearing about theme for many years. Theme is the lesson in stories such as "The Little Red Hen," "The Boy Who Cried Wolf," and a host of other folktales usually read to preschool children. In teaching theme, we guide students to make connections to known stories so that the task of identifying theme will seem somewhat familiar and less foreboding. Marjorie Downer, a retired Benchmark teacher of primary students, loved literature and conveyed a very grown-up attitude about literature to her primary-level students. At the conclusion of every reading lesson she would ask students to comment on whether what they read had a "universal message." She also asked the same question when she read aloud to students. Mrs. Downer's struggling readers seemed flattered to be let in on such a grown-up experience and enjoyed sharing their opinions about how the stories they read, or were read to them, were everyday examples of human nature.

Joanna Williams (2002) presents a straightforward approach to teaching young children how to recognize theme. She describes theme as an idea abstracted from the story context to teach a lesson or merely make an observation about the way people are. She states that theme "operates at the concept level, not the plot level; that is, the lesson or the observation is generalized beyond the specifics of the particular story plot" (p. 128). At Benchmark we teach theme as one way to introduce students to a richer understanding of literature, as well as to introduce students to a common expectation of middle school and high school English courses.

We want students to learn about the concept of theme, then to identify themes in stories and apply those themes to real life. Similar to Williams (2002), we teach that words such as *persistence* and *kindness* are *theme concepts*. Phrases such as *growing up* or *good versus evil* are also theme concepts. A theme is a statement about the material's main concept, such as "People who are persistent are more likely to achieve their goals," or "When you are kind to others, they are more likely to be kind to you." Novels often have more than one theme, so teachers need to be careful not to suggest that there is only one "right" theme, about which students must agree. The deciding point regarding theme is how well a student can substantiate his or her choice of theme with evidence from the text. Examples of theme concepts that Benchmark supervisor Joyce Ostertag introduces to students include:

1. Growing up/searching for truth
   - Changing/evolving as a person
   - Learning about life

2. Survival
   - facing extreme challenge
   - reaching physical, mental, or emotional limits

3. Friendship
   - developing a relationship
   - coping with the loss of a relationship

4. Good versus evil
   - joining a battle between larger forces of good and evil
   - facing moral/spiritual dilemmas

After reading the novel *Sign of the Beaver*, students may summarize that, at the plot level, the novel is about a young boy in colonial times who spends the winter alone in

To enable struggling readers to think deeply about what they read, teachers must explicitly teach relevant comprehension strategies, then ask high-level questions that require students to apply these strategies.

the family cabin located in the Maine wilderness. Thinking more deeply about the novel at the theme level, some students may suggest that the theme concept is "friendship," because Matt makes friends with the Indians, who, in turn, help him. Students might state that the theme is: "Things go better for you when you have friends to help you out." Other students may turn the theme concept of "growing up" into a theme statement such as: "A significant challenge presents a young person with the opportunity to grow up in a hurry." Both themes are appropriate for this novel, because they can be substantiated by evidence from the book and because they meet the criterion for theme: A theme is an idea that turns up over and over again throughout a piece of literature (Roberts, 2003).

In teaching students how to recognize themes, teachers explain what a theme is and relate the task of theme identification to themes in stories teachers have either read to students or are fairly well known in our society (e.g., "Cinderella," "The Tortoise and the Hare"). They explain why it is beneficial for students to know about theme (e.g., "You learn universal truths about life, and you make connections across the book that will make it easier to store information about the book in your brain").

Next, teachers explain when this strategy is useful (e.g., when reading novels by notable authors). Finally, the teacher explains how to do the strategy. Applying the strategy requires the orchestration of many of the strategies students learned and practiced at the primary level. Students survey the text and access background knowledge about the topic and about themes. They predict possible events and themes, and set purposes for reading. As they read, students notice ideas that turn up repeatedly, and they capture these ideas on a recording sheet (including the page number where the idea was found). When a section of the text (often, a chapter) is completed, the reader organizes his or her notes and makes a summary statement about theme. When the entire text is completed, the reader reflects on the chapter theme statements, then discusses with classmates the possible themes of the novel and the evidence that supports his or her selection.

To increase motivation, the teacher often reads aloud the first several chapters of the novel, such as *The Sign of the Beaver*, and, while reading aloud, thinks aloud about clues that might support a theme concept. Students jot down these clues. Once students begin to chime in and supply clues, the teacher realizes she can turn over more responsibility to them for gathering clues. The teacher may ask students to read silently, page by page, sharing clues to theme concepts as they come to them. Finally, teachers totally turn over the reading and gathering of clues to students, followed by a discussion at the end of each chapter.

Teaching Strategies for Self-Regulation

Self-regulation skills and strategies are stressed from the day a student enters Benchmark. Students are taught (and retaught regularly) that they are in charge of how well they use the guidance and instruction given by the staff. It is the staff's job to be in charge of guiding and explaining in a way that makes sense to students. A starting point for self-regulation is to set goals. For example, students may set goals with teachers to take charge of nonproductive aspects of their cognitive styles or to take charge of the setting for study so it will support learning. When students are in the primary grades, teachers take much of the responsibility for helping them set goals that will enhance learning. However, by the intermediate grades teachers tend to describe areas that require improvement and make suggestions about what a student might do to be more successful. However—and this is important—each student is responsible for choosing and monitoring his or her own goal(s). For example, a passive student might set a goal of participating a specified number of times during a discussion, then keep track of how he or she is doing on the goal. Another student who has trouble handing in homework on time might devise a plan with the teacher to overcome this problem. The student might agree to complete half of the assigned homework before playing any computer games or getting on the Internet to engage in instant messaging with friends, as well as agree to sit down at the kitchen table by 7:00 P.M. to complete the homework. Often the teacher designs a chart that the student can use to keep track of progress on his or her goal. We teach our intermediate and middle school students that each of their brains is a chief executive officer (CEO) in charge of a company that has much potential for success and that the company is *them*. If the CEO, their brain, puts forth intelligent effort to direct the company well, then the company will do well.

Like Zimmerman (2001), we believe that "learning is not something that happens *to* students; it is something that happens *by* students" (p. 33). This is the message we share with students. In addition, through mini-experiments and regular self-assessments we demonstrate that the results they produce are the direct product of their thinking and their actions. We also share with students, often via personal stories, the characteristics of a self-regulated student (e.g., a student who can delay immediate gratification for later academic rewards, form an academic personal identity, monitor performance-related feedback, set goals and form expectancies regarding specific academic contexts, and remain attentive despite situational distractions and adverse outcomes). Some of the ways students accomplish self-regulation is by self-talk and by applying strategies (Zimmerman & Schunk, 2001).

CURRENT INSTRUCTION IN BENCHMARK'S MIDDLE SCHOOL

The middle school staff expects that students will continue to implement the strategies introduced and practiced in the lower school, and, to ensure that they do, they cue students when these strategies might be useful. In addition, they introduce more sophisticated forms of the strategies, as well as new strategies, as is discussed in the next section.

Strategies Programs

All of Benchmark's current middle school teachers have been trained by Linda Six and Eleanor Gensemer to use transactional strategies instruction (TSI) when teaching reading, writing, social studies, science, or health. In TSI the teacher explicitly explains, models, scaffolds, and cues the use of strategies that can be applied to complete important school tasks. Teachers in the math department have also been taught to teach using TSI. In fact, the head of the math department, Betsy Cunicelli, was Benchmark's research coordinator when TSI was invented: first, in the middle school, then it spread throughout the school as Benchmark teachers shared their successes with it.

TSI, as we put it together in the late 1980s and beginning of the 1990s (Gaskins, 1988; Pressley, El-Dinary, Gaskins et al., 1992; Gaskins et al., 1993), includes explicit explanations about, and use of, a repertoire of diverse reading, writing, learning, thinking, and problem-solving strategies and the metacognitive strategies that lead to the appropriate use of these strategies. TSI also includes learning and using real-world knowledge and engaging the motivation to put this procedural and declarative knowledge to work. TSI teachers and students jointly construct meaning as they read and discuss. The *transaction* occurs as individual readers approach the text with their own interpretations and understandings and then transform these interpretations and understandings as they work collaboratively with one another to construct meaning. Students' individual backgrounds, experiences, and diverse interpretations affect, and are affected by, one another.

As a result of the transactional nature of these lessons, there is no single correct interpretation, nor is there one best set of strategies that works for everyone in accomplishing the tasks of understanding and learning. It is through cycles of teacher–student transactional dialogues that the class works collaboratively to make sense of tasks and texts and the appropriate strategies to use in accomplishing their task and text goals. An advantage that Benchmark's middle school teachers have over teachers in most settings is that no new students are taken into Benchmark's middle school; therefore, all middle school students have had at least one year of TSI, and most have had many years of it by the time they enter the middle school. As a result, most students enter the middle school with a huge portfolio of strategies.

Knowing that students enter the middle school so well prepared, one would expect that it would be easy for them to put together the strategies needed to complete the projects assigned in their classes. It is not. Completion of projects often proves to be an ordeal for students, parents, and teachers. Therefore, how to help students successfully manage projects is a major goal of the middle school staff and a frequent topic of discussion and teacher collaboration. More than any other single factor, it is probably the difficulty that our students evidence in completing projects that has led me to conclude that there is more to teaching struggling readers than teaching reading. Not only do we teach an incredible repertoire of strategies in the lower school, but we are successful in teaching most of our struggling readers to read at or above grade level, and to be able to write creatively, by the time they enter the middle school. Despite this rich background, completing tasks that require independent application and orchestration of what they know over a period of several days, weeks, or months is overwhelming for the majority of our students. Projects seem to test and strain students' abilities to apply and monitor strategies that need to be organized over time. How we support students through this quagmire is discussed next.

Teaching Strategies for Short-Term and Long-Term Projects

For each project that is assigned, whether it is a 2-day, 1-week, or 3-month project, the teacher provides students with a rubric that describes how the assignment will be evaluated and explicit guidelines for how to proceed through the project, including due dates for each part. Teachers help students monitor completion of projects by requiring them to submit plans, notes, outlines, paragraphs, and the like for feedback on a regular basis. Students are told that they may hand in the completed project early for teacher feedback, and they are welcome to rework the project right up until the moment it is due. Each new project begins with a task analysis.

Task Analysis. When a new task is assigned and the guideline sheet and rubric for the task have been explained, the teacher walks the class through the analyze-the-task procedure outlined in Figure 13.7. First, students are asked to write their interpretation of what the task is. Based on the teacher's explanation, usually just completed, and on the assignment sheet and rubric, students identify the expectations of the task in their own words.

This every-pupil-response (EPR), requesting students to think about the job to be accomplished, can be an eyeopener for both students and teachers. Students often think that they understand what they are supposed to accomplish, yet many discover, when asked to write about the assignment, that they have, at best, only a partial understand-

FIGURE 13.7. Strategies for analyzing the task.

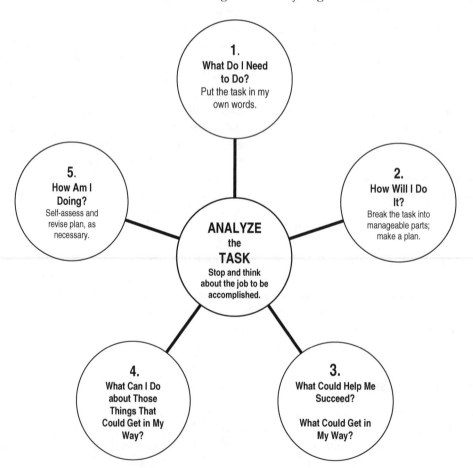

From *Success with Struggling Readers* by Irene Gaskins. Copyright 2005 by The Guilford Press. See copyright page for photocopying limitations.

ing. After composing their interpretation of the task, students give their written inter-pretations to their partners to read. After reading each other's written interpretation, the members of each partnership discuss any differences in interpretation and check the assignment guideline sheet to clarify those differences. The teacher circulates dur-ing these discussions, collaborating with some pairs and suggesting that others check their interpretations of the task with another team.

The next job of the pairs is to break the assigned task into manageable parts and to create a written plan for completing the project. As they work on their plans, and in col-laboration with their teacher and peers, students also consider and list possible road-blocks to success, such as specific person, situation, task, or text variables. They ask themselves, "What are some factors about myself, the situation at home or school, the task (especially scheduling the parts of the task to meet deadlines), or the available texts that could get in the way of my satisfactorily completing this project?" Road-blocks are listed with a plan for overcoming the roadblocks—a plan that usually fea-tures some of their strengths. The last phase is to make a plan for assessing progress toward completion of the project and for determining whether the plan needs to be revised.

Self-Assessment. Students in the middle school are asked to self-assess most of the written work that they complete, as has been discussed in previous chapters. Their basis for self-assessment is the knowledge they have gained during their years at Benchmark about cognition, metacognition, and motivation and the strategies they can use to take charge of these areas. One of the keys to success in managing a project over time is establishing, and then monitoring, the incremental steps or goals that eventually lead to accomplishment of the project objective. Mastering the disciplines of self-assessing progress toward one's goals and taking action to stay on schedule results in tools that will be of great advantage throughout life—because, after all, life is a series of projects.

Teaching Strategies for Literary Analysis and Thematic Essays

In Benchmark's 1991 book (Gaskins & Elliot), we tell how Sharon Rauch introduced her students to "identifying the theme," a strategy they would use to keep track of infor-mation as they read a new novel. She defined *theme* as a label for a group or category of important ideas and explained that the important events in a story are related to theme. She asked her students why they thought a reader would look for themes when read-ing a novel. Students suggested that readers look for themes as a way to become actively involved in their reading and to think at a deeper level than just the surface facts in the novel. Mrs. Rauch told the group that the strategy of identifying the theme could be used in thinking about any good literature.

After reading several chapters of a book both in class and as homework, Mrs. Rauch's students brainstormed themes they remembered from books they had read during previous years and made predictions about themes that might be developed in the book they were reading. Next, they made a chart with a column for each of the themes they predicted. As they read the next day, students filled in events from the book that would support each of the theme categories. During discussion, based on their categorized notes, students suggested that one of the themes of the book was probably going to be "survival" because that was the category where they had put most of their notes. To support this theme, students cited specific instances in which the main character was able to survive. Mrs. Rauch asked them what message they thought the author was giving about survival. They concluded that the author's message was that having friends helps one survive. Mrs. Rauch also asked students if they had additional ideas or events listed under other themes, such as "good versus evil," "growing up," or "real versus supernatural." A few more ideas were shared.

Mrs. Rauch reminded students that any time they read good literature, they can look for themes. She reviewed the five steps they had learned to use. These steps are listed in Figure 13.8.

Over a decade later Benchmark's middle school teachers continue to teach their students how to identify themes. The major difference is that, due to a strong decoding program and a continually developing strategies program, our middle school students tend to be reading at higher levels than they were a decade ago. Therefore they are identifying themes in more sophisticated novels—and they love it. Students view identifying a theme as a mystery that they can solve if they are attentive to subtle clues in the text. One middle school student told me that the best part of learning about theme is his group's daily discussion about the chapter or chapters assigned for homework. Students arrive at the discussion table armed with notes jotted in columns that have possible themes as headings. Students share their nominee for the book's theme, then use their notes to provide evidence from the text to support it. (Benchmark teachers were using the term *evidence-based* long before No Child Left Behind legislation made the term popular.) Students enjoy debating possible themes and hold one another accountable for appropriate evidence, with many trips made back to the text to prove their points. (Notes contain the page number of the evidence.)

Mrs. Reisinger teaches theme as a vehicle for teaching second-year middle school students how to write clear, effective paragraphs. In order for students to recognize their growth in writing during the year, she asks students to read the same novel in September and again in late May, and on both occasions they are required to write a thematic essay about the novel. Students have been discussing and writing about

FIGURE 13.8. How to look for themes in literature.

How to Look for Themes in Literature	
SURVEY	Survey the title and chapter headings in search of clues to the theme.
BRAINSTORM	Brainstorm and predict possible themes based on background knowledge about the title, chapter headings, or other clues.
CHART	Set up a chart of possible themes to keep track of clues from the text.
READ	Read and gather clues.
CONNECT	Connect and summarize clues into a thematic essay.

From *Success with Struggling Readers* by Irene Gaskins. Copyright 2005 by The Guilford Press. See copyright page for photocopying limitations.

theme since their lower school years at Benchmark, so the September assignment is not regarded as too daunting. Nevertheless, the difference in their writing between fall and spring is amazing. How does she do it?

Mrs. Reisinger begins by explaining the rationale for taking notes and participating in group discussions of the novels the class analyzes for theme. She explains that their first thematic essay will be written in groups of three—one essay and one grade for each group. The grade each member earns will be the result of group cooperation and collaboration. Mrs. Reisinger goes on to point out the value of reading the assigned chapters nightly and coming to class prepared with notes for their group discussion. She also explicitly explains and models how to take notes related to theme and how to gain the most from participating in group discussions. Her framework for a paragraph on theme, shown in Figure 13.9, is the guideline she gives her class for writing their thematic paragraph on the novels they read. This paragraph is later expanded into a three-paragraph theme essay during the winter, then into a five-paragraph essay, usually by March of the school year. The framework is taken home each night and brought to school each day until it is well worn. Hardly a day goes by that Mrs. Reisinger or the students do not refer to it as they move from group writing of essays to individual writing, with a great deal of teacher and group support, and finally to essays written as independently as each student can handle.

On the day after the introduction of the project, and after students have read and taken notes about the first several chapters of the novel, she calls on several students to join her as the demonstration group. She tells the class that she will model how to participate in a discussion about theme. She demonstrates strategies for deciding which of

FIGURE 13.9. Framework for a paragraph on theme (as developed by Kristina Reisinger).

Introduction Sentence: States author, title,* and genre** of work.
Thesis Statement (TS): States theme, as shown through main character (MC).
(EX) 1st Supporting Statement (SS-1): States how the MC is in the beginning.
(EX) 1st Developing Statement (DS-1): Proves and explains SS-1 through quote or example.
—transition words—
(EX) 2nd Supporting Statement (SS-2): States the event/realization that makes the MC grow or change.
(EX) 2nd Developing Statement (DS-2): Proves and explains SS-2 through quote or example.
—transition words—
(EX) 3rd Supporting Statement (SS-3): States the lesson the MC can now apply or has learned as a result of event/realization.
(EX) 3rd Developing Statement (DS-3): Proves and explains SS-3 through quote or example.
Concluding Thesis Statement: Restates theme, as shown through MC.

*Short-story titles are set in quotation marks: "To Build a Fire," by Jack London
**Genre options include realistic fiction, historical fiction, fantasy, utopian fiction, science fiction, mystery, detective, and allegory.
EX, exposition; included only as needed so the reader can understand and follow along as the author explains the TS.

From *Success with Struggling Readers* by Irene Gaskins. Copyright 2005 by The Guilford Press. See copyright page for photocopying limitations.

the statements she makes, and those made by students, are closer to the truth, often using exact quotes from the text. She questions members of her group when she does not understand or agree with what they say, and she compares statements they make based on information in the text. Most importantly, she verbally reflects what she hears group members say to be sure she has interpreted correctly what she thought she heard. She models how to give group members feedback. Mrs. Reisinger is firm in her requirement that each student must take personal responsibility for the contents of the group's final essay. If a student does not agree with the final theme or supporting quotes, it is his or her job to disagree and provide reasons.

During the project Mrs. Reisinger repeatedly tells students that what she is asking them to do is hard: "This is even hard for us as adults! You shouldn't expect this kind of thinking to come easy. However, the challenge can be made easier by collaborating well—by listening with an open mind, by understanding what others are saying, and questioning them when you don't understand."

Students may hand in their paragraphs for feedback at any time throughout the year prior to the project's due date. Mrs. Reisinger meets with the group or individual after she has read the essay and gives students very specific feedback about the one aspect of the essay that needs the most work, or several aspects, if this amount of feedback would not seem overwhelming.

SUMMARY

Strategy instruction at Benchmark has an almost mystical aura to it because the use of strategies changes the lives of struggling readers—it changes struggling readers into successful students. Benchmark students know that when they apply strategies, their likelihood of success is high. This chapter told the story of the gradual progression of strategy instruction at Benchmark from first through eighth grade. The basic strategies introduced and practiced in our youngest classes provide the foundation for strategy instruction throughout the grades. Becoming strategic begins with several skills: surveying, accessing background knowledge, predicting, and setting a purpose, followed by learning to summarize, and make inferences.

Each of these strategies is expanded as students move to the intermediate grades. For example, students learn in greater depth how to take notes about important ideas, a strategy actually begun in the primary grades as part of the summarizing strategy. They learn to collect notes using charts and planning sheets and to organize those notes using concept maps, outlines, two-column note-taking schemes, and other organizational tools. Surveying the text and setting purposes point the way for note taking. Students also learn to make pictures in their minds (imagery) and how to identify themes in literature. Self-regulation is another huge category of strategies that receives attention in one form or another from the day a student enters Benchmark until the day he or she leaves. This emphasis is related to the important role of volition and the need to teach students metacognitive strategies to take charge of their learning, thinking, and problem solving.

The middle school emphasizes TSI as a way to orchestrate all the productive strategies students have learned (and perhaps invented) during their time at Benchmark. This approach is begun in the primary grades, but it comes to fruition in the middle school. The goal is for students to learn to independently apply and orchestrate the strategies they need to take charge of person, situation, task, and text variables to satisfactorily complete both short-term and long-term assignments. Two important aspects of achieving this goal are students' abilities to implement the analyze-the-task strategy and their ability to self-assess. Literary analysis and thematic essays are also introduced as one more way to prepare students for high school.

One of the greatest gifts a teacher can give his or her students is explicit explanations of how to complete the tasks that are assigned. The provision of explicit explanations, modeling, scaffolding, and ongoing opportunities for meaningful application of strategies paves the road to success for struggling readers.

CHAPTER 14

Rationale for Teaching Concepts, Essential Understandings, and Knowledge Structures

In this chapter I provide an overview of the Benchmark staff's and my current musings about how to teach declarative knowledge. We are not nearly as far along in our development of this conceptually based approach to teaching as we are in our understanding of how to teach struggling readers how to read and succeed in academic settings. We do, however, know that we are onto something exciting—a way of teaching students to learn that enables them to remember and understand big ideas and generate new knowledge as well. What we worry about is that this approach to learning may be so unconventional that our graduates will be discouraged from putting it into practice in many mainstream classrooms, despite their having experienced success with it while at Benchmark.

Psychologists usually refer to two basic kinds of knowledge, procedural and declarative. Procedural knowledge, the knowledge of how to do things, was discussed in Chapters 10 through 13. Declarative knowledge is the knowledge of *what*. It includes vocabulary knowledge, world and domain knowledge, linguistic knowledge, discourse knowledge, cognitive and metacognitive strategy knowledge, knowledge of the structure of domains, and even beliefs.

Knowledge is the grist for the mill of thought. It is the material one uses to think. All knowledge, however, does not have the same value for creating "lifelong learners, thinkers, and problem solvers," which is the goal of Benchmark School. A question we asked ourselves was, "Should we be teaching students the facts of the content areas such as social studies and science, or should we be teaching them essential understandings?" We wondered, "What kind of knowledge will be most valuable for students in the learning, thinking, and problem solving they will do in the future?"

Benchmark's research seminar studied these questions during the 1990s and concluded that, to achieve our goal of creating lifelong learners, thinkers, and problem solvers, we must focus on concepts and essential understandings and the knowledge structures they form (Shulman & Quinlan, 1996). This is in contrast to survey courses, with their breadth of coverage and memorization of facts, that are typical of classrooms at the beginning of the 21st century. In this chapter, I share our rationale for teaching students the concepts, essential understandings, and knowledge structures of content areas.

WHY TEACH CONCEPTS, ESSENTIAL UNDERSTANDINGS, AND KNOWLEDGE STRUCTURES?

Educators today are preparing young people for a world that is very different from the world the educators themselves experienced. Thus it stands to reason that the education experienced by today's young people must be different (Thornburg, 2002). Unfortunately, for the vast majority of students, it is not (Oakes & Lipton, 1999). "Less is more" is the mantra often heard but rarely heeded. Teachers still try to teach students all they think they will need to know to enjoy a fulfilling and successful life—an impossible task in view of the knowledge explosion of recent decades. For some time now, reformers have advocated that instruction be based on the realities of the 21st century and on research about how people learn (Brady, 1989). It is not appropriate now, if it ever was, to have acquisition of knowledge as the goal of schooling. Instead, the goal must be to provide students with the tools and essential understandings that provide a foundation for lifelong learning.

The ability and motivation to engage in lifelong learning is essential because as much as half of what is taught in classrooms today may be irrelevant or inaccurate by the time today's students enter the work world. Furthermore, new information is emerging at an exponential rate. Just one example is the tremendous rate of change in technology that makes it important to be able to learn an entirely new system as quickly as possible. Many jobs of the future have yet to be invented; thus young people will need to be learning as jobs are being invented. As Thornburg (2002) states: "The only certainty is change. The challenge for educational institutions is to prepare their students for the years to come without knowing exactly what the future holds" (p. 84). Lifelong learning is the only effective coping strategy for change.

Undoubtedly, some students will become lifelong learners by disposition, and they will figure out, on their own, the skills, strategies, and core concepts they need. However, figuring out skills, strategies, and concepts on their own is not a familiar scenario for children who have struggled with learning to read. Those of us who teach struggling readers need to search for ways to explicitly teach students how to acquire the knowledge, skills, strategies, and dispositions they need to become lifelong learners. In this chapter I review and explore factors related to achieving this goal, with particular emphasis on two areas we have not previously explored: understanding the structure of the concepts and essential understandings that comprise each knowledge domain, and knowing how these knowledge-domain structures are related to text and genre structures of diverse texts and hypertexts.

Strategies instruction received major emphasis at Benchmark during the late 1980s and early 1990s, although the seeds of a conceptually based program in social studies and science were also being sown. During school year 1990–1991 Eleanor Gensemer and I co-taught a social studies class composed of sixth and seventh graders who were

reading on third- through fifth-reader levels. The class began the year reading and discussing the first chapter of a middle school American history text, a chapter about
Native Americans. The chapter was divided into the regions of the United States in
which Native Americans lived (i.e., Northeast, Southeast, Plains, Northwest, Southwest). This regional approach, supplemented by a host of easy-reading books about
Native Americans, provided the focus and content for our course. In preparation for
comparing the Native Americans from different regions, we discussed with students
the geographic characteristics of the region in which each group lived. By November,
someone suggested that the geography of a region seemed to determine the way each
Native American group lived. Students shared that wooded mountains and rivers
bounded by the Atlantic Ocean provided the impetus for birch bark canoes, clothes
made of animal skins, and fishing and hunting, whereas the sun-baked clay cliffs and
arid land of the Southwest led to quite a different way of life with cliff dwellings, pueb-
los, and some farming.

It seemed to be a revelation to these middle school students that all Native Americans did not live in tepees and hunt buffalo. The revelation for their teachers was the
power of a conceptually focused principle. We decided to test the hypothesis that the
geography of a region influences how people live. We did this by studying the geography of the region where the Mayan culture once flourished (Yucatan and Guatemala).
After studying the geography of the region, and without reading about the Mayans,
students predicted that the Mayans would develop an advanced society because geographic conditions were so favorable. As students read about the Mayans, they
delighted in locating evidence that confirmed their prediction. Students wondered
whether the notion of relating geography to the way people lived was true only of
Native Americans, so in January we decided to put American history aside and study
the geography of the region bounded by the Tigris and Euphrates Rivers. We had spent
only a few days investigating the geography when students correctly predicted the
development of an advanced civilization in this area once known as Babylonia.

Our students had combined two concepts, geography and adaptation, to form the
principle, or essential understanding, that geography influences the way people live
and the civilization that develops in a specific region. It was now the beginning of February. Our students were motivated by their discovery and wanted to study other
regions of the world. For the remainder of the year students applied the concept that
geography influences the way people live as we studied the geography and development of Egypt, the Middle East, Greece, and Italy. Rather than memorize facts about
history, students constructed their own history of ancient civilizations based on an
essential understanding about the two concepts of geography and adaptation. And,
because this history was based on one core understanding or principle that acted as a
magnet for major concepts, these students were able to reconstruct and remember the
concepts time and time again. Topics and text were no longer at the center of instruction, concepts and essential understandings were. Students were not the only ones
developing essential understandings. We were too!

About the same time our notion of core understandings was emerging, we read
What's Worth Teaching by Marion Brady (1989). He reminded us that learning theorists
believe that teaching for understanding requires the building of conceptual structures
and that "certain very powerful ideas should be introduced early and developed year
after year" (p. 2). Brady went on to state that "great thinkers have said for centuries that

everything is related to everything else, yet we organize instruction so as to send just the opposite message" (p. 2). We also read *Elementary School Science for the '90's* by Loucks-Horsley and her colleagues (Loucks-Horsley et al., 1990). Again we found the admonition to focus on concepts because they "provide a framework for elementary science curriculums, which students can use to integrate facts and experiences. They promote greater understanding from fewer topics, through depth rather than breadth" (p. 17). Interestingly, similar views have been expressed more recently (e.g., Linn, Songer, & Eylon, 1996; Penner, 2001–2002). In fact, these current researchers lament that not much has changed in the past decade. As Penner (2001–2002) notes, science instruction "typically focuses on accumulating facts and formulas" (p. 1).

In 1991–1992, with renewed funding from the James S. McDonnell Foundation to develop a learning, thinking, and problem-solving curriculum in science, we initiated a conceptually based approach to science for two middle school classes. The essential understandings emphasized the first year included "energy and matter are neither created nor destroyed" and "all systems are interrelated; a change in one affects the rest." We were excited to learn at the end of the first year of this project that students' conceptual understanding and application of specific science principles had increased significantly (Gaskins et al., 1994).

The following year I collaborated with science coordinator Joyce Ostertag to extend the project to develop a schoolwide science curriculum, organized around a few essential understandings, that would help students understand the relationships and themes that undergird scientific knowledge. The goal of the curriculum was for students to view science as connected and organized, rather than as a basket of facts to be memorized and dumped on an exam sheet. Our curriculum goal would be accomplished by identifying a few essential understandings to serve as focal points for collaborative problem solving and discussions about information students constructed from texts, experiments, and other resources. We wanted students to realize that learning is aided by organizing, connecting, and restructuring knowledge around powerful ideas. For example, students discovered that they were able to solve a fictitious health problem located in one body system (circulatory) when they applied the principle, learned in a science ecosystems unit, that "all systems are interrelated; a change in one system affects the rest" (Gaskins, Satlow, Hyson, Ostertag, & Six, 1994). As the principle suggests, a problem in the circulatory system is likely to affect other body systems, just as problems in other body systems are likely to affect the circulatory system.

A particularly helpful resource during our initial attempt to develop a science curriculum around essential concepts and understandings (principles) was Rutherford and Ahlgren's (1990) book *Science for All Americans*. The common concepts they recommended introducing in science classes were *systems*, *models*, *constancy* and *change*, and *scale*. We expanded these to design a science curriculum around six concepts: *systems*, *adaptations*, *conservation*, *constancy*, *models*, and *classification*. The essential understandings derived from these concepts, around which our science curriculum was developed, are outlined in Figure 14.1.

Teaching with an emphasis on concepts and essential understandings just made good sense to us. Therefore, at the conclusion of our second 3-year James S. McDonnell research and development project, we decided to develop a schoolwide, conceptually based approach to teaching social studies. During the year 1997–1998, regularly scheduled staff meetings were held to study professional literature related to important con-

FIGURE 14.1. Essential understandings in science.

Systems	Adaptations	Conservation	Constancy	Models	Classification
Each part of a system has a special job to keep the whole system functioning. The parts of a system are interdependent; a change in one part will affect the whole system. Technology can be used as part of a system to keep it functioning.	Cells/organisms have special parts and behaviors to help them survive. All living things need to have food and oxygen, to protect themselves from their environment and their enemies, and to reproduce. Organisms grow and develop over time.	Matter and energy within a system can transfer and change form, but total levels of matter and energy remain the same. Matter and energy cannot be created or destroyed. The surface of the earth is always changing. Everything on earth operates in cycles.	Matter and energy have characteristic properties and behaviors.	Models can explain behavior: Microlevel behavior explains macro-level behavior. All matter is made of molecules; a molecular model can explain behavior of matter and energy. A wave model can explain behavior of energy. An electron model can explain behavior of electricity. Plate tectonics can explain changes on earth. A model of cells can explain growth.	Actions and objects have similarities and differences; thus, they can be grouped in categories.

From *Success with Struggling Readers* by Irene Gaskins. Copyright 2005 by The Guilford Press. See copyright page for photocopying limitations.

cepts in social studies and history and to identify essential understandings that we would like to develop in our grades 1–8 social studies program. Once again Joyce Ostertag played a leadership role in developing this program. Some of the essential understandings discussed in our lower school social studies program can be found in Figure 14.2.

In addition, we decided to look at history through six lenses (concepts) or points of view similar to those recommended by Leinhardt and colleagues (Leinhardt, Stainton, Virji, & Odoroff, 1994). We labeled our lenses (1) values and beliefs, (2) social factors, (3) technology, (4) economics, (5) government, and (6) geography. Leinhardt et al.'s lenses included political, social, scientific, and economic domains. (Leinhardt et al. define

FIGURE 14.2. Essential understandings in social studies.

	1. People's ideas change the way people live.
	2. Groups of people have the same basic needs that are met in different ways.
	3. Geography affects the way we live.
	4. People explore new lands for economic reasons.
	5. Inventions lead to changes in society.
	6. Strongly held values and beliefs cause people to take action that brings about change.
	7. Differences in values and beliefs often lead to conflict.
	8. When groups of people need or want the same resources, these needs and wants often lead to conflict.
	9. What is happening within a country determines its relationship with other countries and people.
	10. Government is necessary to balance the needs of the individual with the good of the people.

From *Success with Struggling Readers* by Irene Gaskins. Copyright 2005 by The Guilford Press. See copyright page for photocopying limitations.

history as "a discipline that is framed by chronology and geography" [p. 156], whereas we include geography as one of our lenses.) Our goal was to create an analytic, constructivist, problem-solving approach to developing essential understandings about history's stories, time frames, and places.

STUDENT OUTCOMES AND NEXT STEPS

During the 18 years since we initiated a strategies-across-the-curriculum program for struggling readers, followed closely by a conceptually based approach to teaching in the content areas, we continued to follow the progress of our graduates as they moved on to high school and college (see, e.g., Murphy, 1996.) We have discovered that our graduates stand out in the minds of their teachers in their receiving schools (i.e., schools they attend after graduating from our program) as good self-advocates and as exceptionally strategic learners. Most of our graduates, particularly those in the past 18 years, have been more successful as learners and students than is predicted for children who have struggled with learning to read. Still, we wonder if they could have been even more successful. Realizing that knowledge is a conceptual scaffold for subsequent learning (Alexander, 2000), we now wonder if we spent enough time guiding students in how to build and recognize knowledge structures and in how to apply cognitive and metacognitive strategies to a wide variety of text structures.

Currently, we are revisiting our approach for helping students construct knowledge by asking the question: "What should we be doing more of, or differently, to provide students with a framework for lifelong learning?" Our hunch is that we could enhance students' learning by doing a more precise job of choosing and introducing students to the concepts, essential understandings, and characteristic structures of each domain, such as the domains of physical science, biology, history, social studies, and literature. Looking at concepts, essential understandings, and characteristic domain structures would fit with what we know about the brain as a pattern seeker. The purpose of the remainder of this chapter is to explore the hunch that there is more we can do to help students discover and apply concepts, essential understandings, and the inherent structures in knowledge as they read and learn from a plethora of text types.

A REVIEW OF THE LITERATURE

Learning and Understanding

What learning and understanding goals do we have in mind when we say we want students to become lifelong learners? Can we say that students have learned something when they are able to tell us a lot of information about a topic? Probably not, for it is the quality and discipline of thought processes, not the amount of information about a subject, that separates the expert from the nonexpert (Strong, Silver, & Perini, 2001). Learning is about something more than knowing a lot. Admittedly, an important first step in learning is being able to locate relevant information. However, learning is also about much more than locating or retrieving information. Learning is about building multiple representations of each concept and generating useful, sophisticated, and personally meaningful connections between and among concepts (Caine & Caine, 1994).

Learning means being able to explain, exemplify, generalize, analogize. It also involves manipulating knowledge, including the classification, organization, storage, and retrieval of knowledge (Prawat, 1991).

Genuine learning, or learning with understanding, is demonstrated by (1) explaining a concept in one's own words, (2) including novelty in one's explanation, (3) exceeding the information given, and (4) relating the new information to other information. What counts most in demonstrating understanding is knowing how to *use* knowledge (Perkins, 1991).

Learning with understanding requires both knowledge of concepts and knowledge of strategies for taking charge of thinking processes and affect (Alexander & Jetton, 2000; Bransford, Brown, & Cocking, 2000; Prawat, 1993). I have dealt extensively with strategic processing and affect in earlier chapters; here I concentrate on the concepts and structure of domains of knowledge. My goal is to gain insight into what the staff can share with students that will allow them to discover the secrets that each domain holds.

Concepts

A concept is "a category or class of things with shared commonalities" (Tomlison, 1998, p. 5). Stated another way, a person's concept of something is his or her understanding of it, which often corresponds to a larger societal conception; it is a rule for deciding whether an item is a member of a particular category (Pressley, 1995). In a book about designing curriculum around concepts, Erickson (2001) defines concept as "a mental construct that is timeless, universal, and abstract" (p. 25) and explains that concepts are a higher level of abstraction than facts.

Others have developed programs based on concepts (e.g., Guthrie et al., 1996). However, in these projects the goal was to use concepts that were common to several content areas to integrate several areas of the curriculum. In addition, the focus was on conceptual themes rather than on developing essential understandings.

What concepts should we teach? Are the concepts we have chosen powerful concepts for developing the essential understandings that will provide a foundation for lifelong learning? We are currently addressing these questions. Rutherford and Ahlgren (1990) suggest four concepts that "transcend disciplinary boundaries": These are systems, models, constancy and change, and scale. Tomlinson (1998) lists 11 generic concepts, only two of which are the same as those suggested by Rutherford and Ahlgren (1990). A third set of possibilities is provided by Erickson (2001), who includes concepts that are common to science, social studies, and literature. Surprisingly, only one of Erickson's concepts makes the list of generic concepts suggested in the other two sources (see Figure 14.3 for a comparison).

Are there major concepts that are generic and transcend disciplinary boundaries? If there are, it might be beneficial to expect students to demonstrate an understanding of these concepts as they relate to each domain. However, mastery of just the few generic concepts that may transcend boundaries does not appear to be a sufficient guideline for selecting concepts that students should understand. Of greater interest to us at Benchmark are concepts that are unique to each domain, for we believe that to have power in a domain, students must thoroughly understand essential domain-specific concepts (Tomlinson et al., 2002).

FIGURE 14.3. Concepts that may transcend disciplinary boundaries.

Rutherford & Ahlgren (1990)	Tomlinson (1998)	Erickson (2001)
Systems	Systems	
Constancy and change	Change	Change
Models		
Scale		
	Interdependence	
	Pattern	
	Group and individual	
	Values	
	Structure and function	
	Freedom and responsibility	
	Relationships	
	Power	
	Conflict	
		Cause–effect
		Order
		Interaction
		Evolution
		Cycle

From *Success with Struggling Readers* by Irene Gaskins. Copyright 2005 by The Guilford Press. See copyright page for photocopying limitations.

What are some examples of domain-specific concepts? Tomlinson (1998) suggests such concepts as tempo in music, perspective in art, pollution in science, right to privacy in government, characterization in literature, and culture in social studies. Erickson (2001) suggests that *energy, matter, equilibrium,* and *force* are concepts unique to science, while also including *systems* and *population* as important concepts for both science and social studies. Some subject-specific concepts Erickson includes for social studies are *culture, civilization, migration/immigration, conflict/cooperation, innovation,* and *beliefs/values.*

Acknowledging that (1) each domain of knowledge is organized around mostly unique concepts and the essential understandings judged by experts in that field to be at the core of that domain (Alexander & Jetton, 2000) and (2) that each domain of knowledge has its own idiosyncratic organizational properties (Bransford et al., 2000) suggests that we should be teaching these concepts, principles, and organizational properties. It would appear that to understand a domain, students need information about the conceptual underpinnings of the domain and the principles that tie the concepts together (Odden & Kelley, 2002), as well as to understand how knowledge is structured in the domain (Caine & Caine, 1994; Shulman, 1986). Some would even suggest that each domain requires a different mindset and different strategies (Donald, 2002).

Essential Understandings

A domain is a network of big ideas or concepts. An important learning goal is for the student to build a domain-specific conceptual framework by looking for the connections between concepts. These connections form the essential understandings or principles that tie the concepts together. A principle is a statement of truth about a concept—a rule that governs how the concept functions (Tomlinson, 1998). Two examples of principles suggested by Tomlinson (1998) are "Authors use characters to establish points of view" and "Change has both a cause and an effect" (p. 6). A few principles or essential understandings suggested by Erickson (2001) for a first-grade social studies program include "Values and beliefs guide the decisions in a family," "Family members work to meet needs and wants," and "Rules establish order in a family" (p. 119). Examples of principles for a fourth-grade social studies unit include "Differing values and economic concerns and/or interests can create tension and conflict between individuals, groups, or nations"; "Incentives, values, traditions, and habits influence economic decisions"; and "The physical environment affects where and how people in a region live" (pp. 123–124). What we have discussed above as principles, sometimes called essential understandings or enduring understandings, form the framework of a domain. The ability to use the core principles of a domain reflects the highest level of understanding; thus it stands to reason that learning core principles should be the goal of instruction in each domain.

Structures of Knowledge Domains

In addition to learning core principles, we want students to know that knowledge has structure (Perkins, 1986) and to learn how structures of knowledge differ among domains, influence learning, and what processes of thinking are important in each.

Knowledge Structures

The knowledge structure of a domain is composed of concepts and their relationships. This structure differs according to the domain, discipline, or content area. The knowledge structures described here are based on the research of Donald (2002). For example, the structure of the sciences, such as physics and chemistry, tends to be hierarchical, with branches from more to less important concepts and with more links between them than found in most domains, suggesting tighter relationships, whereas in the social sciences, webs or clusters of concepts link to a pivotal concept. In the humanities, a linear or loose block is more common, and concepts tend to stand on their own.

Although the sciences tend to be more tightly structured than other disciplines, content areas within the sciences also differ in structure. For example, physics and chemistry concepts are tightly structured, yet "a physicist's scientific background is based on deductive solutions (law to particular instances), whereas the chemist's is based on inductive solutions (instances to law)" (Donald, 2002, p. 98). Biology, on the other hand, is more divergent in the phenomena it studies, its methods, and its knowledge structures.

The humanities embrace history and literature. English literature is usually regarded as a soft, limitless, or unbounded discipline. This discipline is organized around the "production of consensual knowledge arrived at through contention rather than the empirical testing of theories as in the sciences" (Donald, 2002, p. 236). Literature goes beyond the cognitive and includes affective aspects of interaction and emotion. Contrary to most other domains, in literary studies the meaning of the text lies in the individual. A piece of literature also yields different insights depending on the questions put to it. The unit of analysis in literature is the text—in most disciplines, it is the concept.

More important than memorizing facts is searching for the essential understandings that are at the core of each content area, as these girls are doing in a math class.

Relationship between Structures and Learning

To understand a discipline, one must first understand the conceptual framework. The structure of each discipline cues students to important concepts and their relationships. The kinds of relationships are cues to the thought processes or strategies required to comprehend the material. The key concepts provide ideational scaffolding for learning. The goal of discussions and activities in the content areas should be to help students develop a conceptual framework for the content area being studied. For example, students should see tightly structured topics, such as physical science, as a coherent system, rather than attempt to memorize facts as if the discipline were a collection of isolated pieces.

As a result of different structures for different content areas, *knowing* takes on different meanings in each discipline. Therefore, students need to be flexible in their approach to each academic discipline. One thinking process or approach will not fit all content areas. For example, in the domain of literature, a text may yield different insights to different people; however, in a more tightly structured content area, such as physics or chemistry, the content leaves little room for debate. In literature the texts do not contain all the elements needed for understanding; thus the reader must infer as well as integrate separate textual elements. In more tightly structured disciplines, such as the sciences, important ideas are more salient and consistently agreed upon.

Not only do disciplines differ in structure, they differ in the kind of language used, the preferred criteria for validating knowledge, and the most pronounced method of inquiry (Donald, 2002). These differences make it apparent that students will need to know how to learn differently in each discipline, and they will need to understand each discipline by learning the structure, perspectives, and processes of the discipline.

Match between Thinking Processes and Structures of Knowledge

Because all disciplines do not have the same structure, learning and knowing take on different meanings in different contexts, and students must be guided to recognize these differences. However, common to all disciplines is the fact that students need to be actively and deeply engaged, learn the vocabulary of each discipline, and demonstrate reflectivity. Additional keys to success in all disciplines include motivation, self-regulation, and control over the learning environment. Most disciplines are organized around concepts and their relationships, necessitating that students search for and understand these patterns of conceptual relationships. Students also need to acquire discipline-specific thinking processes that enable them to understand tightly and logically structured, as well as loosely structured, disciplines. For example, because the sciences tend to be hierarchical in structure, it makes sense to learn concepts in order. In contrast, the social sciences tend to be organized around key concepts; thus learning can be enhanced by recognizing those key concepts and understanding the relationships between concepts, as is done in constructing a concept map. In the humanities the focus tends to be on individual concepts, with links (if any) that are less obvious.

One striking difference between the disciplines is the degree to which idiosyncratic interpretation of text is tolerated. In literature, much of the meaning of the text lies in the individual, whereas in other disciplines, meaning is judged by much more stringent rules. The unit of analysis in most disciplines is the concept. In literature the unit of analysis is larger and more complex; it is the text, "a unit of thought that allows us to organize experience" (Donald, 2002, p. 242). Text encompasses the idea of logical structure or schema. The openness of text structure in literature contrasts with most content-area domains. Because literature texts do not contain all the elements needed for their comprehension, the reader must infer from his or her world knowledge in order to make sense of the material. In literature there is no explicit or systematic framework that links the terms used in critical discourse to well-defined properties of text (Donald, 2002). Literary theory can provide a working framework for the analysis of text, but the framework consists of open and nondiscrete procedures rather than rigorous methods used in the sciences. Furthermore, understanding literature is made more challenging by the fact that students often lack the Biblical and classical background upon which the domain is predicated.

So how does one match thinking processes to reading literature? Donald (2002) suggests that understanding literature requires "close reading, following the steps of an argument, and modeling different forms of literary criticism" (p. 270). In contrast, one approach to learning history is to interpret events from the viewpoints of political, social, scientific, and economic perspectives, as framed by time and geography (Leinhardt et al., 1994). In the case of the sciences, the approach involves understanding principles and the hierarchical framework more than interpreting the text, as occurs in the humanities.

Knowledge Structure, Genre Structure, and Text Structure

Currently researchers speak of at least three kinds of structures when they talk about the rules of organization underlying written forms: (1) domain-specific knowledge structure, (2) genre structure, and (3) text structure. Text structure has the most longevity in schools. In the past, educators have suggested that students, especially those in fourth grade and above, should be taught the "commonly found" text structures of nonfiction texts. Editors Harris and Hodges (1995) identify these as expository, problem–solution, cause–effect, comparison–contrast, description, and sequence. Teachers often comment that authors of content-area texts alternate the type of text structure a dizzying number of times within a chapter or text, causing them to question whether teaching students to identify text structures is a worthwhile endeavor. This is not to say that there are not educators who still see a value in teaching text structure, suggesting that we should keep an open mind. For example, Rhoder (2002) extols the value of being able to identify, represent, and use the structure of a text. There is an implication that any piece of expository text has one text structure. The three structures a school text might have, according to Rhoder, are cause and effect, compare and contrast, and time order. She introduces the text structure strategy using "well-organized, tightly written texts" (p. 502). At Benchmark we have tried that, too; but, as stated above, students rarely encounter well-organized, tightly-written texts.

In contrast to those who support a text-structure view, genre theorists believe the purpose of the text (e.g., procedural, narrative, explanatory) determines the organization of the entire text. The genres of nonfiction text, especially of science trade books written for the primary grades, is a relatively new interest among researchers. For example, the research of Smolkin and Donovan (e.g., Donovan & Smolkin, 2001; Smolkin & Donovan, 2002) and Duke and colleagues (Duke, 2000; Purcell-Gates & Duke, 2001; Pearson & Duke, 2002) suggests there may be value in students being aware of the characteristics that differentiate genres within nonfiction, and even within a specific domain of nonfiction such as science.

Langer (2001), in her study of middle school and high school students who "beat the odds," reported that teachers guided students to make connections between important concepts as a way of helping them develop well-organized knowledge. The focus of her study was the conceptual structures of knowledge. Langer's research suggests that it may be important for teachers to guide students to be aware of and understand concepts, essential understandings, and domain-specific knowledge structures.

Do students need to be aware of all three structures discussed—knowledge, genre, and text? We think not, particularly if the goal is to understand concepts and essential understandings. We have a hunch that teaching students text structures, as defined in Harris and Hodges (1995), might have the least payoff for our students. We see value in teaching genre structures as a scaffold for writing and wonder whether teaching genre structures via writing instruction would contribute to students' understanding and use of concepts. One point on which we are sure is that we want to teach students to look for the organizing concepts, essential understandings, and domain-specific knowledge structures from which they can construct conceptual networks. This conceptual approach would seem to move students away from text as authority to students as authority in understanding and using knowledge.

POSSIBILITIES FOR INSTRUCTION

This review of the literature suggests that there probably is more that could be done in U.S. classrooms to prepare students to be lifelong learners. Certainly an explicit teaching of concepts and strategies is essential. However, an area of instruction that has not received much classroom attention is that of making students aware of how concepts and essential understandings are organized in each knowledge domain and how to use an awareness of knowledge structures to read and learn in a plethora of text types. In fact, we have only begun this process in earnest at Benchmark during the past decade.

Most educators would agree that an important goal of instruction is to teach in a way that guides students to become aware of major concepts and their connections in specific domains. However, the recommendations for how to accomplish this are many, and there is no definitive research upon which to base a decision. For example, in teaching literature, Silva and Delgado-Larocco (1993) suggest developing conceptually related literature units with the goal of helping students better understand the literary piece, themselves, and the world around them. They suggest that, through the study of literature that has similar conceptual generalizations, universal generalizations are developed. This approach focuses on the identification of concepts and universal generalizations rather than activities. The goal of such a literature unit is for students to construct and test universal generalizations as well as to develop a better understanding of themselves and the world around them.

In teaching social studies integrated with language arts, Roser and Keehn (2002) suggest a topic-driven approach in which fourth-grade students learn about the Texas Revolution (a social studies topic) by reading and discussing topic-related literature in a book-club fashion. These discussions lead to student-generated questions that are researched and discussed in small inquiry groups, using informational texts. The goal of the Roser–Keehn project was to use discussion to foster good thinking; specifically, for students to be willing to question, suspend judgment, entertain alternative views, tolerate ambiguity, raise the level of discourse, and pose and support hypotheses. These are all laudable goals, but the Roser–Keehn approach would not be an example of a conceptually driven program; instead, it is topic driven.

From each of these approaches what might we recommend to our teachers as steps toward developing lifelong learners? In our presentation of the Texas Revolution, students gained information about Sam Houston by integrating the study of literature and social studies. They also put into practice some very important thinking and reasoning strategies. In the Silva and Delgado-Larocco (1993) units, students addressed the universality of the notion of *self-concept* by reading books with a similar theme. Which, if either, program to emulate depends on the teacher's goal. If the goal is introducing students to the concepts, skills, strategies, and dispositions of lifelong learners, while also developing an awareness of the structure of knowledge and how to navigate different genre, neither of these approaches goes far enough, yet each has its strengths. One introduces students to concepts, whereas the other focuses on thoughtful discussion. As Langer (2001) commented, it is a matter of "What counts as knowing" (p. 843). One decision is between a focus on facts and concepts. The other is whether to focus on students' abilities to think about and use new knowledge. Langer (2001) speaks of helping students learn to better approximate expert thinking, such as "thinking like an historian," and contrasts it with a focus on "higher levels of cognitive manipulation of the material" (p. 843). Is one goal more important than the other? Is there research that suggests which approach will provide students with the best foundation for becoming lifelong learners? Donovan and Smolkin's work (2001) would suggest that stories may not be the best way to develop conceptual networks about important concepts in science and social studies.

Perhaps as suggested by Smolkin and Donovan (2002), a good way to introduce young children to the intricacies of informational text genres is to have interactive read-alouds using informational text. In this approach it is the teacher's responses to students that determine the effectiveness of the approach. The goal is that "children's initiations, efforts at meaning, are *extended* and key points of comprehension *revealed* by their teachers" (p. 145). The goal is to build on the connections children make between the text and their lives, schemas, and other texts to extend their reasoning. It is the belief of these authors that "different types of texts call for different types (and amounts) of comprehension activity" (p. 148).

Clearly there are many opinions and not enough empirical data to make definitive statements about the best way to teach declarative knowledge. However, grounded in research-based principles of learning, the Benchmark staff is currently developing a program for teaching in the content areas that has at its core three ingredients: concepts, essential understandings, and knowledge structures. This approach contrasts with those based on thematic units across domains. We question whether such units are the best way to teach declarative knowledge, in view of the fact that it is the unique concepts, understandings, and knowledge structures of a domain that support organizing and learning in a domain.

SUMMARY

In this chapter I explored the rationale for replacing detail-oriented, traditional ways of teaching in the content areas with an approach that emphasizes concepts, essential understandings, and knowledge structures. This approach fits with what we know about the brain as a pattern seeker. Furthermore, it is a well-established principle of learning that students remember more of what they learn if they are taught to look for, and organize information around, essential understandings and knowledge structures. Benchmark students find this approach motivating and feel they have been let in on an important secret of learning. They regard an essential understanding as a magnet for related information and therefore find learning in the content areas less effortful than it was in the past. They are learning what psychologists have known for some time, that the most durable form of knowledge is at the conceptual level (Prawat, 1989).

Included in this chapter was a review of the literature regarding the efforts of others to explore the use of concepts, essential understandings, and knowledge structures as frameworks for learning. Although there certainly is no consensus, there is also no doubt that educators and researchers see promise in conceptually based teaching. We not only foresee the promise, we have experienced it. An added bonus is that our students find that conceptually-based teaching provides a more interesting way to learn than the approaches to learning declarative knowledge they experienced in the past.

Afterword

Five Major Insights from 45 Years of Teaching Struggling Readers

As a result of learning from, and working with, hundreds of top researchers and classroom teachers during the past 45 years, I have had a unique opportunity to learn about what works in teaching struggling readers. There is no doubt that Benchmark enjoys the success that it does with struggling readers because my staff and I have been able to stand on the shoulders of the giants in the field of reading. In this chapter I share five major insights that I have gained from my years as a reading teacher, psychologist, and director of a school for struggling readers. They are insights that have had a profound impact on practice at Benchmark School. I hope they will impact your practice, as well.

TEACHERS, NOT MATERIALS, DETERMINE SUCCESS IN LEARNING TO READ

Looking back on my first experiences as a teacher of reading, I am now absolutely convinced that many children learn to read *in spite of* teachers. How else can I explain the success of the children I taught? In my early days as a reading teacher I wanted to believe that as long as I put hours into planning and followed the basal manual, I was doing the best I could for my students. That rationalization, however, did not prevent me from worrying and wondering about those students who were not making progress in learning to read.

In my first year teaching reading in a school near the oil refineries on the Delaware River, I struck up a friendship with the first-grade teacher who taught in the room next to mine. I had heard that *all* of her students learned to read by the time they left her class. I wanted to find out how she did this and what materials she used. Her answers to my initial inquiries surprised me. Mrs. T said that she had studied many teachers' manuals and theories of how to teach reading and used a few of the ideas from each.

Her belief was that, if she exposed her students to many different approaches to learning to read, each student would implement the approach that worked for him or her.

Mrs. T shared a few other secrets as well. One was that, except for the 45 minutes
she devoted to math, she taught reading and writing for the entire day. I was pledged
to secrecy about the fact that she had not yet taken from her shelves the social studies
and science texts she inherited from the first-grade teacher who had preceded her. I
remember that when I visited Mrs. T on several occasions during her afternoon recess
period, I found 8 or 10 students in the classroom busily writing—not because they had
to, but because they asked to stay in to finish what they were writing. Mrs. T's first
graders loved to write—and they loved to read to one another what they had written!

Other of Mrs. T's secrets included the caring relationship that she had with each
student and the vast amount of reading each student completed every day. Clearly
each of her students felt safe and knew that he or she was a reader who was special to
Mrs. T. It was not unusual for Mrs. T to send one or two of her students to my classroom to read to me, sometimes from a story they had written and sometimes from an
old basal reader. Mrs. T collected discarded beginning reading materials and used them
as anthologies. The reading material did not matter to her, as long as it was written at a
level her students could handle independently. The goal for each student was to do a
lot of reading.

Even at this early stage of my development as a teacher, it was beginning to dawn
on me that teachers, not materials, determine children's success in learning to read.
This fact was confirmed by the First Grade Reading Studies (Bond & Dykstra, 1967)
and later by the Beating the Odds studies (Taylor, Pearson, Clark, & Walpole, 2000).
Successful teachers such as Mrs. T establish positive relationships with their students;
they know a lot about educational research, theory, and child development; and they
continue to learn. They instinctively know that there is no one best way to teach reading. They use a variety of methods and materials and provide explicit and scaffolded
instruction that is paced to each student's rate of learning and geared to where each
student is and how he or she learns.

CHILDREN FALL BEHIND IN READING
FOR MANY DIFFERENT REASONS

There is almost never just one reason why a child is struggling in reading. Some students struggle in learning to read because there is a mismatch between how they learn
and the way they are taught. For example, in the early years of Benchmark School, most
of the local school districts were using synthetic approaches to teaching decoding in
first grade. Students were taught the match between sounds and letters by participating in drills, memorizing rules, and completing workbook or worksheet exercises. I had
a son in first grade at the time who has a great ear for sound differences in language.
He easily mastered the sound–letter matches and their accompanying rules and was
reading stacks of preprimers by Thanksgiving. Unfortunately, some of his equally intelligent classmates, and students in other local first grades, were not experiencing similar
success in learning to read using a synthetic phonics program. They seemed unable to
hear sound differences in words, particularly for vowels (e.g., the differences between

the vowel sounds in *car* and *cat*; *school* and *look*). At that time, we jokingly called Benchmark a school for fallout from synthetic phonics.

However, this was not the only difficulty these students exhibited. There was no doubt that the problems our struggling readers were having in learning to read were the result of person, situation, task, and text variables interacting to cause and exacerbate difficulties in learning to read. For example, we seemed to have more than our share of students who exhibited maladaptive cognitive styles. Some were inattentive, others were passive, some were inflexible, and still others were impulsive or lacked persistence. We also enrolled some students who were attentive, actively involved, flexible, reflective, and persistent, yet still exhibited severe difficulty in learning to read. Our students were actually more different than alike!

THERE IS MORE TO TEACHING STRUGGLING READERS THAN TEACHING READING

Teaching struggling readers how to decode and comprehend well does not ensure that they will succeed when placed back in the mainstream. In fact, it is not unusual for "recovered" students who have achieved the median in reading of their regular classroom peers to regress when returned to mainstream classrooms. One reason this regression occurs is because it takes years of scaffolded practice for newly acquired skills and strategies to become automatic, particularly as applied to reading in the content areas.

Another reason that students who once struggled in reading have difficulty successfully returning to the mainstream is because programs for struggling readers tend

The number of words read correlates with progress in reading; therefore, students make frequent trips to the library to stock up on books.

to deal only with deficits in reading skills and strategies. Our theory at Benchmark is that for struggling readers ultimately to meet with success in the mainstream, teachers must not only teach reading, but they must deal with what got a student in trouble in the first place, as well as the student's response to that difficulty. The "what got a student in trouble in the first place" is most often an interaction between a number of person, situation, task, and text variables. For example, it may be as simple as an interaction between the approach used in teaching decoding and the way a student processes sounds. On the other hand, it may be as complicated as an interaction between some aspect of the student's temperament and much that is not going right in the student's classroom and home environments. The possibilities for what got a student in trouble in the first place are much more numerous than merely the need for a second chance to begin again at the beginning of learning to read—although that does seem to be the only problem for a few of our students.

Once Benchmark students appear to function well in the application of reading and writing skills, there are two key characteristics they need to demonstrate in order to be successful in the mainstream; self-regulation and self-advocacy. By *self-regulation* I mean knowing and using the strategies of metacognition, including self-monitoring mental processing and taking action to repair confusion in reading, understanding, and learning. As part of this process, students regulate strategies, motivation, volition, affect, and style. By *self-advocacy* I mean that students know when they need support and are willing to take action to obtain the help that they need. For example, when a concept is discussed and a student does not understand it, he or she is willing to risk asking for clarification in class, or to stay after class to discuss the concern with the teacher, or to collaborate with peers to develop an understanding of the concept. Students who are self-advocates ask for and pursue whatever support they need to understand, learn, and complete projects well and on time. Often that means calling on others for help.

Expert educators become experts by continually seeking evidence-based answers to questions about how to better meet the needs of their students.

THERE ARE NO QUICK FIXES

Catching up is a slow, arduous process—one that is facilitated by a teacher who implements research-based practices. Catching up should include the notion that to be able to function at the median or higher in the class to which a student returns, the student must be able to successfully apply reading and writing strategies to understanding and learning in all areas of the curriculum. Merely learning to read on level will never be enough. It is how well students can apply their reading and writing abilities to learning that makes the essential difference for school success.

Although there are no quick fixes, there are research-based instructional practices that, if applied regularly, substantially increase the likelihood that students will learn how to read, write, and think well and will function successfully when they return to regular classrooms. These practices and the rationale for each are listed in Figure 15.1.

BECOMING A TEACHER IS A LIFELONG PROCESS

A teaching certificate marks the beginning of the lifelong process of becoming a teacher. Expert teachers become experts because they are always honing their skills. They collaborate with other teachers and attend conferences and other meetings of educators to learn from researchers in the fields of reading, psychology, and cognition. They regularly read, and discuss with colleagues, professional books and journals and seek answers to questions about how to better meet the needs of their students. The inevitable outgrowth of these professional development activities that are based on research about what works in classrooms is better instruction for children.

SUMMARY

Five important insights, gained from 45 years of teaching struggling readers, are:

1. Teachers, not materials, determine success in learning to read.
2. Children fall behind in reading for many different reasons.
3. There is more to teaching struggling readers than teaching reading.
4. There are no quick fixes; catching up is a slow, arduous process that can be best facilitated by the implementation of research-based practices.
5. A teaching certificate marks the beginning of the lifelong process of becoming a teacher.

FIGURE 15.1. Research-based instructional practices.

Educational Practice	Rationale
1. Provide opportunities for students to read many words each day.	1. The number of words read correlates with progress in reading.
2. Teach explicitly and systematically, including modeling and scaffolding.	2. Children learn what they are taught explicitly.
3. Communicate with parents about their child's progress.	3. Support is one of the reasons struggling readers overcome their difficulties.
4. Teach students to segment words into sounds and to match sounds to letters.	4. Phonemic awareness and decoding provide an essential foundation for reading.
5. Design every-pupil-response (EPR) activities.	5. Time on task correlates with progress.
6. Attend to motivational needs, including affiliation, competence, and autonomy.	6. Motivation and volition are essential to learning to read and to using what is read.
7. Provide opportunities for interaction, transaction, and collaboration.	7. Learning is a social process and requires active involvement.
8. Expect students to ask for clarification and apply critical analysis.	8. Information that is deeply processed is more likely to be understood and applied.
9. Teach and practice processes and strategies in authentic contexts.	9. Strategies, skills, and concepts that are not applied are easily forgotten.
10. Provide rubrics and constructive feedback.	10. Use of rubrics and feedback scaffolds students' understanding of how to perform tasks.
11. Pace instruction and provide repeated practice in relation to each students' rate of learning and differences in skills and strategies.	11. When instruction is too difficult, children struggle and fail.
12. Attach what is to be read to what students know.	12. Attaching what is already known to what is being learned enhances understanding and remembering.
13. Teach students how to organize what they read.	13. Organized knowledge is easier to recall and use than random information.
14. Provide repeated practice.	14. Achieving automaticity and expertise requires practice.

From *Success with Struggling Readers* by Irene Gaskins. Copyright 2005 by The Guilford Press. See copyright page for photocopying limitations.

References

Abowitz, K. K. (2000). A pragmatist revisioning of resistance theory. *American Educational Research Journal, 37*, 877–907.

Ackerman, P. L., & Beier, M. E. (2003). Trait complexes, cognitive investment, and domain knowledge. In R. J. Sternberg & E. L. Grigorenko (Eds.), *Perspectives on the psychology of abilities, competencies, and expertise* (pp. 1–30). Cambridge, UK: Cambridge University Press.

Adams, M. J. (1990). *Beginning to read: Thinking and learning about print*. Cambridge, MA: MIT Press.

Alderman, M. K. (2004). *Motivation for achievement: Possibilities for teaching and learning* (2nd ed.). Mahwah, NJ: Erlbaum.

Alexander, P. A. (2000). Toward a model of academic development: Schooling and the acquisition of knowledge. *Educational researcher, 29*(2), 28–33, 44.

Alexander, P. A., & Jetton, T. L. (2000). Learning from text: A multidimensional and developmental perspective. In J. Kamil, P. Mosenthal, P. Pearson, & R. Barr (Eds.), *Handbook of reading research* (Vol. 3, pp. 285–310). Mahwah, NJ: Erlbaum.

Alexander, P. A., Schallert, D. L., & Hare, V. C. (1991). Coming to terms: How researchers in learning and literacy talk about knowledge. *Review of Educational Research, 61*, 315–343.

Allington, R. L. (1983). The reading instruction provided readers of differing reading abilities. *Elementary School Journal, 83*, 548–559.

Anderson, J. R., Greeno, J. G., Reder, L. M., & Simon, H. A. (2000). Perspectives on learning, thinking, and activity. *Educational Researcher, 29*, 11–13.

Anderson, R. C., & Pearson, P. D. (1984). A schema-theoretic view of basic processes in reading comprehension. In P. D. Pearson (Ed.), *Handbook of reading research*, (pp. 255–291). New York: Longman.

Barr, R., & Dreeben, R. (1983). *How schools work*. Chicago. University of Chicago Press.

Bear, D. R., Invernizzi, M., Templeton, S., & Johnston, F. (1996). *Words their way: Word study for phonics, vocabulary, and spelling*. Upper Saddle River, NJ: Merrill.

Bempechat, J. (1998). *Against the odds: How "at-risk" students exceed expectations*. San Francisco: Jossey-Bass.

Bereiter, C. (2002). *Education and mind in the knowledge age*. Mahwah, NJ: Erlbaum.

Bereiter, C., & Scardamalia, M. (1993). *Surpassing ourselves: An inquiry into the nature and implications of expertise*. Chicago: Open Court.

Bloom, B. S., Engelhart, M. D., Furst, E. J., Hill, W. H., & Krathwohl, E. R. (Eds.) (1956). *Taxonomy of educational objectives: The classification of educational goals. Handbook I: Cognitive domain.* New York: David McKay.

Bond, G. L., & Dykstra, R. (1967). The cooperative research program in first-grade reading instruction. *Reading Research Quarterly, 2,* 10–142.

Bosworth, K. (1995). Caring for others and being cared for: Students talk about caring in school. *Phi Delta Kappan, 76,* 686–693.

Brady, M. (1989). *What's worth teaching? Selecting, organizing, and integrating knowledge.* Albany, NY: State University of New York Press.

Brandt, R. (1998). *Powerful learning.* Alexandria, VA: Association for Supervision and Curriculum Development.

Bransford, J., Brown, A., & Cocking, R. (Eds.). (2000). *How people learn: Brain, mind, experience, and school* (exp. Ed.). Washington, DC: National Academy Press.

Brophy, J. E., & Good, T. L. (1974). *Teacher–student relationships: Causes and consequences.* New York: Holt, Rinehart & Winston.

Brown, A. L., & Palincsar, A. S. (1982). Inducing strategic learning from texts by means of informed, self-control training. *Topics in Learning and Learning Disabilities, 2*(1), 1–18.

Butler, R. (2000). What learners want to know: The role of achievement goals in shaping information seeking, learning, and interest. In C. Sansone & J. Harackiewicz (Eds.), *Intrinsic and extrinsic motivation: The search for optimal motivation and performance* (pp. 161–194). San Diego, CA: Academic Press.

Caine, R. N., & Caine, G. (1994). *Making connections: Teaching and the human brain.* Alexandria, VA: ASCD.

Calderhead, J. (1996). Teachers: Beliefs and knowledge. In D. Berliner & R. Calfee (Eds.), *Handbook of educational psychology* (pp. 709–725). New York: Simon & Schuster Macmillan.

Calfee, R., & Drum, P. (1986). Research on teaching reading. In M. Wittrock (Ed.), *Handbook of research on teaching* (3rd Ed., pp. 804–849). New York: Macmillan.

Carey, W. B. (1997). *Understanding your child's temperament.* New York: Macmillan.

Carroll, J. B. (1993). *Human cognitive abilities: A survey of factor-analytic studies.* Cambridge, UK: Cambridge University Press.

Ceci, S. J. (1996). *On intelligence: A bioecological treatise on intellectual development* (exp. Ed.). Cambridge, MA: Harvard University Press.

Center, Y., Wheldall, K., Freeman, L., Outhred, L., & McNaught, M. (1995). An evaluation of Reading Recovery. *Reading Research Quarterly, 30,* 240–263.

Chess, S., & Thomas, A. (1999). *Goodness of fit: Clinical applications from infancy through adult life.* Philadelphia: Brunner/Mazel.

Cronbach, L. (Ed.). (2002). *Remaking the concept of aptitude: Extending the legacy of Richard E. Snow.* Mahwah, NJ: Erlbaum.

Csikszentmihalyi, M., & Schenider, B. (2000). *Becoming adult: How teenagers prepare for the world of work.* New York: Basic Books.

Cunningham, P. M. (1975–1976). Investigating a synthesized theory of mediated word identification. *Reading Research Quarterly, 11,* 127–143.

Cunningham, P. M. (2000). *Phonics they use: Words for reading and writing* (3rd Ed.). New York: Longman.

Damasio, A. R. (2000). Thinking about belief: Concluding remarks. In D. L. Schacter & E. Scarry (Eds.), *Memory, brain, and belief* (pp. 325–333). Cambridge, MA: Harvard University Press.

Deci, E. L. (with Flaste, R.). (1995). *Why we do what we do: The dynamics of personal autonomy.* New York: Putnam.

Dembo, M. H., & Eaton, M. J. (2000). Self-regulation of academic learning in middle-level schools. *The Elementary School Journal, 100,* 473–490.

Donald, J. G. (2002). *Learning to think: Disciplinary perspectives.* San Francisco: Jossey-Bass.

Donovan, C. A., & Smolkin, L. B. (2001). Genre and other factors influencing teachers' book selections for science instruction. *Reading Research Quarterly, 36*, 412–440.

Duffy, G. G. (2003). *Explaining reading: A resource for teaching concepts, skills, and strategies*. New York: Guilford Press.

Duffy, G. G., Roehler, L., & Herrmann, B. A. (1988). Modeling mental processes helps poor readers become strategic readers. *The Reading Teacher, 41*, 762–767.

Duffy, G. G., Roehler, L., Sivan, E., Rackliffe, G., Book, C., Meloth, M., Vavrus, L., Wesselman, R., Putnam, J., & Bassiri, D. (1987). Effects of explaining the reasoning associated with using reading strategies. *Reading Research Quarterly, 22*, 347–368.

Duke, N. K. (2000). 3. 6 minutes per day: The scarcity of informational texts in first grade. *Reading Research Quarterly, 35*, 202–224.

Durkin, D. (1978–1979). What classroom observations reveal about reading comprehension instruction. *Reading Research Quarterly, 14*, 481–533.

Ehri, L. C. (1991). Development of the ability to read words. In R. Barr, J. Kamil, P. Mosenthal, & P. Pearson (Eds.), *Handbook of reading research* (Vol. II, pp. 383–417). New York: Longman.

Ehri, L. C. (1995). Phases of development in reading words. *Journal of Research in Reading, 18*, 116–125.

Eichenbaum, H., & Bodkin, J. A. (2000). Belief and knowledge as distinct forms of memory. In D. L. Schacter & E. Scarry (Eds.), *Memory, brain, and belief* (pp. 176–207). Cambridge, MA: Harvard University Press.

Erickson, H. L. (2001). *Stirring the head, heart, and soul: Redefining curriculum and instruction* (2nd Ed.). Thousand Oaks, CA: Corwin Press.

Fischer, K. W., & Tose, L. T. (2001). Webs of skill: How students learn. *Educational Leadership, 59*, 6–12.

Fowler, C., Napps, S., & Feldman, L. (1985). Relations among regular and irregular morphologically related words in the lexicon as revealed by repetition priming. *Memory and Cognition, 13*, 241–255.

Fry, F. B., Fountoukidis, D. L., & Polk, J. K. (1985). *The new reading teacher's book of lists*. Englewood Cliffs, NJ: Prentice-Hall.

Gardner, H. (1983). *Frames of mind: The theory of multiple intelligence*. New York: Basic Books.

Gardner, H. (1999). *Intelligence reframed: Multiple intelligence for the 21st century*. New York: Basic Books.

Garner, R. (1987). *Metacognition and reading comprehension*. Norwood, NJ: Ablex.

Gaskins, I. W. (1970). *Characteristics that differentiate dyslexics from nondyslexic poor readers*. Unpublished doctoral dissertation, University of Pennsylvania, Philadelphia.

Gaskins, I. W. (1980). *The Benchmark story: The first ten years, 1970/1980*. Media, PA: Benchmark Press.

Gaskins, I. W. (1982). A writing program for poor readers and writers and the rest of the class, too. *Language Arts, 59*, 854–861.

Gaskins, I. W. (1984). There's more to a reading problem than poor reading. *Journal of Learning Disabilities, 17*, 467–471.

Gaskins, I. W. (1988). Teachers as thinking coaches: Creating strategic learners and problem solvers. *Reading, Writing, and Learning Disabilities, 4*, 35–48.

Gaskins, I. W. (1991). And it works for them too! In J. T. Feeley, C. C. Strickland, & S. B. Wepner (Eds.), *Process reading and writing: A literature-based approach* (pp. 160–170). New York: Teachers College Press.

Gaskins, I. W. (1994). Classroom applications of cognitive science: Teaching poor readers how to learn, think, and problem solve. In K. McGilly (Ed.), *Classroom lessons* (pp. 129–154). Cambridge, MA: MIT Press.

Gaskins, I. W. (1998). There's more to teaching at-risk and delayed readers than good reading instruction. *The Reading Teacher, 51*, 534–547.

Gaskins, I. W. (1999). A multidimensional reading program. *The Reading Teacher, 53,* 162–164.

Gaskins, I. W. (2000). *Word Detectives Intermediate Program (A).* Media, PA: Benchmark Press.

Gaskins, I. W. (2002). *Word Detectives Intermediate Program (B).* Media, PA: Benchmark Press.

Gaskins, I. W. (2003). Taking charge of reader, text, activity, and context variables. In A. Sweet & C. Snow (Eds.), *Rethinking reading comprehension* (pp. 141–165). New York: Guilford Press.

Gaskins, I. W. (2004). Word Detectives. *Educational Leadership, 61,* 70–73.

Gaskins, I. W., Anderson, R. C., Pressley, M., Cunicelli, E. A., & Satlow, E. (1993). Six teachers' dialogue during cognitive process instruction. *Elementary School Journal, 93,* 277–304.

Gaskins, I. W., & Baron, J. (1985). Teaching poor readers to cope with maladaptive cognitive styles: A training program. *Journal of Learning Disabilities, 18,* 390–394.

Gaskins, I. W., Cress, C., O'Hara, C., & Donnelly, K. (1996). *Word Detectives: Benchmark extended word identification program for beginning readers.* Media, PA: Benchmark Press.

Gaskins, I. W., Downer, M. A., Anderson, R. C., Cunningham, P. M., Gaskins, R. W., Schommer, M., and the Teachers of Benchmark School. (1988). A metacognitive approach to phonics: Using what you know to decode what you don't know. *Remedial and Special Education, 9,* 36–41, 66.

Gaskins, I. W., Downer, M. A., & Gaskins, R. W. (1986). *Introduction to the Benchmark School word identification/vocabulary development program.* Media, PA: Benchmark Press.

Gaskins, I. W., Ehri, L. C., Cress, C., O'Hara, C., & Donnelly, K. (1996–1997). Procedures for word learning: Making discoveries about words. *The Reading Teacher, 50,* 312–327.

Gaskins, I. W., Ehri, L. C., Cress, C., O'Hara, C., & Donnelly, K. (1997). Analyzing words and making discoveries about the alphabetic system: Activities for beginning readers. *Language Arts, 74,* 172–184.

Gaskins, I. W., & Elliot, T. T. (1991). *Implementing cognitive strategy instruction across the school: The Benchmark manual for teachers.* Cambridge, MA: Brookline Books.

Gaskins, I. W., Guthrie, J. T., Satlow, E., Ostertag, J., Six, L., Byrne, J., & Connor, B. (1994). Integrating instruction of science, reading, and writing: Goals, teacher development, and assessment. *Journal of Research in Science Teaching, 31,* 1039–1056.

Gaskins, I. W., Rauch, S., Gensemer, E., Cunicelli, E., O'Hara, C., Six, L., & Scott, T. (1997). Scaffolding the development of intelligence among children who are delayed in learning to read. In K. Hogan & M. Pressley (Eds.), *Scaffolding student learning: Instructional approaches and issues* (pp. 43–73). Cambridge, MA: Brookline Books.

Gaskins, I. W., & Satlow, E. (2004). *Roadblocks to becoming a proficient reader: Implications for instruction.* Manuscript submitted for publication.

Gaskins, I. W., Satlow, E., Hyson, D., Ostertag, J., & Six, L. (1994). Classroom talk about text: Learning in science class. *Journal of Reading, 37,* 558–565.

Gaskins, R. W. (1996). "That's just how it was": The effect of issue-related emotional involvement on reading comprehension. *Reading Research Quarterly, 31,* 386–405.

Gaskins, R. W., Gaskins, I. W., Anderson, R. C., & Schommer, M. (1995). The reciprocal relationship between research and development: An example involving a decoding strand for poor readers. *Journal of Reading Behavior, 27,* 337–377.

Gee, J. P. (2003). *What video games have to teach us about learning and literacy.* New York: Palgrave Macmillan.

Gibson, E. J., & Levin, H. (1975). *The psychology of reading.* Cambridge, MA: MIT Press.

Glushko, R. J. (1979). The organization and activation of orthographic knowledge in reading aloud. *Journal of Experimental Psychology: Human Perception and Performance, 5,* 674–691.

Goldenberg, C. (2001). Making schools work for low-income families in the 21st century. In S. Neuman & D. Dickinson (Eds.), *Handbook of early literacy research* (pp. 211–231). New York: Guilford Press.

Goldstein, L. S. (1999). The relational zone: The role of caring relationships in the co-construction of mind. *American Educational Research Journal, 36,* 647–673.

Gollub, J. P., Bertenthal, M. W., Labov, J. B., & Curtis, P. C. (Eds.). (2002). *Learning and understand-ing: Improving advanced study of mathematics and science in U. S. high schools.* Washington, DC: National Academy Press.

Goslin, D. A. (2003). *Engaging minds: Motivation and learning in America's schools.* Lanham, MD: Scarecrow Press.

Graves, D. H. (1975). An examination of the writing processes of seven-year-old children. *Research in the Teaching of English, 9,* 227–241.

Greeno, J. G., Collins, A. M., & Resnick, L. B. (1996). Cognition and learning. In D. Berliner & R. Calfee (Eds.), *Handbook of educational psychology* (pp. 63–84). New York: Macmillan.

Guthrie, J. T., Van Meter, P., McCann, A. D., Wigfield, A., Bennett, L., Poundstone, C. C., Rice, M. E., Faibisch, F. M., Hunt, B., & Mitchell, A. M. (1996). Growth of literacy engagement: Changes in motivations and strategies during concept-oriented reading instruction. *Reading Research Quarterly, 31,* 306–333.

Hammill, D. (1972). Training visual perceptual processes. *Journal of Learning Disabilities, 5,* 552–559.

Hammill, D., Goodman, L., & Widerholt, J. L. (1974). Visual processes: Can we train them? *The Reading Teacher, 27,* 469–478.

Harackiewicz, J. M., & Sansone, C. (2000). Rewarding competence: The importance of goals in the study of intrinsic motivation. In C. Sansone & J. Harackiewicz (Eds.), *Intrinsic and extrinsic motivation: The search for optimal motivation and performance* (pp. 79–103). San Diego, CA: Academic Press.

Harris, T. L., & Hodges, R. E. (Eds.). (1995). *The literacy dictionary: The vocabulary of reading and writing.* Newark, DE: International Reading Association.

Hatano, G., & Oura, Y. (2003). Commentary: Reconceptualizing school learning using insight from expertise research. *Educational Researcher, 32*(8), 26–29.

Hiebert, E. H. (1994). Reading Recovery in the United States: What differences does it make to an age cohort? *Educational Researcher, 23*(9), 15–25.

Hofer, B. K., Yu, S. L., & Pintrich, P. R. (1998). Teaching college students to be self-regulated learn-ers. In D. Schunk & B. Zimmerman (Eds.), *Self-regulated learning: From teaching to self-reflec-tive practice* (pp. 57–85). New York: Guilford Press.

Howe, M. J. A. (1990). *The origins of exceptional abilities.* Cambridge, MA: Blackwell.

Johnson, D. D., & Baumann, J. F. (1984). Word identification. In P. D. Pearson (Ed.), *Handbook of reading research* (pp. 583–608). New York: Longman.

Johnston, F. P. (2001). The utility of phonic generalizations: Let's take another look at Clymer's conclusions. *The Reading Teacher, 55,* 132–143.

Joyce, B., & Weil, M. (with Calhoun, E.). (2004). *Models of teaching* (7th ed.). Boston: Pearson.

Keene, E. O., & Zimmermann, S. (1997). *Mosaic of thought: Teaching comprehension in a readers' workshop.* Portsmouth, NH: Heinemann.

Knowles, T., & Brown, D. F. (2000). *What every middle school teacher should know.* Portsmouth, NH: Heinemann.

Lambert, N. M., & McCombs, B. L. (1998). Introduction: Learner-centered schools and classrooms as a direction for school reform. In N. Lambert & B. McCombs (Eds.), *How students learn: Re-forming school through learner-centered education* (pp. 1–22). Washington, DC: American Psy-chological Association.

Langer, J. A. (2001). Beating the odds: Teaching middle and high school students to read and write well. *American Educational Research Journal, 38,* 837–880.

Lee, V. E., & Smith, J. B. (1999). Social support and achievement for young adolescents in Chi-cago: The role of school academic press. *American Educational Research Journal, 36,* 907–945.

Leinhardt, G., Stainton, C., Virji, S. M., & Odoroff, E. (1994). Learning to reason in history: Mind-lessness to mindfulness. In M. Carretero & J. Voss (Eds.), *Cognitive and instructional processes in history and the social sciences* (pp. 131–158). Hillsdale, NJ: Erlbaum.

Levine, M. (2002). *A mind at a time*. New York: Simon & Schuster.

Levine, M. (2003). *The myth of laziness*. New York: Simon & Schuster.

Linn, M. C., Songer, N. B., & Eylon, B. S. (1996). Shifts and convergences in science learning and instruction. In D. Berliner & R. Calfee (Eds.), *Handbook of educational psychology* (pp. 438–490). New York: Simon & Schuster Macmillan.

Loucks-Horsley, S., Kapitan, R., Carlson, M. D., Kuerbis, P. J., Clark, R. C., Melle, G. M., Sachse, T. P., & Walton, E. (1990). *Elementary school science for the '90's*. Andover, MA: The National Center for Improving Science Education.

Marzano, R. J. (2001). *Designing a new taxonomy of educational objectives*. Thousand Oaks, CA: Corwin Press.

Marzano, R. J. (2003). *What works in schools: Translating research into action*. Alexandria, VA: Association for Supervision and Curriculum Development.

Maslow, A. H. (1968). *Toward a psychology of being* (2nd ed.). New York: van Nostrand.

Matlin, M. W. (2003). *Cognition* (5th Ed.). Hoboken, NJ: Wiley.

McClelland, J. L., & Johnston, J. C. (1977). The role of familiar units in the perception of words and nonwords. *Perception and Psychophysics, 22*, 249–261.

Meier, D. (1995). *The power of their ideas: Lessons for America from a small school in Harlem*. Boston: Beacon Press.

Meltzer, L. (2004). Resilience and learning disabilities: Research on internal and external protective dynamics—introduction to the special series. *Learning Disabilities Research and Practice, 19*(1), 1–2.

Molden, D. C., & Dweck, C. S. (2000). Meaning and motivation. In C. Sansone & J. Harackiewicz (Eds.), *Intrinsic and extrinsic motivation: The search for optimal motivation and performance* (pp. 131–159). San Diego, CA: Academic Press.

Murphy, J. M. (1996). *A follow-up study of delayed readers and an investigation of factors related to their success in young adulthood*. Unpublished doctoral dissertation, University of Pennsylvania, Philadelphia.

National Reading Panel. (2000). *Teaching children to read: An evidence-based assessment of the scientific research literature on reading and its implications for reading instruction*. Washington, DC: National Institute of Child Health and Human Development.

Noddings, N. (1992). *The challenge to care in schools: An alternative approach to education*. New York: Teachers College Press.

Noddings, N. (1998). *Philosophy of education*. Boulder, CO: Westview Press.

Oakes, J., & Lipton, M. (1999). *Teaching to change the world*. Boston: McGraw-Hill College.

Odden, A., & Kelley, C. (2002). *Paying teachers for what they know and do: New and smarter compensation strategies to improve schools* (2nd ed.). Thousand Oaks, CA: Corwin Press.

O'Hara, C., & Gaskins, I. W. (1999). *Word Detectives Transition Program*. Media, PA: Benchmark Press.

Olson, D. R. (2003). *Psychological theory and educational reform: How school remakes mind and society*. Cambridge, UK: Cambridge University Press.

Pearson, P. D. (1993). Teaching and learning reading: A research perspective. *Language Arts, 70*, 502–511.

Pearson, P. D. (1999). A historically based review of preventing reading difficulties in young children. *Reading Research Quarterly, 34*, 231–246.

Pearson, P. D., & Duke, N. D. (2002). Comprehension instruction in the primary grades. In C. Block & M. Pressley (Eds.), *Comprehension instruction: Research-based best practices* (pp. 247–258). New York: Guilford Press.

Penner, D. E. (2001–2002). Cognition, computers, and synthetic science: Building knowledge and meaning through modeling. In W. Secada (Ed.), *Review of research in education* (Vol. 25, pp. 1–35). Washington, DC: American Educational Research Association.

Perfetti, C. A. (1985). *Reading ability*. New York: Oxford University Press.

Perkins, D. N. (1986). *Knowledge as design*. Hillsdale, NJ: Erlbaum.

Perkins, D. N. (1991). Integrating the curriculum: Educating for insight. *Educational Leadership, 49*(2), 4–8.

Perkins, D. (1995). *Outsmarting IQ: The emerging science of learnable intelligence*. New York: Free Press.

Prawat, R. S. (1989). Promoting access to knowledge, strategy, and disposition in students: A research synthesis. *Review of Educational Research, 59*, 1–41.

Prawat, R. S. (1991). The value of ideas: The immersion approach to the development of thinking. *Educational Researcher, 20*(2), 3–10, 30.

Prawat, R. S. (1993). The value of ideas: Problems versus possibilities in learning. *Educational Researcher, 22*(6), 5–16.

Pressley, M. (with McCormick, C. B.). (1995). *Advanced educational psychology: For educators, researchers, and policymakers*. New York: HarperCollins.

Pressley, M. (1998). *Reading instruction that works: The case for balanced teaching*. New York: Guilford Press.

Pressley, M. (2002). *Reading instruction that works: The case for balanced teaching* (2nd ed.). New York: Guilford Press.

Pressley, M., & Block, C. (2002). Summing up: What comprehension instruction could be. In C. Block & M. Pressley (Eds.), *Comprehension instruction: Research-based best practices* (pp. 383–392). New York: Guilford Press.

Pressley, M., El-Dinary, P. M., Gaskins, I. W., Schuder, T., Bergman, J. L., Almasi, J., & Brown, R. (1992). Beyond direct explanation: Transactional instruction of reading comprehension strategies. *Elementary School Journal, 92*, 511–554.

Purcell-Gates, V., & Duke, N. K. (2001, August). *Explicit explanation/teaching of informational text genres: A model for research*. Paper presented at the Crossing Borders: Connecting Science and Literacy Conference, Baltimore, MD.

Purkey, W. W. (2000). *What students say to themselves: Internal dialogue and school success*. Thousand Oaks, CA: Corwin Press.

RAND Reading Study Group. (2002). *Reading for understanding: Toward an R & D program in reading comprehension*. Santa Monica, CA: RAND.

Renninger, K. A., & Hidi, S. (2001). Student interest and achievement: Developmental issues raised by a case study. In A. Wigfield & J. Eccles (Eds.), *Development of achievement motivation* (pp. 173–195). San Diego, CA: Academic Press.

Reynolds, R., Taylor, M., Steffensen, M., Shirey, L., & Anderson, R. (1982). Cultural schemata and reading comprehension. *Reading Research Quarterly, 17*, 353–366.

Rhoder, C. (2002). Mindful reading: Strategy training that facilitates transfer. *Journal of Adolescent and Adult Literacy, 45*, 498–512.

Roberts, E. V. (2003). *Writing about literature* (10th ed.). Upper Saddle River, NJ: Prentice Hall.

Roeser, R. W., Eccles , J. S., & Sameroff, A. J. (2000). School as a context of early adolescents' academic and social–emotional development: A summary of research findings. *Elementary School Journal, 100*, 443–471.

Rogoff, B. (1990). *Apprenticeship in thinking: Cognitive development in social context*. New York: Oxford University Press.

Rosenshine, B. (1979). Content, time, and direct instruction. In P. Peterson & H. Walberg (Eds.), *Research on teaching: Concepts, findings, and implications*. Berkeley, CA: McCutchan.

Rosenshine, B., & Berliner, D. C. (1978). Academic engaged time. *British Journal of Teacher Education, 4*, 3–16.

Rosenshine, B., & Furst, N. (1973). The use of direct observation to study teaching. In R. M. W. Travers (Ed.), *Second handbook of research on teaching*. Chicago: Rand McNally.

Roser, N. L., & Keehn, S. (2002). Fostering thought, talk, and inquiry: Linking literature and social studies. *The Reading Teacher, 55*, 416–426.

Rutherford, F. J., & Ahlgren, A. (1990). *Science for all Americans*. New York: Oxford University Press.

Ryan, R. M., & Deci, E. L. (2000). When rewards compete with nature: The undermining of intrinsic motivation and self-regulation. In C. Sansone & J. Harackiewicz (Eds.), *Intrinsic and extrinsic motivation: The search for optimal motivation and performance* (pp. 13–54). San Diego, CA: Academic Press.

Sansone, C., & Harackiewicz, J. (2000). Looking beyond rewards: The problem and promise of intrinsic motivation. In C. Sansone & J. Harackiewicz (Eds.), *Intrinsic and extrinsic motivation: The search for optimal motivation and performance* (pp. 1–9). San Diego, CA: Academic Press.

Sarason, S. (2004). And what do you mean by learning? Portsmouth, NH: Heinemann.

Seligman, M. E. (1975). *Helplessness: On depression and death*. San Francisco: Freeman.

Seligman, M. E. (1990). *Learned optimism*. New York: Knopf.

Seligman, M. E. (2003). *Authentic happiness: Using the new positive psychology to realize your potential for lasting fulfillment*. New York: Free Press.

Shanahan, T., & Barr, R. (1995). Reading Recovery: An independent evaluation of the effects of an early instructional intervention for at-risk learners. *Reading Research Quarterly, 30*, 958–996.

Shaywitz, S. (2003). *Overcoming dyslexia: A new and complete science-based program for reading problems at any level*. New York: Knopf.

Shepard, L. A. (2000). The role of assessment in a learning culture. *Educational Researcher, 20*(7), 4–14.

Shulman, L. S. (1986). *Educational Researcher, 15*(2), 4–14.

Shulman, L. S., & Quinlan, L. M. (1996). The comparative psychology of school subjects. In D. Berliner & R. Calfee (Eds.), *Handbook of educational psychology* (pp. 399–422). New York: Simon & Schuster Macmillan.

Silva, C., & Delgado-Larocco, E. L. (1993). Facilitating learning through interconnections: A concept approach to core literature units. *Language Arts, 70*, 469–474.

Silverman, S. L., & Casazza, M. E. (2000). *Learning and development: Making connections to enhance teaching*. San Francisco: Jossey-Bass.

Simonton, D. K. (1994). *Greatness: Who makes history and why*. New York: Guilford Press.

Smolkin, L. B., & Donovan, C. A. (2002). "Oh excellent, excellent question!": Developmental differences and comprehension acquisition. In C. Block & M. Pressley (Eds.), *Comprehension instruction: Research-based best practices* (pp. 140–157). New York: Guilford Press.

Snow, R. E., Corno, L., & Jackson, D. (1996). Individual differences in affective and conative functions. In D. Berliner & R. Calfee (Eds.), *Handbook of educational psychology* (pp. 243–310). New York: Simon & Schuster Macmillan.

Stallings, J. A., & Kaskowitz, D. (1974). *Follow-through classroom observation evaluation, 1972–73*. Menlo Park, CA: Stanford Research Institute.

Stanovich, K. E. (1988). Explaining the differences between the dyslexic and the garden-variety poor reader: The phonological-core variable-difference model. *Journal of Learning Disabilities, 21*, 590–612.

Stanovich, K. E. (2002). Rationality, intelligence, and levels of analysis in cognitive science. In R. Sternberg, *Why smart people can be so stupid* (pp. 120–158). New Haven, CN: Yale University Press.

Sternberg, R. J. (1998). Abilities are forms of developing expertise. *Educational Researcher, 27*(3), 11–30.

Sternberg, R. J. (2003). What is an "expert student"? *Educational Researcher, 32*(8), 5–9.

Strickland, D. S. (1998). *Teaching phonics today: A primer for educators*. Newark, DE: International Reading Association.

Strickland, D. S., Ganske, K., & Monroe, J. K. (2002). *Supporting struggling readers and writers: Strategies for classroom intervention 3–6*. Portland, ME: Stenhouse.

Strickland, D., & Snow, C. (2002). *Preparing our teachers: Opportunities for better reading instruction*. Washington, DC: Joseph Henry Press.

Strong, R. W., Silver, H. F., & Perini, M. J. (2001). *Teaching what matters most*. Alexandria, VA: Association for Supervision and Curriculum Development.

Taylor, B. M., Pearson, P. D., Clark, K., & Walpole, S. (2000). Effective schools and accomplished teachers: Lessons about primary-grade reading instruction in low-income schools. *Elementary School Journal, 101*, 121–165.

Tharp, R. G., & Gallimore, R. (1988). *Rousing minds to life: Teaching, learning, and schooling in social context*. New York: Cambridge University Press.

Thomas, A., & Chess, S. (1977). *Temperament and development*. New York: Brunner/Mazel.

Thornburg, D. (2002). *The new basics: Education and the future of work in the telematic age*. Alexandria, VA: Association for Supervision and Curriculum Development.

Tomlinson, C. A. (1998). For integration and differentiation choose concepts over topics. *Middle School Journal, 30*(2), 3–8.

Tomlinson, C. A., Kaplan, S. N., Renzulli, J. S., Purcell, J., Leppien, J., & Burns, D. (2002). *The parallel curriculum: A design to develop high potential and challenge high-ability learners*. Thousand Oaks, CA: Corwin Press.

Torgesen, J. K. (1985). Memory processes in reading disabled children *Journal of Learning Disabilities, 18*, 350–357.

Torgesen, J. K., & Burgess, S. R. (1998). Consistency of reading-related phonological processes throughout early childhood: Evidence from longitudinal-correlational and instructional studies. In J. Metsala & L. Ehri (Eds.), *Reading acquisition* (pp. 307–342). Hillsdale, NJ: Erlbaum.

Vellutino, F. R., & Scanlon, D. M. (1984). Converging perspectives in the study of the reading process: Reactions to the papers presented by Morrison, Siegel and Ryan, and Stanovich. *Remedial and Special Education, 5*, 39–44.

Vosniadou, S., & Brewer, W. F. (1989). *The concept of the earth's shape: A study of conceptual change in childhood*. Unpublished paper. Center for the Study of Reading, University of Illinois, Champaign, IL.

Vygotsky, L. S. (1978). *Mind in society: The development of higher psychological processes* (M. Cole, V. John-Steiner, & E. Souberman, Eds. and Trans.). Cambridge, MA: Harvard University Press.

Wertsch, J. V. (1991). *Voices of the mind: A sociocultural approach to mediated action*. Cambridge, MA: Harvard University Press.

Williams, J. P. (2002). Using the theme scheme to improve story comprehension. In C. Block & M. Pressley (Eds.), *Comprehension instruction: Research-based best practices* (pp. 126–139). New York: Guilford Press.

Wolman, B. B. (Ed.). (1989). *Dictionary of behavioral science* (2nd Ed.). San Diego, CA: Academic Press.

Zimmerman, B. J. (1990). Self-regulating academic learning and achievement: The emergence of a social cognitive perspective. *Educational Psychology Review, 2*, 173–201.

Zimmerman, B. J. (1998). Developing self-fulfilling cycles of academic regulation: An analysis of exemplary instructional models. In D. H. Schunk & B. J. Zimmerman (Eds.), *Self-regulated learning: From teaching to self-reflective practice* (pp. 1–19). New York: Guilford Press.

Zimmerman, B. J. (2001). Theories of self-regulated learning and academic achievement: An overview and analysis. In B. J. Zimmerman & D. H. Schunk (Eds.), *Self-regulated learning and academic achievement: Theoretical perspectives* (2nd Ed., pp. 1–37). Mahwah, NJ: Erlbaum.

Zimmerman, B. J., & Campillo, M. (2003). Motivating self-regulated problem solvers. In J. E. Davidson & R. J. Sternberg (Eds.), *The psychology of problem solving*. Cambridge, UK: Cambridge University Press.

Zimmerman, B. J., & Schunk, D. H. (2001). Reflections on theories of self-regulated learning and academic achievement. In D. Schunk & B. J. Zimmerman (Eds.), *Self-regulated learning: From teaching to self-reflective practice* (pp. 289–307). New York: Guilford Press.

Index